THE POPE AND I

The POPE AND I

HOW THE LIFELONG FRIENDSHIP BETWEEN
A POLISH JEW AND JOHN PAUL II
ADVANCED THE CAUSE OF
JEWISH-CHRISTIAN RELATIONS

JERZY KLUGER

WITH GIANFRANCO DI SIMONE

TRANSLATED BY MATTHEW SHERRY

ORBIS BOOKS
Maryknoll, New York 10545

Founded in 1970, Orbis Books endeavors to publish works that enlighten the mind, nourish the spirit, and challenge the conscience. The publishing arm of the Maryknoll Fathers and Brothers, Orbis seeks to explore the global dimensions of the Christian faith and mission, to invite dialogue with diverse cultures and religious traditions, and to serve the cause of reconciliation and peace. The books published reflect the views of their authors and do not represent the official position of the Maryknoll Society. To learn more about Maryknoll and Orbis Books, please visit our website at www.maryknollsociety.org.

Library of Congress Cataloging-in-Publication Data
Kluger, Jerzy.
    The Pope and I : how the lifelong friendship between a Polish Jew and John Paul II advanced Jewish-Christian relations / by Jerzy Kluger with Gianfranco Di Simone ; translated by Matthew Sherry.
        p.   cm.
    ISBN 978-1-57075-970-3 (cloth)
    ISBN 978-1-60833-130-7 (ebook)
    ISBN 978-1-62698-009-9 (pbk)
    1. John Paul II, Pope, 1920–2005 – Friends and associates. 2. Kluger, Jerzy – Friends and associates. 3. Popes – Biography. 4. Jews – Poland – Biography. 5. Catholic Church – Relations – Judaism. 6. Judaism – Relations – Catholic Church. I. Di Simone, Gianfranco. II. Title.
BX1378.5.K5813   2012
282.092 – dc23
[B]   2011160504

CONTENTS

FOREWORD

T his is the poignant story of a friendship between a Polish Catholic and a Jew from a small town in Poland, a friendship deepened
by the great human tragedies that swirled around it in their youth
and the international controversies that defined so much of their mature
years together. It is the story of young Karol "Lolek" Wojtyła, and Jerzy
"Jurek" Kluger, the story of a pope and of a survivor of the *Shoah*, as told
from the perspective of the latter. As such, the background for the remark-
able friendship narrated here is nothing less than the entire history of
the ancient, covenantal relationship between the Christian Church and
the Jewish People, a relationship, many Jews and Christians today attest,
that can illumine and deepen our understanding of the larger relationship
between humanity and its Creator, the One God, the God of Israel.

The opening paragraph of this foreword may seem to many readers to
be an exercise in hyperbole, but I can assure them, after nearly a lifetime of
study and involvement in the Jewish-Christian dialogue, that it is not. The
boy Lolek, of course, was to become Blessed Pope John Paul II, arguably
one of the handful of most significant figures in Christian-Jewish relations
since the time of the Apostles and certainly one of the most positive, with
the goal of improving the relationship between Catholics and Jews a chief,
defining feature of his relatively long pontificate. Indeed, no pope in history spoke more often or more positively about Jews and Judaism, or acted
more decisively and symbolically to embed his words into the life of the
Church, than did John Paul.* He was the first pope since Saint Peter to visit
and to pray with Jews in the Great Synagogue of Rome (1986), the first to
visit Auschwitz and to meet and dialogue substantively on American soil
with representatives of the world's largest Jewish community (1987), and
the first to make a personal pilgrimage and official state visit to the state
of Israel (2000). These actions and the developing clarity and depth of his

---

*See Eugene J. Fisher and Leon Klenicki, editors, *The Saint for Shalom: How Pope John
Paul II Transformed Catholic-Jewish Relations* (New York: Crossroad, 2011).

teachings on how we Catholics are as Church to understand theologically our ongoing relations with God's People, the Jews, one may say without exaggeration, have forever changed that relationship, in the process bettering the ability of the Church and the Jewish People to witness, together, to the One God and to God's loving Will for all humanity, drawing on the Scriptures we share and our own distinct yet interrelated traditions of interpreting them.

Though fraught with large historical and theological implications, the story told by Jurek of his friendship, lost and found, with the Catholic boy Lolek, is at the same time a deeply personal one, here narrated in simple and engaging language that draws in the reader and enables us as readers to feel that we are sitting at the table with them, whether in the Vatican or in the papal summer residence, Castel Gandolfo, enjoying the pasta, the Italian wine, a sip of vodka, reminiscences of their youth, and hopes for the present and future of Catholics and Jews alike. This memoir is both illuminating for those who wish to understand why John Paul was so deeply motivated to further the Catholic-Jewish dialogue, and a good read, communicating sometimes complex truths with human warmth and a dollop of humor.

When it became known that one of the pope's best friends in Rome was a Polish Jew who had known Wojtyła from boyhood, of course, the larger Jewish community reached out to Jurek in the understandable hope that he might be able and willing to communicate Jewish concerns to the leader of the Church, which of course he was and did, relying on the equally open and willing ears of the pope in so doing. One of the key Jewish leaders in Rome to contact Kluger with this in mind was Józef Lichten, himself originally a Polish Jew who had for many years been in charge of interfaith relations for the Anti-Defamation League (then of B'nai B'rith), especially with Catholics, and who had retired to live in Rome. In my own capacity working in Catholic-Jewish relations for the U.S. Conference of Catholic Bishops, I had come myself to know Joe Lichten as a colleague and a friend, knowledgeable and positive toward Jewish relations with Catholics, so I can appreciate how appropriate he was as a mentor for Jurek in this regard, just as this memoir depicts him to have been.

In the discussions between Kluger and Lichten, also often over pasta and good wine, the latter gives the former quite digestible lessons in Jewish-Christian history and in the current controversies of the day, whether matters evocative of the Holocaust, such as the convent of nuns built adjacent to the death camp of Auschwitz, or the need, from the Jewish viewpoint, for the Holy See to exchange ambassadors with the state of Israel and thus make manifest for all the recognition by the Church of the existence of Israel as a Jewish state, indeed as a safe haven for Jewish survivors of the *Shoah* and for Jews of future generations who may need what the European Jews of the Second World War did not have, a refuge from persecution whether by Christians or others. This book, then, is informative not only about the psychology and inner spirituality of a great pope, but also about the larger issues that faced the Church in his time, and which no less face the Church today.

Eugene J. Fisher
Distinguished Professor of
Catholic-Jewish Studies
Saint Leo University

PREFACE

I first met Jerzy Kluger, known to his friends as Jurek, about fifteen years ago through an introduction by a mutual friend. He was anxious to arrange for the publication of a short piece by the Polish prelate, Cardinal Andrzej Deskur, a close friend of Pope John Paul II. I was able to arrange for its publication in a U.S. newspaper and so began our journey together.

Over the years, Jurek and I visited in the United States and Rome on about six occasions, and we communicated via email and occasional phone calls. Sometime in 2007, Jurek's neighbor, a lawyer named Gianfranco Di Simone, suggested that Jurek consider writing a book about his lifelong friendship with Pope John Paul II. While Jurek's memory of events was clear, dates and details had been lost during the closing of his office upon his retirement. Nevertheless, in an excited email in May 2008, Jurek told me of finding his notes "regarding all the meetings I had with John Paul II and other people at the Vatican. The notes include all the details of my numerous meetings with Pope John Paul II and his most important collaborators regarding the Catholic-Jewish relations as well as relations between the Holy See and the state of Israel. All of this is absolutely and completely unedited! They give fantastic details that must be included in the book. Obviously they are all in the Polish language, and I'm translating them into the Italian language for Dr. Di Simone."

With the discovery of this treasure trove, Jurek and Gianfranco began writing *The Pope and I.* Jurek's desire was to publish the book in English, and so this project brought us back together again. Jurek knew I had friends in the book publishing world and I agreed to assist. After the manuscript was delivered, I reached out to my long-time friend Bill Burrows, who had served as managing editor of Orbis Books and who was able to read Italian. Bill liked the book. We then engaged Matt Sherry, who did a masterful job of translating the document into English, and Bob Land, who performed the editorial tasks to make it sing.

Jurek didn't live to see his book in print. He died on the last day of 2011. It was a great joy working with this humble man who had a special devotion to his friend, the pope. Jurek's contribution to Jewish-Catholic relations at the turn of the century, while largely unrecognized, may someday be seen as immense.

It was an honor to call Jurek Kluger my friend.

George B. Irish

CHAPTER I

CHILDHOOD IN WADOWICE

Between Kraków and Bielsko, at the foot of the Beskid mountains on the edge of the Carpathians, stands the little Polish town of Wadowice. And when my memory turns back to my hometown in the mid-1920s, I can still picture it just as it was then: the gravel roads, the horse-drawn carriages, the people passing by on foot or bicycle. And everywhere on the roadsides were the bouquets of white and red roses, a reminder that Poland was back—back in the hands of its own people. It seemed right on script for this nation and its people, so full of passion and just as accustomed to glory and victory as to defeat and foreign domination. The most recent and longest of these periods of outside control had lasted for more than one hundred years, since October 1795, when Poland was divided among the Russian empire, the Austro-Hungarian empire, and Prussia.

This same destiny had pitted the Poles against one another during World War I, forcing them to fight each other in the armies of Germany, Austria, and Russia—a situation that continued until the end of the conflict, when the Central Powers fell and Marshal Józef Piłsudski dissolved the Regency Council and at last proclaimed Poland's independence. That was November 11, 1918. Almost two years later, on August 15, 1920, the Polish army would save Europe from Soviet invasion by driving its troops away from the Polish capital. The effort seemed doomed from the start, because the army commanded by Piłsudski, together with Generals Józef Haller and Wadyslaw Sikorski, had to fight without any allies against an enemy with greater numbers. The victory over the Red Army seemed so incredible to the Poles that it was nicknamed the "Miracle at the Vistula."

During those first years of the 1920s, all attention in Poland was turned to the country's recently regained independence, and Wadowice was no exception. During the previous century, Wadowice had been annexed by the duchy of Zator, in the kingdom of Galicia and Lodomeria, within

1

the orbit of the Hapsburg empire. In the reconstituted Polish state, Wadowice was now the site of the *Powiat*, a sort of administrative center within
its district. Everyone was talking about Piłsudski, not only because he had
restored and defended Poland, but also because he had taken control of the
government. He had led a coup d'etat in Warsaw in 1926, after the various
parties were unable to create a stable government and the country's economic crisis continued to deepen. Although officially he was only the head
of the armed forces, Piłsudski had in reality become the ruler of the country, without much popular opposition. He was hailed almost everywhere in
Poland as the savior of his country, the commander who had renewed its
hope and its military and economic power, the socialist who had restored
public welfare, improving the lives of the working class and guaranteeing
education for the poor. The Jewish Poles called him *wójek Zydowski* (the
uncle of the Jews), and some of them compared him to the Polish King
Casimir III, nicknamed *Wielki* (the Great). The fourteenth-century ruler
had made his kingdom more prosperous than it had ever been and had
allowed the Jews to establish themselves freely and in large numbers all
over the country, considering them "the king's people," on equal footing
with the Catholics.

The Thursday was market day in the Rynek, the main square of Wadowice, and in the morning the merchants from the nearby villages set up
their *stragan*, their booths, carefully displaying their merchandise. It was all
there: tender red meat, exquisite fish—especially *karp* and *szczupak* (carp
and pike), raised in Radocza, Chocznia, and Inwałd—fragrant cheeses,
like *biały ser*, a white cheese made of cow's milk, or *ser szwajacarski*, a sort
of Swiss cheese. There were incomparable fruits (the intense red of the
apples, strawberries, and currants was especially eye-catching), as well as
rye, wheat, barley, potatoes, tobacco, rapeseed, hemp fiber, and sugar beets.
There were plates and glasses, pots and pans, wooden cutlery and stirring
spoons, the plain implements of a simple life.

The Jewish merchants had their own *stragan*, where they sold the
foods prescribed by their Law. These included fish with fins and scales,
unleavened bread and sweets for the *Shabbat*, and the meat of animals that
chew their cud and have cloven hoofs. These animals had to be killed by
having their throats slit, and then their meat was soaked and salted to drain
out all the blood, in keeping with the Torah. Because pork is forbidden in
the kosher diet (although pigs have cloven hoofs, they do not chew their

cud), the Jewish merchants sold *koszerna kiełbasa*, a beef sausage that was not as flavorful as the pork variety, but was still highly prized.

Setting out from Rynek Square, heading down Zatorska Street toward the Choczenka, a little tributary of the Skawa River, one would come to Wadowice's other town square, Targowica. That's where the fair was held, also on Thursdays. Farmers sold their livestock and poultry there, so every Thursday the noise was deafening, a mixture of grunting, braying, whinnying, bellowing, and bleating. There was a ritual to the buying and selling, with the farmers spending a long time examining the animals to find the best oxen or the sturdiest horses, and then striking up endless negotiations in order to get the best price.

My family didn't own a car, even though ours was one of the most prosperous families in Wadowice. My father, defense attorney Wilhelm Kluger, didn't consider himself a very good driver. So whenever he had to leave the city for work, he usually rented both car and driver at Leon Foltin's garage. Leon had married the beautiful Zosia, daughter of Anielcia, our family's cook, so he always gave my father the most beautiful car and the best driver.

There were taverns all over Wadowice, and every day, late in the afternoon (but often much earlier), the vodka flowed in surprising quantities, restoring the vigor sapped by the day's work. Watching the men drink, you almost had the impression that a little bit of life was restored with each glass, that their newly warmed blood was again able to flow through their veins because of the therapeutic power of that colorless and—at least to the initiated—odorless liquid. There were many varieties, from Żubrówka, a vodka that took its name from the Żubr, a large bison that grazed in the green fields of Puszcza Białowieska; to the favorite vodka of the Jews, Śliwowica, made from plums and with an unmistakable greenish hue; from Wiborowa to Zamkówka and many others. Some people made their own at home at risk of imprisonment, because private distillation was against the law.

At times, not even my father could exempt himself from the vodka ritual (although he also had another one: he was a great smoker of cigarettes, which he was always rolling up himself using a special tobacco that David Aleksandrowicz—a cousin who lived in Kraków—was getting from Turkey specially for him).

Eventually it was time for me to attend elementary school, and there I discovered that one of my classmates was a boy I had noticed many times before on Sunday in the Rynek together with his father. He was blond and had a very pleasant face.

"What's your name?" I asked.

"Karol Wojtyła," the boy said, "but you can call me Lolek."

"I'm Jerzy Kluger. You can call me Jurek if you want."

My birthday, April 4, 1921, made me about a year younger than Lolek, who was born on May 18, 1920, the very same day on which Piłsudski and his soldiers were celebrating the capture of Kiev in Ukrainian territory. So it may not have been an accident that Lolek was given Jozef, the name of the Polish national hero, as his middle name. His first name, Karol, was the same as that of his father, who had served in the army (first as a non-commissioned officer in the Austrian army and then as a lieutenant in the Polish army).

Lolek and I soon became close friends. We were always together in class—except for the two hours of religious instruction each week, since Lolek was Catholic and I was Jewish. In all the other subjects, from Polish grammar to math, from history to singing, from geography to physical education, we were together. We even lived close to each other. Lolek's house was on Koscielna Street, not far from the Rynek, and I could see it from some of the windows of our house.

Every afternoon after school, we would go to Rynek Square to play together. The square was close to both of our houses, which allowed our parents to keep an eye on us. But something else drew us to that spot: a man named Ćwiék, one of the municipal police officers of Wadowice. We watched him every day as he walked up and down that square in his marvelous brown uniform, constantly tapping the palm of his left hand on the hilt of his sword, capturing our imaginations fully.

"I'm telling you, that sword's a fake, Lolek," I said one afternoon.

"But how could a policeman have a fake weapon?" Lolek replied skeptically.

"Believe me," I insisted. "I'm telling you. Besides, have you ever seen him take it out, even once?"

"Well, no, not really," Lolek admitted. "But that's probably because he's never needed to."

"Oh, come on!" I pressed. "He didn't take it out even during the military parade in the Rynek, when all the other officers were displaying their swords. And you know why?"

"No," Lolek said, "I don't."

"I'll tell you why. It's because his sword's made of wood, that's why!" I declared.

One evening a few weeks later, around dinnertime, we saw Ćwiék dozing on a bench, probably worn out from his constant walking. Next to him, on the same bench, was the sword, sheathed as usual. We decided to get a look, once and for all, at that weapon. I went to pull on the hilt while Lolek tugged at the scabbard. The sword refused to budge, so we pulled harder—too hard. We both went tumbling to the ground, together with the sword, which made an unmistakable metallic sound that jolted the soldier from his slumber. Ćwiék was more than just a little angry, and we had to endure some harsh words before we went home, but we were happy all the same. We finally solved the mystery of the sword.

My family's home, on Zatorska Street, was one of the most elegant buildings in Wadowice. Ebel's trattoria was outside the main entrance, and so was Lisko's pastry shop, which was later sold to a man named Hagen-huber. The pastry shop made *kremówki* (a custard-filled puff pastry sand-wich), which Lolek loved. Also beneath our house, but on the side facing the Rynek, were a fabric store and a tavern. The tavern had once been run by my mother's parents, when they had the *propinacja*, which had given them exclusive rights to make and sell distilled spirits in their district when it was part of the Austro-Hungarian empire. The granting of that right, a kind of monopoly over alcoholic beverages in the province, was worth a fortune to Mother's family while it lasted. But the privilege could no lon-ger be exercised under the new Polish state, so the tavern had been rented out. My family owned many properties at the time, including more than one hundred rental homes in Wadowice alone, without counting our fam-ily's vast land holdings.

My mother's mother, Anna Goldberg, took the last name of her deceased husband, Izrael Huppert, who had been president of the Jewish community in Wadowice during the early 1900s, when the local syna-gogue was built according to the design of Karol Korn, a famous archi-tect from Bielsko. The fact that my grandmother belonged to an extremely wealthy family was clear from her maiden name, Goldberg. The reason that this was clearly a rich family's name had to do with a law passed under Austrian domination. The law banned Jews from using their patronym (as in the case of a character in *Pan Tadeusz* by Adam Mickiewicz, Jankiel, whose patronym was Ben Isaac [son of Isaac]) and required them to use last names instead. Last names were literally bought from the Starosta, a sort of city hall, and some were more expensive than others. The most expensive were the ones that contained the word "gold," like Goldberg, but also Goldberger or Goldmann. After the most expensive came a wide range of last names without any meaning at all, like Huppert or Korn. These meaningless names were also fairly expensive, because in the long list of last names that had some sort of meaning, even if one could pay more for a flattering name (like Kluger, from *klug* [wise]), there were many less dignified names, like Hosenduft, which literally means "trouser smell." Such a name could easily give someone the wrong idea.

Grandma Huppert had nine children, including Rozalia, my mother. By the time I'd made friends with Lolek, all of my mother's siblings had married, except for the youngest, my uncle Wiktor Huppert, who lived in Warsaw. He had established himself there as one of the city's most prestigious lawyers, another reason why Grandma was unable to imagine him without a good wife by his side. "It wouldn't take much for you to get engaged to a young lady from a good family," she would tell Uncle Wiktor—now in his forties—every time he went to visit her in Wadowice. "And when you do, make sure you don't wait too long before marrying her!" Naturally, when she spoke of a wife for her son, Grandma Huppert was thinking of a Jewish woman.

In addition to being an excellent lawyer, my father was also president of the Jewish community in Wadowice. He had received his education through high school in Wadowice, after which he went to Vienna and then to Kraków, where he became a law student at the Jagiellonian University, the oldest in the country. The Jagiellonian University had been founded in 1364 by King Casimir the Great, and was named to commemorate the dynasty of the Jagiellonian kings of Poland. In Kraków, Father began to be influenced by the socialist ideas of the Bund, the Jewish socialist party, which rejected communism as an enemy of the Polish state, but also rejected Zionism, because it meant abandoning one's country.

Father also learned to speak Yiddish, the language of European Jews, in Kraków. Yiddish originated in medieval German, but was influenced by Hebrew, Aramaic, and the other languages spoken by the Ashkenazi Jews, including the Romance languages, Polish, and Russian; in its written form, Yiddish continues to use the ancient Hebrew alphabet.

Father enrolled in the Polish socialist party (Polska Partja Socjal-
istyczna), in which he became known for his speaking ability. This natural talent shone through even when he spoke in Yiddish, a language that
he found especially helpful when he had to talk to blue-collar Jewish
workers. He became a soldier in the Austro-Hungarian army, training
in light artillery on Lake Balaton in Hungary, and fought against the
Russians during the First World War. This also meant fighting against
Poles from areas that had been annexed by tsarist Russia, something
he couldn't fathom. Shortly after this, after becoming an officer, he
decided in Kraków to bind his fate with that of Józef Piłsudski, probably to avoid further betraying his socialist ideals. Piłsudski already had
the reputation of a prophet because of his proclamation that Poland
would soon come back to life. My father entered Piłsudski's legions,
which were being formed clandestinely, but which were growing by
attracting the best men. After the war, Father returned to Wadowice,
where he married Rozalia Huppert and had two children. I was the first
child; my sister, Tesia, was two and a half years younger than me.

Most striking about my sister was her refined grace, together with
her sharp and well-trained mind. Tesia had always been the best student in
her class. Helena Szczepanska, her teacher, always reminded me about this
when I went to look for Lolek at his house. She would meet me in front
of the gate, and she always had the same sharp words for me: "Why aren't
you at home studying, like your sister, Tesia? If you want to be head of the
class like her, you need to hit the books, Jurek."

But Tesia's virtues were not limited to the austere pleasure of study.
She was also an excellent tennis player. At first, the sport had been a diver-
sion for her, but she showed such a natural talent for it that she soon
became the strongest player in Wadowice, and not only among the women.
One of my classmates, Stanisław Banas, sometimes invited Tesia and me
to spend the hot summer afternoons at his family's house in Radocza. It
had a tennis court, and every now and then Tesia would practice there.
Stanisław and I would watch her tenacious efforts to transmit power and
movement to the ball, to make it obey her every command. Stanisław commented that if Tesia continued playing that way, nothing would keep her
from becoming a champion. He had no idea that he truly was predicting
the future, because it wasn't long before she was noticed at a tournament
by Jadwiga Jędrzejowska, nicknamed "Jadzia," the most famous female

tennis player in all of Poland. Jadzia had been a finalist at the Grand Slam three times, and she decided that Tesia would be her sparring partner. My family, of course, was overjoyed to hear the news. Grandma Huppert was especially proud. She was the one who had installed, at the *Sokół* (a sort of public gym in Wadowice), a wooden barrier where her niece could practice her volleys. Mother was also pleased. Like Tesia, Mother loved tennis, even though she played the old-fashioned way: only the forehand, no backhand.

A short distance from Zatorska Street was Kościelna Street, where Lolek lived together with his family in a small house. It had a kitchen, a small bedroom and living room, and a bathroom. The owner of their building was a man named Chaim Bałamut. He was Jewish, and had run as a candidate for president of the Jewish community of Wadowice during the same year in which my father had been elected. Lolek's mother, Emilia Kaczorowska, was the fifth of eight children born to a man named Feliks, a craftsman who made coverings for carriages. Emilia's husband, Karol Wojtyła, was originally from Lipnik, a small town near the city of Bielsko Biała. His father, Maciej, Lolek's grandfather, was a master tailor there, and taught his art to his son. Karol worked as a tailor until he enrolled in the army, first under Austria and then in the Polish army, and he was greatly disappointed when he had to leave for health reasons in 1927. Since he was a captain when he retired, practically everyone called him by that title in Wadowice. He had three children, but the only girl, Olga, died soon after she was born, in 1914. His first son, Edmund, was born in 1906, while Karol was much younger, having been born in 1920.

When Lolek and I played with our classmates, our favorite game was Cowboys and Indians. We got the idea from the novels of Karol May, a famous writer of Westerns. One of his novels was *Old Shatterhand*, named after the title character, who could break rocks with his fists. The other main character was the Indian chief Winnetou. The two men were rivals, but they also respected one another. Lolek and I often pretended to be Old Shatterhand and Winnetou. Lolek in particular would recite entire passages from the book, obviously having learned the whole thing by heart, and I loved listening to him. We would also play with model airplanes, which we made from balsa wood. The challenge was to see who could make his plane go the farthest, using rubber bands to launch them from the same starting point. Lolek was not very good at making models, so his airplanes never went far. I, however, worked well with my hands. My planes had just the right wing design, so they readily took to the air, free from the bonds of gravity, and always went farther than Lolek's.

In 1929, when Lolek was about nine years old, he was struck by tragedy. His mother, Emilia, died from an infection of her heart and kidneys. The loss was extremely painful for the entire family. After the death, I would spend many afternoons at Lolek's house, partly so we could both keep his father company. Lolek didn't want to leave his father alone, seeing how deeply saddened he was after his mother's death. By now the two of them were all alone in Wadowice, because Edmund had moved to Kraków to complete his medical studies at the Jagiellonian University. I was perfectly happy to spend time at Lolek's because it gave me the chance to listen to Captain Wojtyła, who spun his marvelous stories with all of the drama and excitement of a play. Many of his stories were about their country, about its tumultuous upheavals when it was still a great empire— and when Lolek and I listened to him, hypnotized by his penetrating eyes, we saw in our imaginations the vast plains of Poland being torn apart by the invading armies; from the captain's unique storytelling gift, we felt the warmth of the soldiers' bodies, we saw the unflinching Cossack fighters and the resigned determination in the eyes of the Turks, we heard the war cry of the Swedes, we smelled the putrid odor of defeat, and we saw the lifeless bodies after the frenzy of the battle.

In fact, even though he did not have a formal education, Captain Wojtyła was self-taught in history and literature, being an avid reader, and my father never concealed his profound respect for the captain. Actually, because the captain had gained all of his knowledge outside of school, which he never had the opportunity to attend, that seemed to make him ever more worthy of admiration.

Most of the stories that Lolek's father told were inspired by the famous Polish author Henryk Sienkiewicz, who had recounted the hardship and triumph of Poland's history in a trilogy that Captain Wojtyła had collected together with many other books. These volumes made up the little library that he kept in the living room, on a shelf set against one of the walls. The library had a little bit of everything, from Żeromski's *Doktór Piotr* to Mickiewicz's *Pan Tadeusz*; from Słowacki's *Poezje* to Norwid's *Promethidion*, and many others—including the works of a man named Zegadłowicz, an author originally from Wadowice who had been a classmate of my father.

Among all these books was Sienkiewicz's *Quo Vadis?* for which the author was awarded a Nobel Prize in literature at the beginning of the twentieth century. As for the Latin title, Lolek told me that it had been inspired by one of the stories about the life of Saint Peter. According to the account, the apostle was walking down the Appian Way together with Nazarius, leaving Rome in the direction of Campania, having decided to establish the Church elsewhere because Christians were being massacred in the eternal city. But along the way, Jesus appeared to Peter, who threw himself at his feet, saying, "Quo vadis, Domine?" (Where are you going, Lord?). Jesus answered that he was going to Rome to be crucified a second time, because the apostle was abandoning his people. On hearing these words, Peter decided to turn around and go back.

Overpowered by a desire for reading that Captain Wojtyła's hunger for knowledge had helped to reinforce in us, Lolek and I spent many hours reading Sienkiewicz's books—and not only his. We read practically every book in that library. Mostly we read at the table in the kitchen, in the light from the window facing Koscielna Street. The window also faced the left-hand side of the Church of Wadowice, where there was a sundial with a Latin phrase inscribed beside it: "TEMPUS FUGIT, AETERNITAS MANET" (Time flies, eternity remains). Time really did seem to fly by while we read. Only when the last glimmer of light was flickering away in the kitchen did I know it was time to go home. Even so, I often sat in silence for just a little while longer, watching Lolek's father in the next room, kneeling before the sacred image of the Black Madonna of Częstochowa, Queen of Poland, his hands clasped in prayer, gazing intently at the sword-scarred face of the Virgin.

Every year around springtime, the snow melted away from the vast area around Wadowice. After the intense cold of the winter, those sprawling plains looked like brown and lifeless soil. But with the summer heat, they would again emerge full of lush vegetation, and there was a kind of delightful thrill in the fragrant air, overpowering the senses. Lolek and I would eagerly await the annual plunge back into those golden fields.

One year my excitement over summer vacation was especially strong. After waiting anxiously for the news, I had just learned that I had been accepted into the fifth year of middle school. In order to be admitted, I had to undergo a little examination, and although the test was not especially difficult, I had nonetheless been nervous about the outcome.

The day when the results were released, I ran down Adama Mick-iewicka Street to the Marcin Wadowita school, climbing the stairs to the second floor, where the results had been posted on a wall next to the principal's office. I shouted for joy. At that point, I only had to make sure that Lolek had also been admitted, although it was difficult to imagine the contrary. Once I saw Lolek's name on the list, I decided to bring him the good news personally.

Breathless, I soon came to Koscielna Street. Lolek's father told me that Lolek was not at home, that he had gone to Mass. I headed toward the church and entered that hallowed building. Once inside, I looked around and saw that Lolek was in the sanctuary, serving the Mass. I walked almost all the way down the central nave, looking urgently at my friend, to let him know I had something important to tell him. Lolek fixed his intense eyes on me and gestured for me to be patient and sit down, in order to avoid disturbing the liturgy in any way. I started looking for a place to sit in the pews on the right-hand side, toward the back of the church. Finding an empty spot next to two women, I sat down and quietly listened to the recitation of the Creed and the Our Father. The women stared at me and then began whispering to each other. I knew they were talking about me, but didn't know why. Finally, while Communion was being given out, the one closer to me explained.

"Tell me, young man, aren't you Kluger's son?"

"Yes," I answered.

"But what are you doing here? You are a Jew, and Jews aren't allowed in church!"

My head began spinning, because I had no idea that a Jew could sin by entering a Catholic church. No one in my observant family ever said such a thing; nor had the rabbi, and he was strict. If he ever caught me at the synagogue on the Sabbath with my prayer book open to the wrong page, he always scolded me.

"I'm sorry," I said. "I didn't know." Then I fell silent, almost as a sign of deep contrition, until I heard the priest give the blessing and the faithful respond "Amen," feeling a sense of sudden relief as the women next to me moved toward the exit. I waited a little while longer until the central nave cleared out, and then I quickly went to the pulpit where Lolek was.

"What happened?" Lolek asked.

"We've been admitted to middle school," I said, my voice trembling a little.

"That's not what I meant," Lolek continued. "I wanted to know what the woman sitting next to you said."

"She asked me if I was the son of Wilhelm Kluger, and when I said yes, she told me I wasn't allowed in the church, because I'm a Jew." And I added, "Believe me, Lolek, I didn't know Jews aren't allowed in here."

"What are you talking about?" my friend interrupted, frowning, and then he turned toward the woman, who was at the door. "Doesn't she know that Jews and Catholics are all children of the same God?" he said in a loud voice. The question could be heard clear across the church, and many of the faithful turned around, including the woman herself, who made the sign of the cross and went out. "Jews and Catholics descend from one God, Jurek, who is the God of Abraham," Lolek said, turning again to face me. "You can come here whenever you want."

At the time, Lolek was barely ten years old.

CHAPTER 2

MIDDLE SCHOOL YEARS

Early in the morning, the Rynek was full of eager children, unvarnished adolescents, students perfect in feature and dress, all heading toward Adama Mickiewicza Street, where the Marcin Wadowita middle school and high school stood. Lolek and I wore the distinctive uniform of the Marcin Wadowita school, a blue jacket with a *tarcza* sewn onto the left sleeve, a red patch embroidered with the number identifying which school the student attended. Up through the fourth year of middle school, the patch was blue, like the jacket, but the jacket we wore now was different. The old one had been buttoned up to the neck, with a white kerchief on the inside that was changed when it got dirty. But with the fifth year of middle school, the jacket had only three buttons, and a blue tie had to be worn beneath it. On the shoulders were epaulets indicating the student's grade. In 1930, the year that Lolek and I took the test to graduate to the fifth year, Poland enacted the Reforma Jędrzejewiczów, a school reform that added two years to elementary school, reducing middle school to six years. But because the reform went into effect after our admission to the middle school's fifth year, Lolek and I continued according to the old system of eight years there.

Apart from me, there were only two other Jewish boys in my class, out of more than thirty students. One of these, Zygmunt Zelinger, was behind by a grade, because of a tragedy that had taken place at school. One day, he had fought with another student named Buszek, the son of Wadowice's postmaster. At a certain point, Zygmunt pushed Buszek, who fell and hit his head on the corner of one of the benches fastened to the floor. He died from the injury. This event, already tragic in itself, threatened at a certain point to turn into something more, because some saw it as a Jew killing a Catholic, and the fear was that the Catholics might retaliate. Even my father, as president of the Jewish community of Wadowice, did not conceal his apprehension. Given what was already being said about the Jews, my father realized that nothing could be more insidiously dangerous than such an accusation, and his personal intervention was decisive in persuading everyone that it had simply been a tragic accident.

Almost all the teachers at Marcin Wadowita were Catholic. There were only two Jewish teachers: Professor Raiter, who taught Judaism, and Sabina Rottenberg, called "Sabcia," who taught German on a temporary basis. She was very attractive, and every time she entered the class, after presenting the topic of the day, she sat down with her legs crossed, losing herself in her thoughts. Because she wore a skirt, some of the students (mainly the delinquents) took turns dropping a coin or something else on the floor, bending down to get a look, and then exchanging satisfied chuckles, until she realized what was happening and yelled *Ruhe!* to make them stop.

The students were signaled to put away their textbooks and take out the ones for the next lesson by the ringing of a bell, which was the job of the school janitor, Mr. Pyrek, until a terrible accident in September 1935. During one of the lessons, a metallic sound came from the street, like the braking of a car, and then a dull thud followed by the sound of someone crying out. Everyone went out into the street. Mr. Pyrek was lying there, motionless, covered in his own blood. He had been hit by a driver who had not seen him crossing the street. They tried in vain to revive him, and someone ran to get a doctor, but there was no way to save him. A crowd quickly gathered around the spot of the accident, but at a certain point I realized that Lolek wasn't around anymore. Then I saw him just a moment later, when I heard the ringing of a bell behind me, and turned to see Fr. Kotowiecki, the vicar of the parish of Wadowice, with Lolek beside him in the white vestments that he wore when he served Mass, holding a censer by its chain. And as the incense burned, its spent substance trailing away in the air, Fr. Kotowiecki bent down and administered extreme unction to the unfortunate man, hoping that his soul had not yet left his body. These actions touched me deeply.

During the youthful years spent with Lolek, I had the chance to witness his deep religious faith, which had seemed to support him during the great suffering that his family endured—first with his mother's death, when he was nine years old, and then with another tragedy that struck just a few years later. While his brother Edmund was caring for a scarlet fever patient at Powszechny Hospital in Bielsko, where he worked as a doctor, he caught the disease himself and died a short time later. The loss was extremely painful for Lolek. He relied heavily on prayer and faith and made numerous pilgrimages together with his father, mostly to the shrine of Kalwaria Zebrzydowska, a small-scale reproduction of the holy sites of Jerusalem linked to the life of Jesus and his mother. They also went often to Jasna Góra, where there was a chapel with the image of Our Lady of Częstochowa, the Black Madonna to whom Lolek's father was so devoted. On the day of the janitor's death, I saw once again the proof of my friend's profound spirituality, because as soon as Lolek realized that nothing more could be done for the man's body, he turned his attention to his soul, asking the priest to give him the last rites.

At least once a week, usually on Wednesday afternoon, Professor Gebhardt gathered his students in class to discuss current events. We talked about all sorts of things on those occasions, but one of the most hotly discussed topics was that of the revival of anti-Semitism in Europe. During those meetings, I noticed a certain fanaticism that was stirring in Poland at that time, inspiring in many people a hatred that was increasingly focused on the Jews. This was a genuine threat, because after the diaspora Poland had attracted one of the largest Jewish communities in the world, with more than 3.5 million Jews, second in size only to the one in the United States. Thus, the danger of anti-Semitism was much greater in Poland than in many other European countries. There were seething, delirious articles in *Orędownik* and *Polska Karta*, exclaiming "Na zidow!" (Kill the Jews!). Or one could consider the homilies of Cardinal August Hlond, the primate of Poland, who urged the faithful to undermine Jewish businesses, because he believed they were after economic power. He kept repeating *Bojkot owszem* (On with the boycott). The anti-Semitism was even expressed in a document that had been circulating for some time, *The Protocols of the Elders of Zion,* about a secret plan of the Jews to create a universal alliance for world domination. Because of the extremist ideas that the document contained, at a certain point it was banned from the middle school. One student caught in class reading it was immediately called to the office of the principal, Jan Krolikiewicz, who put strict measures in place.

The *Protocols* was a false document, as had been proven already, inspired by the Okhrana, the secret police of the tsars, and created in an effort to justify the atrocious pogroms unleashed in Russia beginning in 1903. The lies that it contained had made great headway among the fanatical hordes, and even worse, a more horrifying idea would soon be added: that the very blood of the Jewish race was cursed.

Some of the discussions that Professor Gebhardt organized could become very heated. Two of my classmates in particular had no problem accepting some of the anti-Jewish propaganda, and they openly endorsed it. "Should we be surprised by the idea of a Jewish plot?" one of them did not hesitate to observe. "The Jews dominate business just like they do the banks, and the newspapers just like they do politics. It's a race in a clear conflict of interest with our country." While he was saying this, I watched the faces of my other classmates, looking for expressions of disgust or rejection of this dangerous and even obscene slander. I did not conceal my satisfaction when I discovered that the rest of the class did not share this fanaticism. Lolek above all rejected intolerance, frequently drawing on his knowledge of literature to refute it. He knew the writings very well, and that Polish authors celebrated their two great traditions: Catholicism and Judaism. Lolek quoted Andrzej Towiański, a Lithuanian mystical thinker, who was said to have had miraculous powers and had written a book titled *Skład Zasad* in 1848. In it, he had called for respect, fellowship, and aid on behalf of the people of Israel, referring to the Jews as *starsi bracia* (older brothers). Lolek also quoted Adam Mickiewicz and his work *Pan Tadeusz*, which featured a Jewish character named Jankiel, who had spied for the Polish army against the Russians and had narrated the history of Poland to the sound of cimbalom, ending with the singing of the *Mazurek Dabrowskiego*, the country's anthem. "And when the music and singing were over," Lolek would say, "one of the people there spoke out and said that Jankiel was a kindhearted Jew, who loved his country like a true Pole."

In Wadowice, news of the spread of anti-Semitism in Poland was less troubling because it seemed to come from so far away. Apart from an occasional flare-up, relations between Jewish and Catholic students were relaxed. In my class was a Catholic boy named Teofil Bojes, the son of a miner, who came to school every day by train from Woźniki, a village not far from Wadowice. He did this for many years, until an economic crisis forced the mine where his father worked to close, and he could no longer pay for Teofil to ride the train every day. In order to allow him to continue attending school, Teofil was admitted to the Bursa—a sort of dormitory that also had a cafeteria—which accommodated the students who lived far away, lived in places without good transportation links to the city, or were simply poor. The Bursa was financed by a committee formed by the more prosperous families in Wadowice, and my family was among its biggest supporters. In addition, every morning Mother filled a sack with large quantities of the best foods, intended to feed my classmates who were unable to afford a snack. I knew this food was to go to the non-Jews in my class because much of it was food that the Torah forbids the Jews to eat.

This natural compromise between Jews and Catholics was part of everyday life in Wadowice. Mild insinuations were addressed, and every now and then occasional damage was done to Jewish shops and homes, as a feeble demonstration by some group of students from Kraków or by the processions making their way from the villages around Wadowice toward one of the shrines. The word *Żyd*, meaning "Jew," had been written once beneath my father's study, while some Jewish shopkeepers had to endure even more offensive statements. When the procession of the faithful heading to Kalwaria Zebrzydowska went through the city, a few stones were sometimes thrown at the half-closed windows and shuttered shops of Jews. This massive stream of the faithful passed through on foot, starting from the surrounding villages, and even some from very far away. When they reached Wadowice, they took the route from Adama Mickiewicza Street to 3 Maja Street, crossing through the city, and then continued east for another nine miles, toward Klecza, finally reaching the shrine at the foot of Mount Zar. Most of the people went there on Good Friday or in the middle of August for the feast of the Assumption of the Virgin Mary. While they were making these processions, the soldiers of the Twelfth Infantry Regiment stood on guard in Wadowice, charged with preventing any sort of violence in the city. Because they were stationed along the entire route of the procession, giving an impression of absolute order, their presence alone was usually enough to discourage the less tolerant Catholics.

In addition, the commander of the regiment, Colonel Stawarz, was particularly conscientious toward the Jews, contrary to the rumors that had circulated when he arrived in Wadowice, branding him as an anti-Semite. There was so much concern about him among the representatives of the Jewish community that my father, a man of great moderation, refused to attend the reception held at the Kasyno Oficerskie, the officers' club, to welcome the new commander.

"But why have you decided not to go?" Mother asked Father, incredulous. She was especially disappointed that she would not be able to dance the traditional polonaise that she enjoyed so much, but my father was able to convince her all the same.

"Because it appears that the colonel is an anti-Semite," he explained. "And if it's true, the head of the Jewish community and his wife certainly cannot go to celebrate his arrival!"

The ceremony was then postponed until Christmastime. In the following months, those rumors continued to prompt Father to maintain a certain distance from the new officer, until one day by chance they found themselves face to face. It was winter, and the snow was falling so hard that it had mounted up all along the railway tracks, so high the engines couldn't get past. The two men were waiting for the train to Kraków at the station in Wadowice when a voice announced over the public address system that the train was cancelled because of bad weather. Father was planning to go to Foltin's shop and rent his car and driver, but then Colonel Stawarz approached him.

"Are you Wilhelm Kluger, the head of the Jewish community of Wadowice?"

"Yes," my father replied.

"My name is Stawarz, and I am the new commander of the Twelfth Infantry Regiment. A car is coming to pick me up, and if you would like, I would be very happy to offer you a ride to Kraków," the colonel continued, offering his hand to Father as he spoke. My father naturally accepted, and so they rode together to the city, where each went to take care of his own business after arranging to meet again that evening. They had dinner together at Hawelka, one of the best restaurants in Kraków, drinking vodka and talking late into the night. During the long conversation, my father was finally convinced that Stawarz wasn't an anti-Semite at all. They even became close friends, giving Lolek and me the opportunity to take private riflery lessons with the colonel, who had represented Poland at the 1936 Olympics in Berlin.

The cold winter air put an end to the brief reprieve of summer and fall, and the snow began to spread everywhere, down the streets and along the rooftops of Wadowice, over the fields, the forests, and the surrounding hills, dressing the landscape in an unvaried garment—in a soft glow that concealed all of its features.

Lolek and I had learned to ski when we were little boys, going with our friends to Czuma, about half a mile south of the Rynek, toward the mountains, with an unbroken blanket of white stretching from one horizon to the other. Beneath us was a gentle slope, just enough for us to be inspired to tug on our bulky woolen pants and let ourselves slide along for the first time on those wooden slats. Usually the skis were made from *jesion*, the wood of the ash tree, or from more highly prized hickory. The best skis came from Tatar, a woodworker in Klecza.

As we grew older, Lolek and I moved on to the tougher slopes around our area. Lolek's technique was not as good as mine, and I was also afraid of breaking my skis. At a certain point, Lolek even owned a pair of hickory skis, which my grandmother had bought from Tatar for his birthday, although that was not the gift she had originally planned for him. Toward the end of the 1930s, I had been given a motorbike, a 100 cc. Łucznik Setka. Only a few other people in Wadowice had one of these, including my classmates Stanisław Banas, Bogusław Sworzen, and Zrylek Zelinger. Lolek also enjoyed my bike a great deal, and he could often be seen riding on it, either behind me or by himself, when I would lend it to him to go riding in the Rynek. When I told Grandma Huppert that Lolek would also like one, she decided to buy a Łucznik Setka for him, too. But when Lolek's father learned about it, he went to visit my grandmother and pleaded with her not to give the bike to his son, because he was afraid he might fall and hurt himself. So Grandma Huppert, knowing how much Lolek enjoyed skiing, decided to give him a pair of skis made by the best woodworker in Klecza.

Even though I enjoyed skiing and skating and *ferbel*, my greatest passion was ping-pong, which was mostly played at school in the afternoon, because there was a table well suited for the game next to a wall in the library. Lolek was also a good ping-pong player, although not as good as me, and I'd spot him ten points when we played together.

Lolek's passions lay elsewhere. During those years, he had learned Greek, could speak Latin fluently, became increasingly fascinated with literature and philosophy, and charmed his listeners with his sophisticated reflections. The cardinal archbishop of Kraków, Adam Sapieha, once visited our school. The son of a prince, the cardinal was a highly educated and refined man. He had come to administer the sacrament of confirmation, which the Catholic students were receiving in May 1938. It was decided that a speech would be given to welcome him, and that Lolek would be the one to deliver it. It was graduation year for the eighth-graders, and Lolek's words were a happy recollection of those years, the delights of friendship, the teachers they loved so much, the important things they had learned, and the profound meaning of the sacrament that they were about to receive. While he was listening to Lolek speak, Cardinal Sapieha nodded in agreement from his seat next to the principal, his dignified demeanor softening as he was won over by the pupil and his words.

"What is that student's name?" he suddenly asked Mr. Krolikiewicz, nodding toward Lolek with the sort of elegance that was characteristic of him, and covering his mouth as if afraid to interrupt the young speaker.

"His name is Karol Wojtyła, and he's our best student," the principal replied.

When Lolek finished speaking, and while the students and their parents were beginning to move around and talk again, Cardinal Sapieha approached Lolek. The cardinal placed his hand on the boy's cheek and asked him, "What have you decided to do after you graduate? Are you thinking about entering the seminary?"

"No," Lolek replied. "I have decided to study Polish literature and philosophy at the university."

The cardinal's face registered some regret, his eyelids drooping a little and his lips pursed in disappointment. As he turned around, in an almost reproachful tone, he said, "What a shame." And he walked away.

Lolek's great love was the theater, and even as a little boy he had shown great interest in it, bordering on devotion. He was only eight years old when a small amateur company gave him the job of prompter, putting him behind the curtains during rehearsals to feed the actors the right lines. Often he knew the play so well that he didn't need to look at the script. He had an extraordinary memory with a special facility for literary works of all kinds, so much so that he was able to memorize Adam Mickiewicz's epic poem *Pan Tadeusz* from start to finish, reciting it without hesitation when he was just barely twelve years old.

Many other people in Wadowice shared Lolek's passion—one Jewish girl in particular. In his building on Koscielna Street, in addition to the Bałamuts there was another Jewish family, the Beers, who had a daughter named Regina, although everyone called her Ginka. She was very beautiful, and everyone at school was in love with her, including me. I would make my classmates jealous by saying I had seen her the night before while I was leaving Lolek's house and she was returning to hers.

But we all realized we had no place in her thoughts, or at least not the kind we would have liked. Ginka, after all, was a few years older than my crowd, and we were not her only admirers. Swarms of young officials and lawyers buzzed all around her, trying all sorts of outlandish maneuvers just to get her to look at them. In spite of all this, Ginka had a special bond with Lolek, because they both loved the theater and acted on stage together. More than the rest, they were the ones worth watching when they performed, completely caught up in the drama and always demonstrating their surprising talent for acting.

After Ginka graduated, she decided to study medicine at Jagiellonian University. She moved to Kraków with a friend, Marycha Weberówna, the daughter of a doctor in Wadowice. Because they were both Jewish, they had to deal with the rigid rules at the university, according to which only a limited number of places were available for Jewish students in certain faculties, including that of medicine. When finding out about their difficulties being admitted to the university, the principal of the girls' school, Maria Szybalska, decided to help them. If she couldn't do it—she, who during World War I had joined Piłsudski's legions by pretending to be a man, had participated in the Miracle on the Vistula, and had even reached the rank of lieutenant—then no one could. In fact, Principal Szybalska had become a sort of national heroine after the war ended and her story became known. After talking with the right people, she succeeded in having the two Jewish girls admitted to the university, and Ginka's dream of becoming a doctor seemed to be coming true. But as fate would have it, in Kraków Marycha developed a relationship with a young man suspected of being a communist. One night the police broke into the room that Ginka and Marycha were renting, and beneath Marycha's bed they found some communist pamphlets and some flyers calling for protests, all belonging to her boyfriend. He was arrested, and the girls were suspended from the university. Both of them returned to Wadowice. Ginka was deeply disturbed by what had happened, and she was convinced that she and her friend had been suspended because they were Jewish. "The truth is that Poland doesn't want us," she told Lolek once. Meanwhile, a more drastic plan was forming in her mind. In addition to being the Wadowice director of Bank Ludowy—an important Polish financial institution run entirely by Jews but with many Catholic clients—her father was also the vice president of the Zionist Party, so he had many contacts in Palestine. Ginka decided to move there. Kraków was not far away, but Tel Aviv was on the other side of the world, as Lolek knew very well.

On the day of her departure, Ginka went to the Wojtyła home to say good-bye. Captain Wojtyła embraced her and tried to convince her that there were other Catholics in Poland like them, who were not hostile toward Jews. But Lolek said nothing. He was standing in the corner of the living room by the painting of the Black Madonna of Częstochowa. Ginka approached him, and she must have been surprised that her friend wasn't saying a word, because she had become so accustomed to his grand speeches. She understood his silence when she touched his cheek. He was crying.

Although Lolek was very involved in the theater, especially during his last years at school, we continued to spend time together, and we were frequently at each other's home. And because Lolek enjoyed fine music, my father invited Lolek every time my father's string quartet performed. Sometimes our family even offered a series of concerts in which everything was prepared with exquisite care—from the selection of food to the choice of guests, from the embroidered tablecloths to the silver. And then, all lined up in a row, were the crystal glasses full of vodka, which the musicians tossed back after performing each piece, giving Lolek and me the impression that the liquor provided them with the notes the musicians needed for the next selection.

Our house also had a radio, a gramophone, and a variety of vinyl records, mostly opera, plus the records borrowed from my cousin Wanda's father, Bronisław Huppert, who lived on the same floor as we did. Lolek and I especially enjoyed listening to Jan Kiepura, a very famous singer at the time—and a Jew of Polish origin—who in addition to being considered one of the best tenors in the world, equal to Caruso and Gigli, was also an excellent actor. He performed in musical films that were very successful, especially in America. On one occasion in particular Lolek was able to attend a live performance by a tenor. While Colonel Jaklicz—Stawarz's predecessor—was still the commander of the Twelfth Regiment, a man named David Kussawiecki came to Wadowice for his military service. Although Kussawiecki was only twenty-one years old, he was already one of the most important cantors of Jewish prayers, together with two of his brothers. They sang the liturgy in the synagogue of Warsaw, on Tłumacka Street. The Kussawieckis were so famous that even before the war the eldest brother, Moishe, had become a celebrity in New York. As head of the Jewish community of Wadowice, my father asked David Kussawiecki to sing the *Sobotnia Modlitwa*, the Sabbath prayer, at the synagogue. As soon as he accepted, the most important figures in the city were invited, from the head of the county council to the head of the tribunal, from the public prosecutor to the principals of the boys' and girls' schools, plus the professors and many others.

"I would like the captain and Lolek to come to the synagogue on the Sabbath as well," Father told me at one point. I was immediately overjoyed, and I ran to extend the invitation to Lolek. I was not at all concerned that such a proposal, which would require them to enter a Jewish temple, would seem inappropriate to practicing Catholics. I thought again of what Lolek had told me a few years earlier, when I, as a Jew, had set foot in a church, and how my friend had reassured me that this was not a sin, because Jews and Catholics came from the same God. In the same way, I thought that a Catholic would not be committing a sin by setting foot in a synagogue.

The following Sabbath, there was a large assembly at the synagogue. Crossing the threshold of the large central door, one entered a wide space with three galleries, oriented so that the faithful were facing Jerusalem, as prescribed by the Torah. There were rows of benches, with racks on the back to hold the prayer books, about fifteen books for each row. They were the same books that were placed on the *ammùd*, the pulpit, and on the *bimàh*, a platform raised slightly above the floor, although the type in the books opened on the lectern was larger to make it easier for the cantor to read them. On the back wall, behind the pulpit, was the *aròn hakkodeš*, the ark containing the long scrolls of the sacred scriptures, covered with light-colored corduroy with gold embroidery. When the cover was removed, it revealed the white, blue, and silver of those ancient manuscripts, and the rich decorations traced on the sheepskin. In front of the *aròn hakkodeš* stood the *ner tamìd*, the "eternal lamp" that always remained lit, to commemorate the menorah in the Temple of Jerusalem that continued to burn for eight days after the temple was desecrated by the Seleucid marauders. On either side of the *aròn hakkodeš* were rows of seats, traditionally the more important ones placed at the back wall. The people who sat in these seats, including my father, were looking toward the pulpit and therefore toward the main assembly of the faithful. More benches were placed beside the pulpit, set sideways in relation to the others. On one of these—the one on the right, closest to the platform of the *ammùd*—my grandfather Zacharia Kluger used to sit.

Practically every member of the congregation had an assigned place in the synagogue. Apart from Father, who was given a privileged seat because he was president of the Jewish community, and me (I usually sat next to my father), the rest of the Kluger family had their places in the upper balcony, which was reserved for the women. There the female members of the Kluger family had the front middle row, and the central spot belonged to Anna Huppert—that is, when she went to synagogue on the Sabbath, which she hadn't done in a while. Some of the seats were reserved for Jewish soldiers, and there were many of them in the Twelfth Infantry Regiment in Wadowice. Many Catholic soldiers had also come to attend Kussawiecki's performance, accompanied by some of the officers.

The various figures who had been invited found places on the benches that remained available. On this occasion, I sat next to Lolek and his father. The *hazzan*, the cantor, made his entrance, and the temple fell silent. David Kussawiecki was wearing the traditional white *tales* with its blue stripe. Under his robe, you could see the green pants legs of his military uniform. The performance lasted about an hour, during which time the young soldier demonstrated the reason for his fame, intoning the prayers with a powerful, sublime voice. Although much of the audience could only follow the melody, knowing nothing about Hebrew, from the comments I heard when Kussawiecki stopped singing, I was certain that everyone had enjoyed the performance, There was a buzz of excitement inside the temple. "I'm telling you, the way his voice echoed along the ceiling, I saw the chandeliers shaking," one Jewish man said to a group of people as they walked toward the main door. As everyone was leaving, including the many Catholics at the synagogue that day, there was a pure spirit of togetherness in that crowd, the mutual respect between the two communities that seemed to brook no exceptions in Wadowice.

The same togetherness and spirit held true for the students of the Marcin Wadowita school. In the springtime, we finally rediscovered the joys of playing soccer, holding matches of Jews against Catholics, a division that held no significance other than it was just the quickest way to split up the teams. It wasn't a strict rule. For example, when the goalie for the Jewish team—Poldek Golberger, the dentist's son, who lived one floor beneath me—couldn't play, one of the Catholics, usually Lolek, would take his place between the goalposts.

The spirit of competition was so fierce that even though he was not a Jew, Lolek showed no intention of taking it easy on the Catholics when he played goalie for the Jewish side—hurling himself to the ground toward the oncoming shot, his hair disheveled, sometimes taking the blow when a foot caught him instead of the ball. Getting hurt wasn't unusual, because the ground was hard and many of the players wore boots instead of sneakers. Once Lolek was hurt fairly seriously after being hit hard while defending the goal, and my mother and grandmother tended to his injury. Seeing Lolek cross in front of our house with his head bleeding, they forbade him to let his father see him in that condition, and they disinfected the wound before applying a linen bandage to his head.

Graduation exams were in mid-May 1938. One essential condition for being allowed to take them was *dostateczne* (at least a passing grade) in all subjects. Almost everyone in our class took the exams. There were three written tests, one on either Latin or Greek and the others of the student's choosing. The students also selected a fourth subject for an oral exam.

I began considering which subjects I should choose. In the end, I selected Latin, history, and mathematics for the written test, and physics for the oral exam. I had received good grades in all of these subjects, and I was one of the best students in his class in science. At test time, many of my classmates looked to me for help with the answers. Lolek, who sat at the desk in front of mine, had come up with a unique method for getting hints, one ingenious enough to be concealed from the professor. I would use the back of a pencil to trace signs and numbers on Lolek's back, and Lolek was sharp enough to figure out what the tracings were and write them down on his own paper. But when he made the effort, Lolek was very good at mathematics on his own, making calculations and solving equations easily, as proven by his good grades in the subject. His favorite subjects, of course, were literature and language. I had my own preferences; for example, I had never before acquired a taste for Latin or Greek, but now even these appealed to me, now that I was counting down the days to the end of school. It was coming fast.

On the first day of the graduation exams, a gloom came over me. I crossed the Rynek that morning like a lamb going to slaughter. I knew I had to translate a sonnet by Horace, but it turned out that the verses weren't very difficult after all—not for me, anyway. Some of the others had trouble with them, especially the students who had been held back, and after about an hour they all began taking turns going to the bathroom. There, written on a roll of toilet paper, was the translation. No one seemed to be sure who had put the translation there. Maybe it was an indulgent janitor. But everyone knew where it had come from. On Adama Mickiewicza Street, across from Marcin Wadowita, to the right of the courthouse, there was a building where two Jewish sisters lived. They had pear-shaped bodies and had never been beautiful, but they were even less attractive now that they were getting older. They were even starting to grow more noticeable moustaches. Nevertheless, they were sought out as tutors, since they had graduated from teaching school years before and gave excellent lessons in Latin. Some of the students had asked them for help with the translation test, and, strangely, the sisters made no objection.

A relay was set up. One student smuggled the test out of the classroom, and another took it to the sisters. After the translation was brought back, it was placed in the bathroom. I didn't go to look, because I was afraid of getting caught by one of the professors. There was just one verse that I wasn't quite sure of, but Lolek let me copy from his paper, bending to one side so I could see.

I received *bardzo dobrze* (very good) on all of the written tests, meaning that I could skip the oral portions. Now the physics exam was my last obstacle. Lolek also got *bardzo dobrze* on the written exams. When my family found out the results, everyone was a little bit stunned, but not because of Lolek's scores. Lolek was at the top of the class, and because he was such an excellent student they couldn't believe that I had done just as well.

"Come on," Grandma Huppert said happily, after an initial expression of surprise. "Now you just have to take care of physics, and if you pass that, all you have to do is choose your gift!"

I took the exam a few days later, and it wasn't very demanding, since I liked the subject and had prepared well for it. I especially enjoyed mechanics and had decided to study it at the university. When I finally received my diploma, I was even happier than I had imagined I would be. Without caring what anyone thought, I raced down the street like a conquering hero, all the way to my house.

"It's over, it's over!" I exclaimed when I entered the house, repeating it as I ran from one room to the next, until I reached my own bedroom, where I flung myself onto my bed together with my books. I remained there for a moment with my face buried in the pillow, while my mother, grandmother, and sister gathered around the bed. I looked up and saw them standing there, beaming. My mother sat down on the edge of the bed and proudly kissed me.

"Promises must be kept," she said. "What do you want as a gift?"

I had just one wish. "I would like to visit Adas this summer, in Rome," I answered. Adas was my cousin, a few years older than me, handsome, and very successful with the ladies. He had been living in Rome for a few months, working for an important coal company, the Consorzio Robur.

My mother could not disappoint me. "Very well," she said. "I will speak with your father about it, and we will try to send you to visit Adas this summer." Then she hugged me tenderly. "You know," she said, "you're a man now."

Like every year, the *komers*, the graduation dance, was being held at the Kasyno Urzędnicze, the state officials' club on 3 Maja Street. I was absolutely convinced that it would be a great opportunity to win the heart of some girl, because there would be many of them there, buoyant with excitement over their own graduation.

Toward the end of our time at school, my classmates and I had taken dance lessons at Marcin Wadowita, and some of the graduating class were excellent dancers, Lolek among them. Mostly they had been taught the typical Polish dances, like the polonaise and the *Krakówiak*, but they also learned the more classical dances, like the waltz, the tango, and the mazurka. I also knew that I would have no hesitation in making my move, no fear of competing with the many young officers and lawyers who would be at the dance and who seemed to be very attractive to the young ladies. Now that I had come of age, I could make free use of the vodka at the bar, in the little room off the dance floor.

That evening, the hall of the Kasyno Urzędnicze hosted all forty-five of the graduating students of Marcin Wadowita. Four of the students didn't come, because they had failed their exams and didn't have anything to celebrate. The fact that our class was so large was partly explained by the fact that many students had been held back. Some of them were only one year behind. But others had become accustomed to failing, like Bolesław Pomezański, who was two years older than the others, and especially Poldek Zweig, who was four years older.

A little orchestra played in the dance hall, and the first impression was not so different from what I had imagined. There was a sense of contained excitement among the young women, about forty in all, occasionally trying to break through their shyness by darting glances at the handsome soldiers. Those of my classmates who weren't at the bar were moping in the corner away from the girls, as if trying to resist their charm to avoid being hurt if they were rejected. They stood there aloof, defending their dignity—ties neatly knotted, hair nicely combed, some of them even with their shoes lacquered. Spurred on by at least a couple of glasses of vodka, Jędrek Czupryński (the older brother of Tadeusz) came from the bar to break the ice, striding up to one of the beautiful girls and asking to dance with her. She said yes, so some of the others started to come forward—Tadeusz Czupryński, Zrylek Zelinger, Lolek, me, and the rest of our friends—until no one was left just standing around.

Lolek plunged into the action with Halina Krolikiewicz, the daughter of the principal of the boys' school. I paired up with a girl named Olga, with blond hair and a floor-length green silk dress. I quickly realized that I had drunk too much vodka, because as I whirled around the dance floor, everything else seemed to spin as well, and the other dancers became a wheeling blur that I bumped into occasionally. I no longer understood what I was feeling, as my senses were overwhelmed with uncontainable emotion. Even though I didn't quite know what I was saying, my words must have seemed sweet to my partner's ear, to see the way she beamed with happiness—and how beautiful Olga was that night, and how charming were all of the others.

It was a magnificent evening. Shortly after midnight, the young women's fathers started arriving to take their daughters home. Lolek and I watched them go out one by one with their parents, emptying the hall, so that the remaining dancers could really let themselves loose on the half-empty floor. When the last girls left, Lolek and I made our way to the exit, feeling the cool night air on our sweat-dampened foreheads and necks. Lolek wiped his face and ruffled hair with a handkerchief. We felt a sense of exultation, something like a fire still burning within us that showed no sign of dying down, even now that we were leaving, the girls already gone, and the nighttime silence and humidity falling around us. The street was lit by a few lamps and by the moon, like a brilliant pearl in the dark sky gleaming with stars.

"My father and I are moving to Kraków after the summer," Lolek said. "I'll be entering the faculty of philosophy and letters at the Jagiellonian."

I was silent for a moment. Then I said, "You know, I'm also leaving to study, in Warsaw. I'll be entering the engineering faculty, and my uncle Wiktor says I can stay with him. He lives alone, and the house is big." We had reached a point close to both of their houses, where our paths separated, and I knew that the night was ending there.

"We'll always be friends, won't we, Lolek?" I asked a little anxiously.

Lolek just smiled and nodded. Then he embraced his Jewish friend and said goodnight. "Zobaczymy się, Jurek" (We'll meet again, Jurek).

CHAPTER 3

SOMETHING IS CHANGING

As I had been promised, after the graduation I went to Rome to stay with my cousin Adas Josefert. Although he was only a few years older than I, he was the vice-director of Consorzio Robur for Italy. He had a beautiful white Jaguar, with which we set off for Sicily. Together with us there were two American girlfriends of Adas. When we reached Naples, they left us and took the ship coming back to New York. I enjoyed that summer with Adas as I never did before. He was very handsome and athletic (he was a middleweight boxer), and he always had a beautiful girl with him. I hoped to get some advantage from this fact. After a couple of very pleasant months, I returned to Wadowice, where I stayed only a few days. In fact, toward the end of August, I was already in Warsaw.

The building in which my uncle Wiktor Huppert lived was on Jerozolimskie II Avenue. It was close to the Vistula, the river in which, according to ancient legend, the siren Sawa had lived, who together with the Fisherman Wars had given the city its name. The apartment was on the sixth floor, with five rooms and three bathrooms, and almost all of the windows were covered with dark blue damask curtains. When these were opened, the daylight revealed the brilliance of the wood used to make the furniture, the masterful work of Polish craftsmen. The floor, too, was finely decorated.

Although the style of the home was more modern than my home in Wadowice, there was a certain familiarity about it nonetheless, possibly because of the grand piano next to the dining room, in the room that was also used for concerts. Uncle Wiktor would produce intricate melodies from that instrument for his guests, sometimes as accompaniment for a singer.

In order to give me some extra privacy, I was allowed to stay in the quarters next to the office, on the second floor, where there was a bedroom, a little entry hall, and a bathroom. But I stayed there only at night, spending the rest of the day upstairs. I was there at least three times a day—for breakfast, lunch, and dinner, even when my uncle was away, because the servants had been given precise instructions on how to accommodate me.

The Zakrzewski-Huppert law office was famous in Warsaw, although Uncle Wiktor had not practiced law at the start of his career. After he became a lawyer, he was made deputy minister of the treasury. He had to deal with a great number of issues there, some of them extremely delicate, and murmurs began going around that the most important affairs of the treasury department were being given to a Jew, instead of to a Catholic. When Archbishop Adam Sapieha went to him to ask for a salary increase for the professors who gave Catholic religious instruction, Wiktor had to tell him that that someone else would be seeing to the matter. Soon after Uncle Wiktor resigned, the treasury minister at the time, a certain Zakrzewski, decided to resign as well, and the two of them opened a law office together. Their specialty was international contracts, and their office was very successful from the start, becoming one of the most prestigious in Warsaw. One of the most important contracts signed in Poland in those years had been their responsibility: an agreement for the construction of three Polish ocean liners, paid for over a number of years with coal from the mines of the Consorzio Robur. The ships were christened on the Baltic, with the names *Piłsudski*, *Sobieski*, and *Batory*.

Before school started, I had the chance to explore the city that witnessed so much history. After the third partition of Poland at the end of the eighteenth century, Warsaw had been occupied by Prussia. After this, in 1815, it had become the capital of the kingdom of Poland and was governed by the Russian tsar, later becoming the territory of the Russian empire, like much of Poland. Of the three foreign regimes that the Polish Jews had to live under during those years, the tsarist regime was beyond question the most difficult. I thought back to the stories that Captain Wojtyła, Lolek's father, used to tell, when he talked about how in Warsaw the Jews and the Poles had joined forces against the Russians, first in November 1830 and then again in 1863, during the January uprisings that represented the most dramatic insurrection of the century. After their defeat, the Jews who were not killed were sent along with the other Poles to prison in Siberia. The Jewish community in Warsaw was one of the largest in all of Poland. In the year that I arrived, there were more than three hundred thousand Jews in the city.

The car stopped in front of the large wooden gate to the building in which Uncle Wiktor lived. When the servants opened the door, I realized we would not be eating alone. Beside my uncle was a beautiful woman, her chestnut hair elegantly arranged on top of her head, showing off her slender neck and the expensive jewelry lying against her pale skin. She had her hands folded in front of her, resting on her skirt, and as soon as she opened her arms to embrace me, I recognized her. It was Countess Isabella, a member of one of the most aristocratic families in Warsaw. I had already met her a few times, and had frequently heard the family talking about her. The first time I saw her, it was winter, and I was with Mother in the train station of Kalwaria Zebrzydowska, with the car we had rented from Foltin's shop. We were there to pick up Uncle Wiktor. Isabella stepped off the train for just a few moments, because it was about to leave again for Zakopane, where she was going to spend her winter vacation. She had spent much of the journey next to Wiktor, who was going to Wadowice. When I met her, I realized my mother already knew her. I saw her again in passing a few times, always at the train station of Kalwaria, once by myself and then once with my sister, Tesia. In order to avoid meddling in things that didn't concern me, I never asked my family who she was, although occasionally I overheard my grandmother talking about her. I finally understood that her concern about finding a wife for Wiktor was actually two worries in one: she wanted to see him married at last, but she also wanted to put an end to a relationship that—as an observant Jew—she could not accept. Although Isabella was as beautiful, noble, and rich as Grandma Huppert could have wanted, she belonged to a Catholic family. And the approach my grandmother took was somewhat unusual, because although she was against the relationship she was not the kind to cause trouble, much less scandal, and so she practically refused to talk about it. The rest of the family found this funny, and none of us really shared her concerns.

We sat down at the table in Uncle Wiktor's apartment. The countess asked me if I had enjoyed my outing that afternoon, and I said it had been excellent, while I tried to piece back together everything that the chauffeur had explained to me, the names of all those roads and monuments. Isabella was amused as she listened to me talk, and she savored the excellent red wine that accompanied the meal.

"I'm really happy that you're enjoying Warsaw," she said when dessert was about to be served. "And there's still a lot to see and enjoy, even on the outskirts."

"We could all go together. What do you say, Uncle Wiktor?" I asked.

"Of course we will," my uncle replied. "But for now, hurry up and finish that piece of cake so you can go to bed. Unless I'm mistaken, you have some important business tomorrow." Of course. The academic year was starting at the engineering school in Warsaw, and as soon as my uncle reminded me, I was flooded with excitement. While the servants cleared and reset the table, I said goodnight to my uncle and Isabella. I went down to the second-floor apartment and fell asleep, thinking of the wonderful days that lay before me in Warsaw.

The engineering school was about a ten-minute walk from Uncle Wiktor's house. I woke up early that morning in order to get one of the best seats in the lecture hall. The institute had been named after its founders, Wawelberg and Rotwand. In addition to being known for the school, they were especially famous for the construction company that they had owned. Its projects had included the Trans-Siberian Railway—more than fifty-seven hundred miles long. Crossing almost all of Russia from east to west, including Siberia, it was the longest railway in the world.

I took one of the seats in the middle row, near the professor's desk. While I was waiting for the teacher, I introduced myself to some of the other Jewish students.

"You're not from Warsaw, are you?" one of them asked.

"No," I replied. "I'm from Wadowice, near Kraków. I'm staying with my uncle here in Warsaw, the lawyer Wiktor Huppert." While I was talking, I heard a voice from just behind me.

"You're a Jew, Kluger. You can't sit here."

I turned around and saw a few of the students acing me.

"That's your place, Jew," one of them said, pointing to the seats at the very back on the left-hand side. A young Jewish man signaled to me to do what they said.

My reply was risky: "I'm not moving." Just then the professor came, and everyone sat down. The lesson lasted a couple of hours, and by the time it was finished I wasn't thinking much about what those troublemakers had said before. But as soon as the professor had left the room, I was thrown to the floor and then beaten and kicked while my attackers cursed at me. I blacked out.

When I came to a few moments later, someone helped me up. I touched my face and discovered that I was bleeding. The custodians had arrived, and in the meantime the boys who had beaten me had gone.

"Listen to me," said one student, handing me a handkerchief. "Don't cross them. Next time, sit where they told you."

"Never," I replied as I wiped my face with the handkerchief. "But who are they?" I asked.

"They belong to the ND, the National Democracy Party," my classmate replied. "Look, there's just a small group of them here," he continued, "but no one stands up to them." In the meantime, some of my attackers had come back to the classroom, and one of them made a gesture to me that they would get me again later.

They were waiting for me when I left school. In gym class in Wadowice, I had recorded one of the best times in the hundred meters—about thirteen seconds—and I knew that this was the moment to break my record if I wanted to save my skin. I ran without knowing where I was going, turning only briefly to check if my five pursuers were still behind me. Luckily, I managed to shake them off. After I found my way back home, I finally stopped running when I reached the gate on Jerozolimskie II Avenue. I crossed the entrance quickly, keeping my battered face down as I slipped past the doorman, who just waved to me, and then took the stairs two at a time and entered my apartment.

I immediately went to the bathroom, looked in the mirror, and saw that blood was pouring from my nose again. I ran cold water over it for a couple of minutes, which brought some relief, and then I dried my face and lay down in bed.

I thought about what had happened in the lecture hall. I had remained seated where I was, at the price of being humiliated, and the rest of the students had done nothing to stop me from being beaten. I imagined that the same thing would happen if another fight broke out.

Someone knocked at the door. It was a lawyer named Wittman, an apprentice working with my uncle, who told me that if I wanted, we could go later to the club where the attorney was a member, which had a pool. Since that might be a way to stop thinking about what had happened, I agreed. But then Wittman noticed the bruises.

"What happened to your face?" he asked.

I downplayed it: "Too many students, not enough chairs. And no one wanted to stand."

That afternoon, while I was swimming in the outdoor pool at the club overlooking the Vistula, I looked around and saw that the view was much different from the one in Andrychów, near Wadowice, where there was also a club that I went to occasionally. That club had a view of the Bliźniaki mountains, their name meaning "twin" in Polish, because they were identical in form and right next to each other. For a moment, I was seized with nostalgia for my hometown.

Later, when I returned home for dinner, my uncle also noticed the condition of my face and wanted to know what had happened. I told him the truth and saw him growing worried as he listened.

"These are hard times for Jews in Warsaw," he said. "I hope it gets better soon."

I asked my uncle not to say anything to the family, because I didn't want them to worry about me and possibly make me return to Wadowice. I had my heart set on attending engineering school. At last I went to bed.

The following day, the classroom was just as crowded as the day before, with more than one hundred students attending the lecture. I arrived early again, and I was able to take one of the seats at the very front, in the middle. I was approached by the same students who had beaten and chased me the day before.

"You just don't get it, Jew?" one of them said, shoving me. "Your place is back there, with the rest of your kind."

They picked me up bodily from my seat and carried me to the back, to the row on the left, where they threw me to the floor and beat and kicked me again. Since no one helped me that time either, I resigned myself to the thought that the only thing I could do was to sit where I was told. Besides, there weren't enough Jewish students in the school to stand up for ourselves. Just like the experience of Ginka and Marychna, in fact, I encountered a lot of trouble being admitted to the engineering school of Warsaw. The rules were like those at the Jagiellonian: only a few places were set aside for Jewish students, and partly for this reason I hadn't found out until the last minute that I had been accepted. In the following days, however, I noticed that even though I was sitting in the back, the usual students wouldn't leave me alone.

One evening, I went out to dinner with Uncle Wiktor and Isabella, to one of Warsaw's most elegant restaurants. About a dozen other people joined us there, all members of the city's high society—even a deputy minister. Although I had done everything I could to hide the marks that the beatings had left on my face, they were still clearly visible. One of my dinner companions finally became curious enough to ask, "My dear boy, what happened to your face?"

Uncle Wiktor answered for me: "What happened to him is that in Warsaw, Jewish students are having to come to terms with the intolerance of certain fanatics."

"How awful," said one of the women seated at the table, who continued, "and the police? Where are the police?"

"All they do is keep guard outside," Uncle Wiktor said, "to prevent fighting in the streets, even though sometimes it happens anyway. What happens in the classrooms seems to be no concern of theirs."

Embarrassed to find myself the center of conversation, I felt a hand stroke the nape of my neck. It was Isabella, who was sitting right next to me.

"Poor Jurek," she said, looking at me tenderly, with eyes that seemed to me like those of a mother consoling her son. "A third of the people in this city are Jewish, and still things like this are allowed to go on," she added.

Fortunately, although it seemed like the dinner conversation would linger around that one topic, talk did move on to other subjects. One big change in the discussion took place while one of the diners was explaining how concerned he was about the silence that was allowing dangerous anti-Semitic ideas from Germany to spread. At that moment, someone mentioned what Piłsudski had considered a few years earlier in Geneva: the possibility of a preventive war against Germany. Piłsudski had already been very concerned about Germany at the time, in part because the nation was becoming increasingly aggressive in its claims to certain Polish territories. During that dinner I understood, for the first time, the danger that Poland might fight another war.

The following Monday, I was beaten again. That evening, my father came by train to Warsaw to attend to some urgent business. As soon as he saw my condition, the full extent of his concern became clear on his face. Before dinner was served, Father went to the study for a long conversation with Uncle Wiktor. When he came out again he had already made his decision, which he presented when we were all seated.

"Prepare your things, Jurek. Tomorrow evening, when I'm finished with what I have come here to do, you're coming back with me."

The next day Uncle Wiktor and Isabella went with us to the train station in Warsaw to say good-bye.

"Your father told me he's thinking about sending you to study in Nottingham, in England," Isabella said as the passengers began boarding the train. "You'll see, it's going to be an exciting experience," she said, hugging me tightly and enfolding me in a wave of affection. I couldn't speak. For me, leaving Warsaw in this manner was a defeat. When the train departed a short time later, I looked out one of the windows of our train car. As the countryside south of Warsaw began to scroll past my eyes, I suddenly burst into tears.

We traveled through the night, and a car was waiting for us at the Kalwaria station in the morning. When we arrived, Wadowice was gleaming under the high midmorning sun. Fall had begun a little more than a week before, and with nothing important to do, the days that followed seemed too long for me. At such a dark time, it would have been a relief to have friends with me, but not many of them remained in Wadowice, and the few who were still there were busy with their jobs. Zelinger helped his father at the mill; Czuprynski came around now and then, but he was in the army; and even Zweig, who had never wanted to have anything to do with studying, was now diligently helping his father at his coal mining business. One day, while walking down Koscielna Street, I stood for a moment looking at the closed shutters of Lolek's windows. Lolek and his father had moved to Kraków. I wanted to see Lolek again, even though I was ashamed about leaving the university. I resolved to write Lolek as soon as possible, once I found out his new address.

I found a way to pass the time, because our friend Opałko, who worked in Andrichów as an engineer at a textile factory owned by some Jewish Czechoslovakian brothers, the Czeczowiczkas, asked me to come to work there. I enjoyed being around any kind of machinery, and I agreed gladly, although I knew it wouldn't last long. My family had already confirmed that the following year I would go to Nottingham to study at the technical college, which added learning English to my list of things to do.

The factory in Andrichów where I went to work made cotton thread. The cotton balls, which came in to my area already pressed, were sent through one machine that loosened them up, and then through another that carded them. After that, the cotton was spun into thread and dyed. It was tiring work. I had to be at the factory at about eight o'clock each morning and didn't finish until late afternoon. I traveled to Andrichów—about six miles from Wadowice—by bicycle or by train, except for the times someone offered me a ride. Usually this was the engineer Wishik, a very elegant man who worked at the same factory. He was Jewish himself, and my grandmother knew him well. She had often seen him pass beneath her window, always wearing the most beautiful neckties. But we only rode together on the way to the factory, not on the way back. After work Wisyk returned immediately to Wadowice, while I spent a few more hours in Andrichów in the company of Golda, a young Jewish woman who also worked at the factory. Whenever I saw her at the loom, her skin smooth as silk, she reminded me of the beautiful Penelope, the daughter of Icarius and the wife of Odysseus, who avoided betraying her husband by agreeing to marry one of her suitors after she had finished his burial shroud—which she spent the day weaving only to unweave it at night. I spent as much time as I could with her, taking the last train for Wadowice, which came around dinner time. Grandma Huppert never scolded me about this, because I was a man now, but especially because I was spending time with a beautiful Jewish girl.

About a year went by, and I was able to regain the serenity that the experience in Warsaw had taken from me. In the meantime, thousands of rumors were circulating about Poland's future. Germany was continuing to claim ownership of certain territories, including the famous Danzig Corridor, while Poland didn't even consider giving it up. One day, I witnessed an interesting conversation between the engineer Opałko and one of the supervisors, who was readily agreeing with some of his statements.

"They want Gdynia. That's what they want," Opałko said at one point. "It used to be there was nothing there," he continued. "Just a few houses—and those were for the fishermen. Now all kinds of people are living there, and there are almost more wharfs and shipping companies than inhabitants." Naturally, he was referring to the port that had been built in the city on the Baltic, which only a few years after its construction had become the most important port in all of Poland, and one of the most important in Europe, surpassing even Amsterdam, Copenhagen, Le Havre, and Bordeaux. It had two thousand dikes, six wharfs, more than one hundred thousand square meters of docks, and an extensive network of train lines connecting it with every part of the country. Unlike the period immediately after its construction, when just a few ships landed there, in the 1930s there were thousands of them. So it turned out to be a good deal for Poland, which was said to have invested more than $100 million in it. The supervisor kept nodding as Opałko spoke.

The Germans were saying that they had every right to reclaim certain territories. In 1870, when the German empire had been founded, Danzig belonged to Germany and continued to belong to it until Germany lost the First World War and the new map of Europe was drawn in Versailles. The city was made independent, but on one condition: that it leave Poland a corridor of access to the sea. This request was accepted, but the route to the Baltic was created along a strip of land that had once belonged to Germany. When the Poles began to arrive, coexistence was so difficult that many of the Germans who had been living there said they had been forced to emigrate from the region, because they could no longer find work. Germany had previously announced its plan to reclaim its former territory, but now it was trying to speed up the process, saying that it was ready to do whatever it took to get what it wanted. Some people thought there was slim hope of maintaining peace between the two sides in the future.

One evening, a military dispatch was delivered to our house, addressed to my father. Mother handed it to him, while the rest of the family gathered around to find out what it said.

"It says that if Germany attacks, I will need to be in Tarnów by the third day of the fighting," Father announced. Dinner was served just after this, and the most difficult thing for my father was to persuade everyone that the war was just an unfounded rumor.

My sister was the most outspoken about her concerns.

"You shouldn't worry," Father reassured her. "It's normal for reserve officers to receive certain letters. But no general mobilization has been announced." After dinner, however, he took me aside, confiding that if this state of affairs were to continue, the risk of conflict was immediate.

Toward the end of March 1939, after Germany had repeated its request for the restitution of Gdańsk, as well as reaching agreement over the construction of a highway and railway line to connect Germany with eastern Prussia, the Polish government decided to boost its military presence along the corridor and declared that any attempt to change the status of Gdańsk without Poland's consent would mean war. A few months later, a French and British attempt to coax the Soviet Union into an alliance with Poland failed. Instead, Russian foreign minister Vyacheslav Molotov signed a treaty of nonaggression with German foreign minister Joachim von Ribbentrop, astonishing not only Poland and the Western powers, but the entire world.

Germany's ultimatum came at the end of August. Poland would have to send an ambassador with full negotiating power to Berlin to resolve the question of Danzig and the Danzig Corridor. The demand was rejected. War was only a matter of time.

CHAPTER 4

THE PRISONERS OF MARYJSKAJA

"War, war!" someone was shouting in the Rynek down below. The date was September 1, 1939, and the German invasion of Poland had begun at dawn. Just twenty years had passed since the country was last at war, and now it was in another. The radio news broadcasts in those first days said that there was heavy aerial bombing of the Polish military airports, including the Balice airport, near Kraków, and the Mokotów airport in Warsaw.

That's when I saw my father in military uniform. After joining Piłsudski's legions at the end of the First World War, he had been discharged with the rank of artillery captain and added to the reserves.

"Jurek," he said, "you're coming with me. We'll go to Tarnów together."

"And the rest of the family?" I asked.

Father was silent for a moment, because he knew that hundreds of thousands of Jews had been forced to flee from Germany. Then he answered, "I've been talking with the other members of the community. Nothing bad should happen to the women. They'll be safer here at home."

Mother prepared my suitcase, with clean underwear, slacks, and shirts, plus some insulated caps for the cold weather to come.

"Be very careful, my son," she said, hugging me tightly, "and always listen to what your father says."

I then said good-bye to my grandmother and sister.

In the Rynek, a military vehicle was waiting to take us to Kraków, on Stawarz's order. When we reached the square, just before opening the car door, I turned around one last time toward home, and behind the window where Grandma Huppert usually stood I could see my sister. She was crying.

"Bye, Tesia," I called out, waving to her. "Don't worry, we'll see each other soon." I stepped into the car, and it drove away.

When we arrived in Kraków, Father and I went to see some of our relatives: my father's sister Flora, her two daughters Irene and Melita, and her husband, Zilz, who was an engineer. Like many inhabitants of the city, they were preparing to leave and were planning to head east. So we all departed together in two Skoda Superbs. As we made our way, the road was already flanked on both sides by long lines of people on foot. I looked around for Lolek and his father, eager to take them with us far from the advancing German troops, but I couldn't find them among that sea of faces. We were traveling down a one-lane dirt road, and it would have been hard for two vehicles to pass each other—but no one was heading in the opposite direction. At a certain point there was a dull, humming sound coming from up in the sky in the distance, coming closer and closer until it turned into a roar and the sky grew dark with the passage of a squadron of German airplanes. It let loose a hail of machine-gun fire on the unarmed civilians, killing or wounding many of them, while everyone dove to the ground or piled into the ditches at the side of the road to avoid the bullets. Then came the bombs. Just ahead of us, a car was hit and immediately exploded into a ball of flames. The sound of the planes withdrew into the distance again. In surveying that scene, we decided that if we should come under air attack again, we also would take shelter in the ditches along the road.

The air attacks continued over the following days. Once the planes came so close that I could almost see the pilots' faces. Each time, the dead were counted at the roadside. We stopped in Rzeszów for a few hours, before departing for Tarnów. When we arrived, Father decided to continue the journey to Tarnopol together with the Zilz family, because in the meantime he had learned that the Polish military authorities had gathered in that city.

We arrived a few days later, toward the evening. I watched my father talk for a long time with the other officers, and when he returned, he explained that the orders were for all military personnel to go south and cross the border into Romania, where the army would be reorganized. But because Father did not want to leave Polish territory, especially because his whole family was still there, he decided to stay in Tarnopol with the Zilz family. The family's vehicles were commandeered, and after the army personnel had gone, an uncanny silence came over the city.

But of all the consequences that the war might bring, no one could ever have imagined seeing what actually happened when one day, toward the evening, the Red Army arrived from the east. It entered Tarnopol with tanks, heavy artillery drawn by horses, and the infantry, marching or riding on trucks. A voice came over the loudspeakers on the vehicles, repeating a few phrases of propaganda in a mixture of Polish and Russian, announcing the army as the friends of Poland. Shortly after this, the soldiers encamped in the main square of Tarnopol, where they lit a bonfire. Their long brown coats almost touched the ground, the fabric frayed where the hem had been, and their mess kits were always on their shoulders, at the end of a bit of string. When you looked at them, the eyes of those soldiers seemed impenetrable. They spoke very little, but when they did, the heavy odor of their breath, as imposing as the sour smell of their uniforms, immediately permeated the air. That night, I watched them all gather around the fire, and then I heard the voice of the *zapiewajło* (the soloist singer) break out into the old songs of the Russian steppes, while all the others sang the refrain in chorus. To the somber melodies of those songs, I fell asleep.

In the meantime, my father had hidden his uniform. Someone had told him that the Russians were taking the Polish officers prisoner, although the Polish communist propaganda gave no indication of this. Shortly after the arrival of the Red Army, we decided to leave Tarnopol. We traveled by train to Lwow, which had been the capital of Galicia and Lodomeria under the Habsburg empire before being returned to Poland in 1919. Father met there with a merchant who had been one of his clients a long time before, when Father had defended him against the accusation of paying certain suppliers more than others. The merchant was acquitted, and even years later he was still grateful to my father and agreed to rent him a room at a low price. We wrote a letter to the family, telling them that we were doing well and asking them to send more money and a little more clothing for the winter.

After two weeks, the German troops had reached the heart of Poland. As they steadily advanced, many of the people in the cities further to the west decided they were in danger and fled. Without a doubt, this was the explanation for why there were so many more people in Lwow than the normal population of about three hundred thousand, a third of them Jewish. Many of the people who took refuge there were also Jewish. I found my friends Zweig, Zelinger, and Rosenberg, who had left Wadowice just like we had. One afternoon, I also spotted my cousin Adas Josefert walking down the street next to a high-ranking Bolshevik official. Naturally, the official was a woman, in keeping with my cousin's reputation as a ladies' man.

The Red Army had, in fact, established itself in Lwow as well, and the city was now under the communist regime. The signs were everywhere; even the houses were required to change to a new numbering system. A crew had been set up to replace the old address markers with the new ones, and thanks to the connections of cousin Adas, my friends and I were able to earn a little money working on that crew. My father, in the meantime, was at home learning Russian. Some letters came from Wadowice, together with a few packages. They had been sent by my mother, the only member of the family who could write in German in the Gothic script, as the censors required, since she had studied it at the university. Fortunately, everyone was doing well. Since the Germans had entered Wadowice, she said, the city had been directly annexed to the Reich, becoming a full-fledged German territory. On the other side of the Skawa River, to the east, everything had instead become part of the Generalgouvernement, the General Government under Nazi control.

My father and I spent about a year in Lwow. One night we were awakened by Soviet soldiers who entered our room. Once out on the street, an official shouted some questions at us in Russian, and Father, who had learned the language fairly well, answered easily. The official gestured to both of us to get in line with the other people who had been brought down into the street.

"What did he say?" I asked my father.

"He asked me if we were a family, and I said yes, you're my son," he replied.

We and the others were put onto a truck, and half an hour later we were outside one of the train stations of Lwow. A Russian train was waiting for us, which meant that even the train tracks had been replaced in that area of Poland, since the wheels on the Russian trains were set farther apart.

We stepped into one of the many cars, the same kind used to transport merchandise or cattle. Each car had three levels of wooden platforms inside covered with straw, and I immediately understood that these would be our beds during the trip. In a corner to the right, there was a curtain in front of a hole in the floor. That was the bathroom. The walls were also made of wood, and there was a plank that slid back and forth like a door. The surprising thing was that it had not been locked. It was left unlocked not only when we stopped at the station, but also afterward, when we left, without knowing where we were going.

After traveling for a few days, I understood that we were entering the heart of Russia, to the northeast. It was the end of May, and since it was not too cold they left the doors open for most of the day, so we could tell in which direction we were traveling by checking where the sun was in the sky, especially at dawn.

We crossed the Volga and the Dnieper. The endless stretches of black soil outside were almost hypnotic, until after many hours an inhabited village would appear—the farmers with their dark, rough skin; the women in their long sleeveless *sarafan* dresses—and the sight of it would shake off that long monotony. A petty officer in the Polish Air Force who was traveling in the car with us, a man named Szurka, told me that the soil was extremely fertile, so much so that that region of Russia was called the breadbasket of the world.

The train made a few stops during that long trek, and I would see someone jump down from one of the cars and run away, taking advantage of some soldier's distraction. For a moment, I would be overpowered by the desire to run away because of my constant fear of what would happen at the end of that journey. I told my father about this idea. But when I saw a heavily armed soldier marching near our car, marking his rounds with long, regular steps, escaping suddenly seemed like too risky a gamble.

During one of those stops, I met a Jewish girl named Ada. She and her family had been put in the car next to ours, so we spent the rest of that seemingly endless journey together, legs dangling outside of the train, the vast landscape scrolling past us without ever displaying anything new or of particular interest.

After about two weeks, the train stopped in a place called Maryjskaja, and we were all told to get off. The prison camp to which we were taken was not far from the station, so we went on foot, down a road that ran alongside a dense forest of fir trees, thousands of them standing tall in that unknown, unpeopled land. I understood that in the days to come, all of the prisoners would have to come to grips with the magnitude of that terrain, because on the tracks next to their trains I had seen freight wagons loaded with the huge, heavy trunks of the toppled trees.

We arrived at the camp after about half an hour. We prisoners were taken to our barracks, which at least seemed to be well supplied with the bare necessities. There was a massive stove that also served as the fireplace, and there were beds and blankets—stacks and stacks of blankets to help fight off the winter cold. We had rested only fitfully in recent days, but that night we slept well.

The following morning, we were all assembled early in the camp yard and given our assignments, which were not at all different from what I had imagined. The reason that all of those prisoners from Poland and elsewhere were there was to produce as much lumber as possible from the vast stretches of woods all around us. A Russian petty officer named Brakier was in charge of making sure that every one of the work crews reached its quota of trees each day. Doing so guaranteed three meals a day and a salary, and as the trees gradually fell, the train tracks were extended to facilitate removal. It was a hard job all by itself, but it became even harder when winter came. I had never experienced a winter like that. Sometimes the temperatures dropped so low that the prisoners couldn't work at all. The soldiers of the Red Army had a unique method for determining when it was too cold to work: one of them would spit, and if it froze fast enough they knew it was at least minus forty degrees, which meant the prisoners had a day off. In any case, I always did my best to reach the quota, partly because there was a winter bonus, in addition to the food and rubles: *walonki*, boots made from scraps of the special pressed wool of the Russian Tajga, and gloves to help me stay warm in that bitter climate.

In spite of the precautions, incidents still occurred that were connected to the cold temperatures. One of them in particular happened when a four-cylinder Staliniec was brought to Maryjskaja. It was a copy of the Caterpillar D-7 tractor. The offer to drive it was made to any of the prisoners able to do so, and when I said I could, the soldier in charge of finding a driver wanted to evaluate me.

"Show me your hands," he told me. I held them out, and the soldier inspected them carefully.

"A real farmer has rough skin," he said dismissively when he saw that my hands were completely smooth. My father saw the exchange, and he asked Smirnoff—the highest-ranking official at the camp, with whom he was on friendly terms—to give me a chance to drive the tractor. I had learned to drive similar vehicles on the Haberfelds' farm, and I proved to be good enough at it that I was chosen. But one day, while the tractor was crawling smoothly over the icy terrain, the machine began to make a strange noise and then shut down completely. The constant vibrations had knocked one of the exhaust pipes loose, and I had to climb up to reattach it. One of the older prisoners had suggested that I take off the *walonki* while I was in the tractor cab, because the heat from the engine would warm my feet. But I never took them off, and when I climbed off the tractor the sweat inside my boots quickly froze. By nighttime, I could no longer feel my feet. A few years earlier, a Tartar imprisoned at Maryjskaja needed to have the toes of one foot amputated for the same reason. Fortunately, that wasn't necessary in my case, but I did need some time to heal.

In the meantime, the harsh environment was claiming its victims. Illness was common, especially intestinal infections, although a variety of diseases were ravaging the barracks. There was loud coughing all through the night. Some were running high fevers, and every day you could note the progressive gauntness of those unable to reach their quota, which exposed them without exception to rigid dietary restrictions. My gums began to bleed because of a lack of vitamins, and I lost a few teeth. I found a little relief by chewing *machorka*, thin strips peeled from the trunk of the tobacco plant, which was said to have soothing properties. Apart from smoking, it was used for almost everything in the camp; I even tried it once on a leg wound.

One evening I received a package along with a letter. My mother had written, telling me not to worry about them. In a previous letter from my father, she had learned about my infection, so she asked me how that was going. The package contained a few pairs of pants. Deep in the pockets of one of these, wrapped in baker's paper, there were a few red onions and a note: "Eat them raw, my son, they'll do you good. Mummy."

Months went by in Maryjskaja. Winter and disease were taking their toll on the prisoners. The grim faces of the Russian soldiers also became a familiar aspect of the long imprisonment. My father, who now knew how to speak Russian very well, smoked *machorka*, or hand-rolled ciga-rettes, using paper and tobacco that Smirnoff gave him every now and then. Smirnoff had even given me a broken crystal radio receiver, telling me that if I could fix it, it was mine. In middle school, the science profes-sor had taught the students to build a similar apparatus, and I had eagerly applied myself to the lesson. For months, I was completely absorbed in making that radio work again. One summer evening, I was finally able to pick up some scratchy sound, and then soft music fading in and out. I had triumphed. The other prisoners in the barracks, who had been skeptical up until then, gathered around to listen. They had to use an earpiece, passing it from one to the next. At one point a Russian broadcaster came on, so the earpiece was given to my father, the only one who could understand the language well. When he brought it to his ear, what he learned was astonishing. The troops of the Third Reich were penetrating into Soviet territory, their offensive focused mainly on the regions of the Baltic Sea to the north and the Black Sea in the south. The war had taken on another face.

A few days later, almost the entire camp had heard the news. A Tartar who had been imprisoned in Maryjskaja for years covered his toothless mouth to keep the guards from hearing his joyful laughter when he found out. The euphoria united many of the prisoners, especially the Poles, all over the camp. While running down the path that led past the barracks used as the infirmary, I discovered the reason for the celebration when one of the doctors, leaning out of the window to smoke *machorka* and escape the stench of dysentery for a moment, saw me and said, "You happy, kid? You're going free."

The situation of the departing prisoners of Maryjskaja, especially the Polish ones, was truly unusual at that point, because of the way things had changed in just a short span of time. During that summer of 1941, the Polish government in exile in London and a Soviet delegation had reached an initial agreement, followed just a few days later by a genuine military treaty. One of its provisions was the liberation of all Poles from the prisons in forced labor camps, with the intention of forming troops to fight alongside the Red Army in Russia. Lieutenant General Władysław Anders, who had been held at the Lubianka prison in Moscow and who had distinguished himself during his country's war for independence and its fight against the Nazis, was appointed commander of these troops and released.

Members of the NKVD, the Russian secret police, arrived at the camp, and everyone was given a *udostowierienie lićnosti*—a document that would allow us to travel without restrictions anywhere in Russia. It not only permitted us to board trains and ships without spending a single ruble, but it also gave us free access to the Turkish baths at the stations and ports (the heat killed lice) and a free meal. Once the astonishment at learning we were to be freed had passed, there was some confusion about where we needed to go, because it wasn't clear where in Russia the Polish enlistment stations would be located. Colonel Smirnoff then told my father to follow the river to the south, to the Oremburg-Volga region, because the general headquarters in Buzuluk was enlisting Polish soldiers there.

We caught our first train at the station near the camp. It was a freight train, so we traveled in an open-topped wagon. It wasn't the first time that I had ridden on one, because during my long stay at the camp, every now and then I would sneak onto one of the wagons to go to the barracks a few miles from my own. That was where Ada, the beautiful Jewish girl I had met during the journey to Russia, was staying. Together with my father and I were two other prisoners from a village near Wadowice. Even before the outbreak of the war, these other prisoners had made their living as petty thieves, and Father knew them fairly well, because he had obtained acquittal for them at a couple of trials. Still grateful to him, the two thieves decided to look out for us during our journey. The first thing the thieves were able to steal was a sack of sugar, in Yoskar Oła, and they explained to me that it would come in handy during the trip.

When we arrived at the station, we were barely able to make it to the train, because the place was packed with countless people, almost all of them coming from the prison camps. In spite of all the chaos, we made it onto the train. We pushed our way into one of the walkways and made ourselves as comfortable as we could under the circumstances. Some of the people already sitting on the floor were delousing themselves, and the air seemed unbreatheable. I was overjoyed when I was able to make my way to one of the windows.

During the stops that the train made, I noticed that although a few dozen people would get off, larger numbers of people were always pushing to get on, probably Russians and Belarusians, Cossacks and Georgians, Ukrainians and Tartars from Crimea. The journey seemed endless. The following day, toward the evening, we finally reached the Volga. The two thieves were able to persuade a group of sailors to let them get on board a boat that was about to disembark in exchange for the sack of sugar they had stolen the day before, which seemed to be very valuable in the negotiations. As night fell over the murky waters of that river, the overcrowded passengers lost all inhibition, and I decided that it would be a good idea to stay awake and keep watch. Apart from the fact that I could barely see the riverbank going by, my immediate surroundings weren't very reassuring. Groans of pleasure were heard all around me as the men satisfied their natural desires next to the warm female bodies they had gone without for too long. A group of Mongols, their cheekbones high, were off laughing by themselves, because one of them had cut the soles off the shoes of a man overwhelmed by exhaustion. He was a Tartar. When he woke up a little bit later and saw what had happened, a fight broke out, and suddenly all of their knives were gleaming in the moonlight. The Tartar's knife grazed the skin of the thief, and the blood began to flow. He got the soles back. A goat was even butchered to be roasted on the deck, and when its raw flesh met the flames, fragrant clouds of smoke began billowing through the air. The two men who had accompanied us were able to get a piece of the meat—bartering who knows what this time—and the thieves shared it with us. Then it was time for sleep.

The chilly morning air woke us as the dim dawn light drove the darkness away. We traveled down the Volga for about three days, going ashore every once in a while. On the third day, we came to a port where we saw a red and white flag flying, and almost by instinct we headed toward it. My father presented himself to a young officer who immediately began looking for his name on the long list of reserve officers. The officer told Father that he would be joining the *corpus audytorów* (military magistrates), because the most pressing need at the time was to proceed with the complex reorganization of the Polish army. Men were streaming into it from everywhere, and each of them needed to be identified. I had never been in the army, but I had my *census*, my diploma, so I was sent to the officers' school. I had been with my father ever since the beginning of the war, but now it was time to leave him.

The next morning, a train was leaving—no less crowded than the one before—and Father accompanied me to the station. Each of us hoped that the other would not notice his emotions. Father pulled out of his pocket a few rubles he had been able to save and gave them to me. I hid them in my jacket. Then we heard the unmistakable voice of a soldier shouting that it was time to get on the train. We embraced briefly, and I boarded the train. Then I appeared at one of the windows opposite my father.

"I promise, I'm going to become a Polish officer!" I called out. A little smile broke through the sadness on my father's face. Father walked along with the train as it slowly began pulling away. I kept waving as it picked up speed, until finally we couldn't see each other anymore.

CHAPTER 5

HEAVEN ON EARTH

"Welcome to Eden," a young soldier on the truck said to me when he saw me look out onto this new world for the first time. During January and February 1942, the Poles were being transferred to the Asian republics of the Soviet Union, between Kazakhstan, Kyrgyzstan, and Uzbekistan, with the general headquarters set up in Jangi-Jul, between Samarkand and Tashkent. It was a sunny afternoon when I arrived in Kara-Suu, in the Fergana Valley that stretches to the foot of the Himalayas. Those superb mountains, those magnificent forms rising up from the earth and reaching almost to heaven itself, standing outside the boundaries of time, were a perfect emblem of the many virtues of that place, where the wonders of nature seemed to overflow at every turn. The cold, dense glacial waters running through their ancient riverbeds were the main reason for the lushness of that oasis. There the roses were redder, the grass greener, the vines grew higher than could ever have been imagined, and I sunk my teeth deep into the heavy fruit hanging from sturdy branches. One of them must have been like the fruit that led to the original sin, because legend had it that Adam and Eve had lived in that valley.

I soon became friends with a young man named Aleksander Sandig, a Jew from Warsaw who, like me, wanted to become an officer in the Polish army. Sandig excelled in mathematics, one of the essential disciplines of the school. Much of our training was dedicated to military exercises like marching, handling weapons, and also horsemanship, because our unit had no motorized vehicles. The Russians were capable of great feats of horsemanship, and there were many of them in the camp, almost four thousand, compared to just five hundred Polish cadets. I participated very diligently in all of the lessons, partly because I had promised my father that I would become an officer, and I wanted to keep that promise at all costs. So even after days of hard training, when those who were not drinking vodka were playing cards—and some doing both—I would continue my studies alone, apologizing to the others almost as if I was embarrassed. I was even able to discipline myself in an area I had never quite mastered before: self-control with women. The tents of the military camp, in fact, had been set up around an old white building that once had been a hospice for tuberculosis patients, but now it was a nursing school attended by large numbers of young Russian women, and the word was that at least three hundred of them wanted to be dancers for the Bolshoi. They were very tall, and one of the soldiers said they had the longest legs he had ever seen. I reluctantly kept my distance from them, too, especially because the officers at the camp were strict disciplinarians, and also because I was Jewish. I would thus be given less leeway in my conduct than the others.

Whenever I came out of my tent, even during the hottest hours of the day, the shady mountains seemed to exude a pleasant coolness. After the long marches, always conducted at the same tempo, the heels of our boots striking endlessly into the ground, I enjoyed taking off my woolen socks and dangling my legs in the *ariqs* (the furrows). The *kazachi*, the local farming people who were similar to the Tartars in appearance—short and with bowlegs—told me that those streams had been flowing through the valley for more than seven thousand years. Stretched out on the bank, paddling my feet in the water, I would spend hours talking with Sandig—still the head of the class in mathematics—and Rosciszweski, who was from a noble family from eastern Poland and was a few years older than the two of us.

Only a few cadets graduated at the end of the course. I was well aware that, although there were Poles teaching at the school in Kara-Suu, the Russians decided who would be promoted, and they were very demanding. The two armies would be fighting side by side, so the order had come from Moscow that those allies should be trained as thoroughly as possible. General Anders was well aware of this, knowing how well prepared the Russian officers were, especially with their specialized system of military topography, and he had decided that the future artillery officers of the Polish Second Corps should learn the same techniques. Anders came personally from Saratov at the end of the course to congratulate the 156 who had passed, including me. Since I was one of the best in mathematics, although not quite as good as Sandig, I was offered a chance to stay in Kara-Suu for another month to study astronomical topography, a special technique for creating precise terrestrial maps based on the constellations that the Russians in Siberia had developed. During the long nights that followed, I learned to see that the stars that had always seemed scattered chaotically through the sky actually showed a certain consistency in their arrangement, turning the vault of heaven into a firm foundation for my calculations. In order to perform these more quickly, each of the students was given a Marchand, a rotary calculator invented in France about two centuries earlier, and some tables of coefficients. I was also allowed to use a theodolite, a sort of telescope that was essentially identical to the one invented many centuries before by the famous Italian astronomer Galileo Galilei, but had a much smaller margin of error in its astronomical measurements. Using it properly required great expertise, and I was one of the best at handling it.

I spent almost the entire fall in Kara-Suu. Sometimes the training took us on horseback up the rocky ridges of the Pic Lenin, the huge, half-frozen mountain that dominated the valley. There, at an elevation of thirteen thousand feet, the only thing we could hear was the endless whistling of a frigid wind. In the meantime, I had learned from a Polish officer at the camp that an evacuation plan for the troops had been prepared. The rumor was confirmed about ten days later. At the end of November 1942, I obtained permission to go to the camp of Kizyl-Orda, where my cousin David Aleksandrowicz, his wife, Maria, and their three children were prisoners, and I was able to evacuate them. When I returned to the Fergana Valley, my studies in astronomical topography now complete, it was announced that I would be leaving, but I didn't know where I'd be going.

At this point, I discovered that the legends I'd been told about the members of the NKVD, the Russian secret police—that they were almost indestructible beings, having to stay awake for days at a time without ever swerving from their task—turned out to be true. Even when I was pretending to sleep on the train, I could feel their eyes on me at every moment. Their only duty was to keep me in view until we reached the border. At a dock in Krasnovodsk, where I arrived with some of my classmates a few days after we left the school in Kara-Suu, there was a boat waiting to take us to the other side of the Caspian Sea, to Pahlavi, in the former Persia. The sailors pulled up anchor when the sun had started to set. During that westward journey, as I was breathing the thick salt fog up on the deck, I was astonished to see about fifteen of the aspiring dancers for the Bolshoi glide past me. They had evaded the tight security of the NKVD and concealed themselves on the train, and were now strutting around the ship without any more fear, accompanied by some lean young officers who had sacrificed everything else in order to follow them.

After arriving at the port of Pahlavi the following day, we rode a couple of dozen Diamond Ts, American military transport trucks, to our next destination. The drivers were mostly Arabs and Persians, the men most familiar with those roads. They did this for little pay, just enough to support their opium habit. They smoked opium in large quantities, especially during refueling stops, when they could all be seen lighting their *narghilés* and drawing deeply of the water-filtered smoke. They then sat back behind the wheel under the influence of the drug, grinding the gears as they drove along the unpaved mountain roads. Because there were often steep drops to the outside of those narrow lanes, the trucks held as much as possible to the inside track, sometimes scraping against the rocky outcrops.

It was almost evening when we reached Habanya, where we were able to take a shower at the military camp, at which the English had been stationed for a few months, and where they seemed to be almost miraculously sheltered from wartime privations. The officers' mess seemed to be of almost unparalleled elegance, partly because of the dazzling white robes worn by each one of the Persian young men who served the dinner, and everything was of an exotic opulence. We spent that night in the tents, and I made sure that mine was completely closed. Thick clouds of mosquitoes were everywhere, drawn by a well near the camp, and a breeze had begun to blow the dust through the air, lightly at first, but then with increasing force, scraping the sand across my face.

The next morning, an English bomber took us to Iraq, which I learned would be our final destination, at least for the time being. When I stepped off the airplane, the air was so hot that I felt like I was breathing fire into my lungs. Even so, I preferred it to the stale and nauseating air inside the plane. A few hours after we landed, the Diamond Ts brought us to an English military camp near Kirkuk, in the middle of the Iraqi desert. The sun scorched anything exposed to it, so our tents had been sunk into holes about twelve feet deep, which we climbed into and out of using rope ladders.

In these conditions, one had the feeling of drowning in the midst of an ocean of sand. Military life there seemed much different to me compared to my experience in Russia, in Kara-Suu, because now it was my turn at the camp to teach the English what I had learned during those months from the Soviets. The need to study astronomical topography so thoroughly became clear, because just like in Siberia, the only points of reference in that featureless desert were the stars. In addition, the cannon barrels had been worn down through constant use; because precise aim was so important, they needed to be carefully calibrated. So I spent long days working on the artillery, and long nights working out the positions of the stars. The hours of darkness brought an incredibly bitter chill.

One night while I was returning to my tent, I slipped off the ladder and broke my foot. I was taken to the camp hospital, where an English doctor with whiskey on his breath set the foot in a cast. But as the foot continued giving me problems over the next few days, another doctor had to come see me. The second physician was a Polish captain whom I recognized right away. It was Kanarek, a Jew from Kraków who had taught at the Jagiellonian University and who had long been in love with one of my cousins, Irka Zilz. I asked him if there was any news from Poland, but he didn't know much. He replaced the cast that the drunken doctor had put on a few days earlier and ordered me to rest.

I was bored to tears over the days that followed, because I was used to working all day at the camp. I thought about my family a great deal during my recovery. It had been years since I had seen or heard from them, but I had learned from some other officers that my father had been sent to the Middle East, halfway between Tel Aviv and Jerusalem. Since he had a law degree, the Polish army had made him a military judge. I wished that I could at least see him.

One afternoon while I was reminiscing, it suddenly seemed that all of that nostalgia was making me hallucinate, because old friends from middle school appeared before me like ghosts. But it was no hallucination. One of them, Tomas Romański, had found out that I was in Kirkuk and had told the others—Tadeusz Czupryński, Tadeusz Gajczak, Rudolf Kogler, and Zdzisław Bernas—who were also stationed in Iraq. I was overjoyed to see them again. I propped myself up on my elbows and motioned to them to sit down. I needed this visit badly. Skipping the pointless small talk, I asked them if they knew anything about what was happening in Wadowice. Their faces fell, and I insisted on knowing the truth. Kogler—who was still called "Marshal," his nickname from when he had led the school parades—spoke. All of the prewar rumors about Nazi anti-Semitism were, tragically, being proven true. They had blown up the synagogue in Wado-wice, and all of the Jews had been forced to live in the ghetto set up in the eastern part of the city. I no longer felt strong enough to hold back tears. My friends fell silent for a moment.

"And my mother, and Tesia, and Grandma—what do you know about them?" I asked.

"They're living in the ghetto with the others," Romański said, imme-diately adding, "But don't worry, they're fine." They tried to cheer me up again. Czupryński pulled a bottle of vodka from his jacket, cuffed me lightly on the cheek, and handed me the bottle. I drank deeply, and then passed the bottle to my friends. The Germans had destroyed the synagogue during the first days of the occupation, but no one had told me. There had been no mention of it in my mother's letters to my father and me. Maybe she had been trying not to worry us, but German censorship had certainly been involved as well.

"You'll see, we're going to win this war!" Gajczak said with patriotic zeal, after he had taken his pull at the bottle. Then he started singing, "Poland is not lost yet, Poland is not lost yet!" Slowly—and carefully avoid-ing certain topics—they brought a smile back to my face, especially Bernas, when he started doing impressions of our old teachers.

They stayed until almost six o'clock, and then it was time to leave. I didn't know how we might meet again during the war, or if we ever would, but I wanted to keep alive the hope of seeing all of them again in Wadowice, and also my mother, sister, grandmother, and my other friends, including Lolek. And even as we were saying good-bye, Gajczak continued to remind me, "Poland is not lost yet, Poland is not lost yet!"

While I was ardently waiting for all of those things that would mean the end of the war—that would mean victory and safety—in October 1942 I was able to see my father again. Just a few days after my cast had been removed, I decided to take advantage of my remaining medical leave. We—father and son—fell into each other's arms. Father had also learned that the ghetto had been instituted in Wadowice, although he didn't have any detailed news about the family either, since the letters from Mother had stopped. I saw the deep suffering written on my father's face. We were walking outside, beneath a blinding sun, while a group of English tanks went ahead of us on their way to Tel Aviv.

We stopped at a bar to refresh ourselves with a cold drink. At that time, news was continuing to come from Stalingrad, the Russian city named after Stalin, which had been under assault by the Sixth German Army since August. There was ferocious fighting along the Vistula. Frowning, my father confessed that the fate of the war hinged, in part, on that battle, because Stalingrad was a strategic point of defense, and a Soviet defeat would weigh heavily on Russia and all of Europe. But this was not the only battlefront. Another was where we were at the time: North Africa. I told my father that my platoon would soon be sending me somewhere else. In fact, as soon as I returned to Kirkuk, I was sent to Egypt, to Heliopolis, a suburb just outside of Cairo.

I spent my nights in a tent that seemed twice as large as the one I had slept in up until then. At sunrise one morning, following a full moon, an officer pointed toward the northern sky where the faint light of dawn showed an immense cloud of black smoke on the horizon. A few hours later, the news came back that a tremendous battle had been fought there, at El Alamein, about sixty miles from Alexandria. The Germans, led by General Erwin Rommel, had taken the road from Tobruk along the sea toward Cairo, without realizing that the English artillery was pointed at a section of that road. It was early November, and after that massacre the Germans retreated along the coast of Libya, all the way to Tunisia. Those unable to escape were taken prisoner. I saw many of them over the following days, marching along the road to Alexandria.

During my time in Heliopolis, I often went to Cairo, where the open-air market was richly perfumed with the scent of spices. The incessant heat made swimming in the Nile a popular pastime. On El Ma'âdi, an island reached by crossing a wooden trestle set against one bank of the river, there was the elegant Gezirah Club, which was run by the English. On one of these evenings, I had the most pleasant encounter of my entire stay in Egypt. I met Irene, a beautiful Irish woman in her early twenties. She came from a Catholic family and had enrolled in His Majesty's army as a driver, mostly of Jeeps and Diamond Ts. Many of the drivers in the military were women, because they didn't get drunk and had fewer accidents.

Irene and I fell in love. One evening, I whispered into her ear, asking her to spend the rest of her life with me. She accepted. A few days later, we were married in a simple ceremony by an English military chaplain. My father came from Tel Aviv to attend the wedding. It was August 26, 1943. Two days later we also had a wedding in the Catholic church.

CHAPTER 6

FROM MONTE CASSINO
TO AUSCHWITZ

A few months after my marriage to Irene, I had to travel to Taranto on one of the many ships used to deploy Polish soldiers in Italy. Irene had left a few days prior, heading toward Peterhead in northern Scotland, where the Royal Air Force had a base. The war was taking me to Italy, where there were large concentrations of German soldiers in certain strategic areas, which had to be captured at all costs. One of these, which would permit the Allied forces to move from the south toward Rome, was located along the front that ran from the mouth of the Garigliano River on the west coast to the mouth of the Sangro River on the east coast, near a valley with a Benedictine abbey at the top of one of the hills. I was going to Monte Cassino.

It was February 1944 when the ship named the *Batory* swung its heavy flanks into the port of Taranto and the mooring lines were fastened. I came down the long walkway with the crying of the seagulls all around me. Still accustomed to the desert heat, all the young men pulled on their heavy regulation jackets against the chilly morning breeze. The arrival of that ship and the large numbers of soldiers disembarking from it seemed to have raised a great deal of excitement among the local people. Even before the ship reached the shore, the locals were all standing around on the dock, shouting joyfully to the arriving troops.

First we were taken to a camp near a town called Masseria Santa Teresa, a few miles from Taranto on the road to Monopoli. A few weeks later, we arrived at our permanent location, another British camp that had been set up in the area of Mottola. The general headquarters of the Polish Second Corps had also been established there. This time, I didn't sleep in a tent, but in an old farmhouse, one of the many that the farmers in the area had gladly lent to the troops in exchange for some food. During the months I spent there, I was able to rely on a few excellent colleagues, like Lieutenant Wigura, a Polish officer who had graduated with a degree in

astronomy from Warsaw a few years earlier, and Major Michalski, who had
taught astronomy at the university.

When the army was ready, it left toward Venafro, in the Volturno
valley, just a few miles from Monte Cassino. The ancient Benedictine
monastery wasn't there anymore, because English bombers had destroyed
it toward the middle of February in the mistaken belief that there were
Germans hiding there. In reality, the Germans had found another place to
hide, in the damp caverns, full of rats and fleas, that went far back into the
mountainside. Afterward, the Germans established themselves amid the
ruins of the abbey, where they had a vast and deadly arsenal. The area had
become the focal point of the fighting in Italy, and already just a single winter had claimed many victims among the troops who had tried to capture
that position. During the cold months that followed, they had all failed:
the English, the New Zealanders, the Canadians. Not even the Indian
Gurkhas, the soldiers most accustomed to rough terrain, had been able
to break through. The German defense had been carefully planned. There
were soldiers from an Alpine division up on the mountain, as well as the
Green Devils, as the German paratroopers were called. During December 1943, these German units had inflicted heavy losses on the Canadian
divisions in Ortona, in the region of Abruzzo, and because of their great
expertise in fighting they were selected to defend Monte Cassino against
the Allied advance from the south, and also to prevent them from joining
forces with the American troops that had landed a little farther to the
north, in Anzio.

In order to reach Venafro, the vehicles had to cross a stretch of road
that the Polish soldiers had nicknamed *djabeskie przejscie* (devil's point),
because it was extremely exposed to enemy artillery. The first month of
spring had come and gone when I was assigned to the *wzrokowa* battery,
which had to double-check all of the artillery installations, because during the previous attacks it had become clear that many of them were not
aimed properly. To do this, we had to go up Monte Cairo, more than three
thousand feet above sea level. The team rode up the mountain on donkeys,
bringing two theodolites (instruments for precision surveying) plus a large
machine gun in addition to the smaller Thompson submachine guns that
the soldiers carried. I was the only one carrying a pistol. I was accompanied
by two Sicilians, who were good at keeping the donkeys moving up the
path. Every now and then, the distant sound of artillery fire reached that

spot, which was a no man's land. But at one point a shell exploded right next to us, and we all flung ourselves to the ground, where we remained for a few minutes. When we stood back up, the two Sicilians were nowhere to be found, and the donkeys were too spooked to move. One of the Polish soldiers, Chmielewski, passed a lighter under their testicles, and as soon as they felt the heat, they started trotting right along. Fortunately, we didn't come under any more fire, and we didn't see any German soldiers on the way back.

Meanwhile, it had been decided who would be the next to take on the Germans at Monte Cassino. Following the latest failure in March, General Harold Alexander, who commanded the Allied forces in Italy, had designated the Poles as the next to try to take the mountain, partly because of the morale that he knew we would show in the fighting.

General Anders gave the order to attack on the evening of May 11, 1944. Many of his soldiers died in the very first night of fighting. Many others were wounded and taken to the tent hospitals where the doctors did what they could to save their lives, sometimes having no choice but to amputate their ragged limbs. Seeing the bodies of the men in such horrifying condition, one officer let slip the remark that attacking in that way was mass suicide. Anders's plan, which included scaling one side of the mountain, hadn't convinced any of the officers. That side of the mountain was constantly pounded from above by cannon fire, and the guns were well concealed and hard to destroy. Nonetheless, the Germans had been barricaded in Monte Cassino for several months, so it was hoped that their food and ammunition would soon run out.

The order for the second attack came on May 14, and the same price was paid as before. After three days and nights of fighting, the only precaution that some of the Polish soldiers were able to take was that of advancing with handkerchiefs placed around their mouths and noses, to stave off the stench of the decomposing bodies of their fallen companions. The fighting continued until the morning of May 18, when a strange silence suddenly fell over the entire valley. Some of the soldiers thought it was nothing more than a cease-fire. Others hoped that the Germans were retreating. After a few hours, it was clear that in fact they were. Central Command decided to send a platoon of the Lancers of Podolia regiment to reconnoiter the area. I later surveyed the scene from a Jeep and saw up close the carnage from the battle. I went past Masseria Albaneta, the bunker at the foot of the mountain, then past the smoking tanks whose crews had been burned alive. I circled back around on foot, where I felt like I was walking amid an ocean of corpses. Together with some of the others, I explored the caves that had sheltered the Germans and was amazed to find a ping-pong table in one of them. At about eleven o'clock in the morning, our group reached the top of the mountain and the ruins of the ancient abbey, where we raised the Polish flag. While we were going back to the camp, the many lives that had been lost made me think about the stories of Captain Wojtyła, Lolek's father. The bodies of the Polish soldiers lying in their own blood seemed to be those of all the other wars that our country had fought over the centuries for the sake of its freedom. I did what came naturally: I wept. And when the press began spreading the news that the Poles had captured Monte Cassino, clearing the way to Rome, something else came to mind about that date, May 18, 1944. It was my beloved friend Lolek's twenty-fourth birthday.

The battle at Monte Cassino devoured more than a thousand souls. The Sherman and Stuart tanks resumed their advance on Rome, but had to stop at the little town of Piedimonte San Germano, not far from the old monastery along the Via Casilina, where the Germans started shelling them again. The new camp was set up in a little clearing near the convent of Santa Scolastica, where Central Command and all of the liaison officers met to decide on a new plan of action against the Germans, who had blocked the way again. Colonel Zawacki, an expert in geography—who had even visited Alaska and was rumored to have slept in the igloos with the Eskimos—gathered all of the soldiers and told them that anyone who didn't want to be part of the assault should step forward. No one did, so Captain Wenzel started forming the squads.

I was assigned as a lookout to one of the more than two hundred tanks that would take part in the advance. Shortly before the battle, I saw the major who would be riding on his tank tie a yellow and white flag to the top of the long radio antenna. It was the banner of an old cavalry regiment. As soon as I saw it, I tried to convince him to take it down, because it would make us more visible to the German observation points, but the major insisted that it stay. The tanks moved out. When they reached the foot of the mountain, whether by the commanding officer's imprudence or by bad luck, a shell blew up one of the tank's tracks. They had to climb out and dig a hole six feet deep in the ground where they took shelter until night fell. The battle, not nearly as bloody as the one before, ended on May 25 with the Germans' retreat.

In the meantime, Rome had already been liberated by the Americans a month before, and I went there on leave. The last time I had been in Rome was in the summer of 1938, when I had been allowed to stay with my cousin Adas Josefert as a graduation present. The driver stopped on the Via Veneto, in front of the Hotel Flora, where many of the other Polish officers were staying. One of them, a second lieutenant, was just leaving, and I recognized him right away. It was my friend Kogler, and this was the second time we had met during the war. He was leaving for Bologna, one of the cities still under assault by the Germans. I also met my cousin Melita Zilz in Rome, and her husband, Dr. Henryk Szancer, who was a medical officer in the army, with a degree in pharmacology. I went with them to visit the Vatican museums, which I hadn't had time to visit during other trips to Rome, and then to the Trevi Fountain and the Colosseum. Happiness was returning to the faces of the Romans after the withdrawal of the Nazis. I stayed there for about a week and then rejoined my unit in Nettuno.

We remained in Nettuno for more than a month, the time needed to recalibrate the artillery. When we had finished, we resumed our journey toward the Adriatic coast. Other battles had already been fought there, on the Sangro River and then in Ortona, where the Germans who later went to Monte Cassino had strewn mines in anticipation of the Canadian troops. A little farther to the north, Polish troops succeeded in liberating Pescara on June 10, 1944, and I spent a few days in Francavilla al Mare. Our unit then continued along the coast, passing through Roseto degli Abbruzzi, Porto San Giorgio, and Marotta. In the meantime, I had finally been made a second lieutenant.

One of the soldiers of our platoon became ill and was sent to a military hospital in Fano, where he met a Jew named Kurt Rosenberg. When I found out that my friend was there, I immediately went to see him, and we had dinner together. Kurt had fled following the outbreak of the war. From Bielsko, a little city not far from Wadowice, he had gone eastward with his family to Lviv, the last place where we'd seen each other. When the Red Army entered the city, Kurt's father, who was a captain in the Polish army and had not removed his military uniform, was one of the first to be arrested and deported to Russia. Kurt, his mother, and his brother were arrested the following month. While they were traveling on the train, Kurt was able to jump off and get away with two others who had escaped. He made it across the border of Bucovina, which had also been occupied by the Russians, and then crossed into Romania, Yugoslavia, and Croatia. Kurt arrived in Italy in the summer, crossing the border at Trieste, and then continued his journey to Rome, changing his Jewish name to avoid being captured and deported by the Nazis. Until the Americans liberated the city, he had gone by the name of Kazimierz Górski. Like me, Kurt had no idea what had happened to his family, not even about his father. But a horrible rumor had been going around for some time about the Polish officers who had been captured by the Russians—that they had been slaughtered in a forest near Katyń, close to Smolensk, and then buried in a mass grave.

I spent a little time in Ostravetere, a medieval village in the province of Ancona, before continuing toward Cesena, where the army's mission was to free State Highway 76 from the Germans. The road had to be secured for the passage of the Canadian First Corps and the British Fifth Corps, which were needed at the northern front that ran from Massa Carrara on the west coast to Pesaro on the east coast. The camp had been set up in Brisighella, a medieval village in a valley at the foot of three monuments built on the chalky cliffs—a clock tower, a fortress, and a shrine. I spent the whole winter of 1944–45 there, while the battle plans were being devised. When the whole countryside began teeming with grass and flowers, I'd look out at the scenery from the arched windows along the ancient Via del Borgo, the covered walkway that the inhabitants also called the Via degli Asini, after the many stalls that had once housed the donkeys used by the cart drivers.

The Germans in the area no longer had any tanks or airplanes, but they had two infantry divisions on the ground, and although their numbers were reduced there was still a significant risk of falling under their artillery and machine-gun fire. Everyone had been ordered to move very carefully along those roads.

One evening, a lieutenant called on the radio from Forlinpopoli, the headquarters of the Second Artillery Division, about twenty miles east of Brisighella. He was looking for a fourth player for a card game. I went, arriving there about half an hour later, in the sidecar of a motorcycle driven by Chmielewski, the same soldier who had scorched the donkeys' testicles. We played bridge, opening bottle after bottle of Chianti.

Maybe it was because of the wine that we couldn't find our way back. The fog rolled in. I heard German voices telling me to stop and identify myself, so we knew we had come dangerously close to enemy lines. I immediately took off my hat, knocked off Chmielewski's, too, and shouted at him to step on the gas, hard. There was a burst of machine-gun fire, and the terrified driver pulled off some daredevil stunts with that awkwardly balanced vehicle, which had to be steadied repeatedly to keep it from tipping over.

When the fog cleared a little, only a slender crescent moon and the motorcycle's headlight lit up a completely unpaved road, with none of the markers that the Allied soldiers set down to indicate that a road had been cleared of mines. We were in danger of hitting one or of coming across more German soldiers, and now that our hats were gone, it would also have been dangerous to encounter Gurkhas along the way, since they didn't speak the same language, and Chmielewski and I were on a BMW that had been taken from the Germans. Fortunately, we found our way back to Brisighella safe and sound.

By spring of 1945, there were hopes that the war was coming to an end, and troop morale was fairly high. Bologna was liberated on April 21, and the Allies entered the city accompanied by great crowds of people cheering with joy. A few hours later, the Polish flag was raised on the Torre degli Asinelli, the highest point in the city. I found a room at the Hotel Roma. News was coming of the success of the resistance movement in the north, in the cities that the Germans still occupied. At night there were celebrations at the taverns, with some of the drunken citizens heaping gratitude on the soldiers, others offering another round of drinks in honor of those who had fallen in the cause of freedom, while plenty of women clung tightly to the sturdy soldiers. Over the following days, the news coming in from Venice, Genoa, and Milan did nothing but increase the state of excitement. Finally, one morning, a whisper began that gradually swelled into a shout as the word passed through the entire city. Italy was finally free.

Just then, Captain David Kupferman told me to meet him in Castel Bolognese, a little village along Via Emilia between Imola and Faenza. Kupferman had important news for me. The captain was a distant relative, from Kraków. He had just returned from Poland, where he had gone on leave to find out about what had happened to his family. Fortunately, he had found them all safe and sound in Kraków, which had been liberated by the Russians in January. He told me that he had also been in Wadowice to find out about my mother, sister, and grandmother. He learned from some of the inhabitants that the Germans had shut them in the ghetto, together with some relatives on my mother's side of the family: Bronisław Huppert, his wife, Marta, and their daughter, Wanda. The deportations to the concentration camp began at the end of July 1943. The first to be sent there was my grandmother Anna Huppert, but all Kupferman could find out was that the Nazis had taken her to Belzec. One morning about two weeks later, the Nazis came to take the rest of the family. Tesia was separated from the others and put into a black Mercedes, which drove away fast. My mother, uncles, and cousin were loaded onto a truck. For all of them, the destination was the same: Oświęcim—Auschwitz in German. Kupferman went to the camp, already fearing the worst. Looking slowly through the list of survivors, he couldn't find the names he was looking for. Then he returned to Castel Bolognese.

In the meantime, summer was coming to an end.

CHAPTER 7

GOOD-BYE, WADOWICE

he war in Europe was over, and the news from Poland was devastat-
ing. Through my cousin Adas—who had become a member of the
Armja Krajowa, the Polish resistance—I learned more about what
had happened to my relatives. They had all been killed in the gas chambers.

During the weeks that followed, there was more horrifying news.
While the Nazis had been sweeping through Warsaw looking for Jews,
my uncle Wiktor Huppert had shot himself in the temple to avoid being
captured, and when Countess Isabella found out, she threw herself from
the window of her Warsaw home.

I decided not to return to Wadowice. Poland just wasn't the same
after the war. During the conferences that the Allies held in Tehran, Yalta,
and Potsdam, many of the cities on the eastern border were taken from
Poland, while others to the west were added to the country.

It was no mystery that Russia was behind everything that happened
in the country following the Second World War, like the elections held in
January 1947, which the communists won as expected. They had already
been governing Poland, at least since the Polski Komitet Wyzwolenia
Narodovego (the Polish Committee for National Liberation) had been set
up at the behest of the Soviet Union. This committee handed over to the
Russians the administration of the territory liberated from the Germans, a
development that was not especially surprising, considering that even the
manifesto read in Lublin, announcing the nationalization of industry and
the collectivization of agriculture, had been written in Moscow.

After the extermination in the concentration camps, only a few thousand Jews remained in Poland, and some of them immigrated to the West
or to Palestine, because anti-Semitism had not at all vanished from the
country. In Kielce, in July 1946, came the latest in the long series of tragedies for the Jews. Rumors started going around that the Jewish refugees
in the city had committed a ritual murder, unleashing a horrific pogrom in
which many of the Jews were massacred and those who were able to save
themselves were forced to flee.

I finally decided to go to England. My wife Irene was in London, and so was my father, who had been placed on the army's reserve list because of his age. After learning about what had happened to his family, my father also had decided not to go back to Poland, and he split the rent for an apartment in the old neighborhood of Golder's Green with a family from Bielsko. Father was studying to become a barrister, which would allow him to put on his robes again and argue before the English courts. After receiving his license, he secured an important client in Nottingham, Sir Arthur Donald Clay, the owner of the ARC Motor Company. The firm resold heavy equipment—obtaining most of it at military auctions, fixing up the damaged goods, and then selling it to private citizens. At one point I also went to work for the ARC Motor Company.

After the war, I had enrolled in the engineering school in Torino, in Italy, together with a friend named Rosciszweski, with whom I shared a small but dignified apartment in the artists' quarter. After moving to England, I went to finish my studies at the technical college in Nottingham. There I met Mr. Clay, who asked me to work for him, partly because I could speak more than one language, which would be good for business. I made one deal immediately, getting an excellent price for two tractors that I sold to a Swedish farmer. Before long, I was promoted to the position of the company's export manager.

During those years in Nottingham with Irene, we had two daughters, Linda and Lesley. I had received a business offer in Italy, from another old friend, Kurt Rosenberg, who bought military surplus for a company in Ferrara. Kurt proposed that the two of us go into business together. I agreed, and we moved the family to Rome. We bought, fixed, and resold Caterpillar tractors, which were said to have won the war, plus sturdy Jeeps, imposing Diamond-Ts, and lethal Sherman tanks.

My father remained in London. He came to Rome to visit us on a few occasions during those years. We would all go together to meet him at the airport, and afterward we would tour the city. Father knew a lot about the history of Rome, and his granddaughters made him their translator for the many Latin inscriptions on the churches and monuments. Their grandfather knew the language so well that he could even converse in it. When Lolek used to come to our house, my father would hold long conversations with him in Latin, like a couple of ancient Roman senators engaged in some sort of eloquent reflection on the vanities of the world—which were occasionally interrupted by bizarre appearances from Grandma Huppert, who would pass in front of them as she came into and out of the kitchen, telling Anielcia precisely how she should cook the soup.

The last time that my father visited Rome, he was already suffering with lung problems. I saw the signs of the disease burning away in his chest, often making him gasp for breath and interrupting his speech with a nagging cough—a tragedy for one who had always been an orator. Following one of these attacks, I glimpsed some blood on the white handkerchief that Father brought to his mouth. Notwithstanding his coughing, he never stopped smoking his cigarettes, which he rolled himself—although it was no longer the special Turkish tobacco as before the war. I begged him to move to Italy and stay with us, so we could take better care of him, but Father insisted on returning to England. He knew well that his soul would soon leave his diseased body. He died in London a short time later, with no woman at his side. He hadn't wanted any other woman after Mother.

In the meantime, business in Italy was good.

Occasionally Rosenberg and I had to travel outside of Rome for work, usually to clear tractors through customs in port cities like Genoa or Naples. Whenever we traveled toward the south, taking the ancient Appian Way past Monte Cassino, we were flooded with memories of the battle that we had fought in. The abbey had been rebuilt, and the fallen soldiers were buried in a large cemetery there, with many Catholic and Jewish graves. One day, I was taking the road back from Naples with Kurt, who was commenting on a newspaper article that he was reading about an important event taking place in Rome: the Second Vatican Council. The ecumenical council had gathered bishops, patriarchs, and cardinals from all over the world—some knew each other, some were meeting for the first time—and they had been discussing for a few years various questions concerning the Church. The council had been convened by Pope John XXIII, Angelo Roncalli. As pope, he had taken the name last used by Jacques Duèze, who was seventy-six years old when he was elected in Avignon in 1316—only that John XXIII was nicknamed "the good pope," while the first John XXIII didn't have a very good reputation. Dante had even placed him in hell in the *Divine Comedy*.

Not everyone had wanted Vatican II to be held. A significant number of the Council fathers had opposed it from the beginning, saying that it was unnecessary to have another ecumenical council fewer than one hundred years after the first Vatican Council. Pope Pius IX had convened Vatican I in 1868, and its results included the dogma of papal infallibility in matters of faith and morals. So when John XXIII died in 1963, less than a year after the Council had been opened, its opponents called for it to be disbanded. But the new bishop of Rome, Pope Paul VI, disagreed, saying that "the windows must be opened to let fresh air into the church," and he ordered that the Council should continue.

The third session of Vatican II was under way, and the article that had caught Kurt's attention was about an address given by a young Polish archbishop, very different from anything that anyone else had been saying. This young archbishop claimed that the Church needed to open up to the atheists and the communist countries, while the other Council fathers wanted only to preach the gospel to the faithful and opposed any change.

"He's brave, this Polish archbishop," Kurt commented as he read, "but I don't think they'll listen to him."

"How do you know?" I asked.

"Common sense," Kurt replied. And then he added, "He's Polish, and a progressive, too!"

"What difference does it make if he's Polish and progressive?" I responded, confused.

"The Roman curia is conservative and traditionalist, and it'll do everything it can to block certain reforms," Kurt said.

"But it's the bishops at the Council who will decide," I noted, "and not the curia. And there are thousands of them, from all over the world."

"Yeah, yeah," Kurt answered, sure of himself, "but you'll see. The conservatives will get up from their seats—the best in the house—and they'll have their say, those theologians, preachers, and respectable types used to the soft life at the bishop's mansion. And they'll convince everyone that change, innovation, openness to the world is just a bunch of trash, and the only valid teachings are the established ones, including the one that says the pope is never wrong. You'll see, this council will be exactly like the others."

I was silent for a moment, taking in my friend's pessimism. Then I said, "Maybe it's like you say, but who's that Polish archbishop you were telling me about? What's his name?"

Kurt opened the paper again. "Karol Wojtyła."

CHAPTER 8

THE BOOK OF MEMORY

E veryone at the Kluger home saw the joy and amazement on my face as soon as the nun on the phone told me that the person I was looking for—the archbishop of Kraków, Karol Wojtyła—was in fact staying at the place I had called, a Polish convent not far from the Vatican. I had found the number in the phone book, among some other Polish institutes in Rome. But the nun told me that the archbishop was out working at the Council, and it wasn't known when he would return.

"Should I give him a message when he comes back?" she asked.

"Please," I replied. "Tell him that Jerzy Kluger called." I also left my telephone number.

When I hung up the phone, my daughters asked me who the archbishop was. I simply told them that he was an old friend and that we hadn't seen each other for many years. Then Irene finally remembered where she had heard that name. I'd mentioned it with love and reverence on the rare occasions when I had spoken to her about Wadowice.

The phone rang about an hour later. My voice was trembling when I answered, and the other people in the room (Kurt Rosenberg was one of them) started huddling around me, curious. The person on the other side of the phone said that he was Karol Wojtyła, the archbishop of Kraków, and asked to speak with the engineer Jerzy Kluger. That voice was as unmistakable as ever.

"That's me," I said. "I'm Jurek. How are you?"

"You're Jurek? Jurek Kluger?"

"Yes, it's me, Karol, it's really me. How are you?" I asked again, emotionally.

"I'm doing well, but tell me about you. How many times I've prayed that you were still alive! Where are you?"

"I'm in Rome, too. I live here now."

"Good, great. I mean, now we can get together. Can you come here, or do you want me to come to you?"

71

"I'll be there right away."

"But do you have the address? Do you know where I am? I'm at a convent on Via Pietro Cavallini. Write down this address—"

"Yes, don't worry, I have the address. That was in the phone book, too."

"Then I'll be waiting for you. How long will it take you?"

"Just the time to get the car and drive there."

"I'll be waiting for you, Jurek. I'll be waiting for you."

Kurt Rosenberg, who had overheard the conversation, didn't have his own car with him and said that he would be glad to take a taxi home, not wanting me to be delayed. But I insisted on driving Kurt home, which was on my way anyway. During the drive, while I was wrapped up in intense childhood memories, Kurt sat next to me in respectful silence.

Half an hour later, after dropping Kurt off at his apartment, I arrived at the address I'd written down from the phone book. Via Pietro Cavallini was just a stone's throw from the river. After I rang the bell, I heard the sound of a key from behind the gate, and then the gate creaked as a sister struggled to pull it open. She had chubby cheeks and penetrating eyes.

"Good evening," she said.

I introduced myself. "I am Jerzy Kluger, and I am here to see Archbishop Wojtyła."

The sister motioned for me to follow her to a room on the right-hand side of a small hallway. She was very serious about her job.

"His Excellency Archbishop Karol Wojtyła will be with you soon," she reassured me, asking me to wait patiently there. She introduced herself and spoke warmly with me for a few moments before telling me that she had to return to her duties. I felt a strong sense of agitation, almost as if it had been pulled up from deep within me by the room's silence and sparse furnishings (a few chairs, and some missionary tracts in Polish on a table), and I fidgeted a little to distract myself. Turning around, I saw an image of the Black Madonna of Częstochowa on the wall, and I began to scrutinize the face. I'd seen it many times before, when I'd gone to Lolek's house as a boy. I began to call up memories connected to that image, the times my friend had knelt before it to pray, the times when Lolek and his father had gone to the shrine where the ancient image of the Madonna was displayed. It was kept behind a massive golden plate that was removed each day so that the faithful could venerate the image, while a band played a hymn written by an Italian composer. Those pilgrimages became more frequent after the terrible loss of Lolek's mother, Emilia, and of his brother, Edmund. Following those deaths, I would often find Lolek in church, absorbed in prayer, wearing the white vestment that he put on to serve Mass. When I saw Lolek like this, I almost had the feeling that I was spying on him, so I would quickly go to the courtyard to wait for him.

When I heard the sound of footsteps outside, I had a sudden impulse to get up and leave the room. When I did, I saw three men in long robes coming down a spiral marble staircase. The eyes of the figure in the middle lit up when he saw me, and he hurried forward, almost falling down. God, how good it was to see Lolek—Karol—as clumsy as ever, and how good to see him again after almost thirty years. He came toward me with his arms open and hugged me tightly.

"Jurek," he said, "my dear Jurek, you're really alive!"

My heart was racing. I tried to speak, but realized that nothing was coming out of my mouth. I could barely manage a whisper when I was introduced to the others, who had kept their distance out of respect. Karol introduced them to me as the primate of Poland, Cardinal Stefan Wyszyński, and the archbishop of Philadelphia, John Joseph Król. The latter's last name meant "king" in Polish, and Karol made a little joke. "Nomen, omen," he said in Latin—"a name, a promise"—and everyone laughed.

They told me that they were in Rome to participate in Vatican Council II, which would keep them in the city for a few more days. After this, they would go back home—the United States for Król, Poland for Wyszyński and Wojtyła. Then Cardinal Wyszyński explained that they could only hope that their passports would be renewed for their following trips to Rome for the Council. It might have seemed that he was joking, but the risk was real. The Berlin Wall had been built, the Cold War was under way, and there was constant interference with the activities of the Polish Church. Many of the country's bishops had been refused permission to leave to attend the Council.

"Well, then," Cardinal Wyszyński said, "I suppose you two have a lot of catching up to do after all these years, so we should leave you alone." Archbishop Król nodded in agreement, and the two men said goodnight and walked away. I watched as they passed through the door at the end of the hallway, struck by the tranquility that seemed to emanate from them.

"So, then," Karol said, "where should we go?"

"You decide, Your Excellency," I replied, smiling.

My friend didn't miss a beat. "Do you want to go for a walk?"

"Why not?"

We made our way to the gate. The sun was just beginning to set as we headed toward the Tiber. Karol said that just after the war, he had been told about the terrible tragedy that had struck my family.

"I was horrified when I found out," he said. "I also heard that when they had the chance to escape the ghetto," he continued, referring to my mother and sister, "they refused to save themselves, because it would mean leaving your grandmother alone. May God bless their souls!"

Then I heard that Karol's father had died during the invasion, while Karol was working for a factory. One evening, on returning to their humid basement apartment near the river, he had noticed that the house was strangely quiet. He had brought home a dried fruit compote and a meat pie for his father, but the captain didn't make a sound as Karol approached, his body almost entirely wrapped in blankets, which were still warm. Karol admitted to me that it was very painful not to have been with his father at the moment of his death, and just as he was saying that, it came to mind that I had suffered exactly the same kind of pain over my own father's death. Karol told me that after his father's death, while he was still doing manual labor and acting on the stage, he had decided to become a priest. Like the others who had made the same decision during wartime, he had become a clandestine seminarian.

We continued along the embankment beside the Tiber, at the foot of the imposing Castel Sant'Angelo. Karol was happy to learn that not all of my relatives had died after being deported to Auschwitz. The Haberfelds, for example, had survived. When my uncle Emil Haberfeld came to Wadowice in his luxurious Bentley, which he usually parked in the Rynek, I had been allowed to sit behind the wheel and was even allowed to invite a friend into the car, usually Lolek. Whenever Emil's son Gerhard came to the city, we all had a lot of fun pretending that we were driving a powerful blue Bugatti.

I told Karol about some of my other relatives who had survived the war—such as the Aleksandrowiczes, who had been interned in a Russian prison camp in Kizyl-Orda. One of my cousins, who like my mother was named Rozalia, had been married in a fairy-tale wedding to David Aleksandrowicz, a member of one of the richest families in Poland. Karol had met her. Karol also remembered her father, Mr. Groner, who ran a restaurant on Grodzka Street in Kraków, where the students of Marcin Wadowita usually ate lunch during their field trips to the city, tipping the waiter so that he would fill their water glasses with vodka.

We stopped at a cafe to have coffee. The people inside showed a certain reverence toward the archbishop, and I even found myself being somewhat formal toward him. Karol noticed this and told me, "I want you to call me 'Lolek,' at least when we're alone, and not 'Your Excellency.'" We finished our coffee and continued down the street.

Lolek wanted me to fill him in on what had happened since we had last seen each other. I told him about how my father and I had left Wadowice when Poland was invaded, joining all of the others heading east. I told him about the people who died during the air raids. I talked about reaching Lwow, and how one afternoon the Red Army entered the city, with its dizzying array of men and vehicles. I tried to describe the Russian countryside, which I had seen scrolling in front of me from the train I had traveled in as a prisoner, and then about how cold that region was, and how even the spit was turned into glittering crystals of ice. I told Lolek of the joy I had felt when I was set free, and the emotion of putting on my uniform for the first time, in Kara-Suu, where it was said that Adam and Eve had been created. I explained to Lolek about the single star that burns in the daytime in the African desert, baking everything in its heat, and of the many stars that shine in the night when the air turns cold. I continued, talking about Italy and about the courage of the Polish soldiers, and about how I had heard the people shouting in the streets that the war was over, and the joy I had felt, and then about my suffering when I learned about what had happened to my family. I explained my move to England, where I lived for more than a decade before returning to Italy and Rome with my wife and two daughters.

Lolek listened in silence, noticing that after I told the story about leaving Wadowice, I didn't mention the city again. "So you haven't returned to Wadowice since, have you?" Lolek asked me.

We were walking down a street full of people, in an ancient Roman neighborhood in front of the Vatican walls, and an elderly woman came out of one of the shops.

"Enjoy your walk, Your Excellency!" she shouted, almost as if impelled by her faith when she recognized his vestments. He waved to her and gave her a blessing. When he turned back to me, I gave him his answer.

"You're wrong, Lolek," I said. "I go back every night, when I fall asleep."

It was dark when we returned to Via Pietro Cavallini. We said goodnight with the promise to see each other again soon, just as we had done so many years before. The Council was still meeting in Rome, so Lolek would be returning for that. I watched my friend walk to the gate of the convent, then turn around to wave good-bye again before disappearing behind the heavy door.

About a month went by. The phone rang one evening at our house, and Irene answered. The priest on the other end asked to speak with the engineer Jerzy Kluger. Irene was smiling when she came to get me. When I picked up the phone, the priest told me that he had a message from His Excellency Karol Wojtyła. Lolek was in Rome and was inviting me to come to the Polish convent the following day, at about six o'clock in the evening, when he would be finished for the day with his work at the Vatican.

"Of course, of course," I replied cordially. "If His Excellency wishes to see me, then see me he shall."

The next day, when I rang the bell, Karol himself came to open the gate. After we greeted each other, Karol took me by the arm and we set off the same way we had gone the time before. I noticed that my friend was holding something in his right hand, an object wrapped in something like packing paper. We were soon at a bridge by the river. We could hear the chattering of some fishermen from below.

"Here," Karol said, handing me the package. "It's for you."

"What is it?" I asked.

"You'll see. Open it."

I touched it, thinking it was probably a book. I recognized it as soon as I unwrapped it. Just as I had thought, it was a book, but not just any book. Lolek had presented me with the *Modlitewnik Machsor*, the book of Jewish prayers, with a side-by-side translation in Polish. It was mine, the one I had studied and then used on the Sabbath at the synagogue, still handsomely bound after so many years, although the pages had begun to yellow. Paging through it, I found my old notes penned in it, and a caricature of the rabbi. My fingers were trembling.

"How did you get it?" I asked Lolek.

"Mrs. Szczepanska gave it to me," he said. "She's the one who had it."

He then handed me a letter. It had been written by Mrs. Szczepanska, in her own hand. She and my mother had always been friends. They
had gone to teachers' school together, and had gone on to receive degrees
in education from the Jagiellonian. When the first deportations of Jews
from the ghetto of Wadowice to the concentration camps had begun, possibly sensing that the end was near, Mother had given the book to her
friend, asking her to give it back to her son if she ever saw him again. Lolek
knew Mrs. Szczepanska very well, because she had taken care of him and
his brother, Edmund, after the death of their mother, Emilia, and Lolek
had told Mrs. Szczepanska that he had found Jurek safe and sound in
Rome. Finally, she could keep the promise she had made so long ago. She
had entrusted the book to Lolek, asking him to give it to me. And now I
was holding tightly in my hands that valuable gift, the last that my mother
had given me.

CHAPTER 9

A SLAVIC POPE

I n the meantime, Vatican II continued, and Jewish-Christian relations were among the topics discussed. In 1959 Pope John XXIII had
ordered that the word *perfidis* (faithless) be removed from the prayer
Pro perfidis Judaeis, which had been recited for centuries in the Latin liturgy for Good Friday, because the Church held the Jews responsible for
the death of Jesus Christ. The pope's action left no doubts about his inten-
tions for the Council in this regard. An elderly Jewish professor, Jules Isaac,
came all the way from France to thank him in person for this gesture. Isaac
was the author of a book titled *L'enseignement du mépris* (Teaching of Contempt), meaning the contempt toward the Jews that the Church had kept
alive for too long.

"Your Holiness," Isaac said to the pope, "this teaching is profoundly
anti-Christian, and it must be condemned."

"I understand, I understand," the pope replied.

When it was time for his guest to leave, the pope smiled and told
him that these delicate questions would be handled by Cardinal Agos-
tino Bea, recently appointed as the new rector of the Pontifical Biblical
Institute and also in charge of relations with the chosen people of the
Old Testament. Isaac went to see him and made an official request that
the discussions at the Council should also include relations between Jews
and Christians, because in his opinion there had to be dialogue between
these two peoples, and not hostility. Isaac was supported in this approach
by Nahum Goldmann, president of the World Jewish Congress, and
Cardinal Bea assured both of them that the subject would certainly be
discussed at the upcoming Council. Everyone went away content and
satisfied. But when the proposal was presented in committee, it was
rejected out of the fear that speaking in favor of the Jews might provoke
war in the Middle East. Many Jewish figures then appealed to the pope,
and John XXIII intervened personally to have the subject readmitted to
the Council discussions.

The "good pope John" died on June 3, 1962, but his initiative con-tinued as before. His successor, archbishop of Milan Giovanni Battista Montini, who took the name Paul VI, moved the Council forward just as his predecessor had wanted. Moreover, he helped Bea to explain and justify the need for a decree on the Jews, convinced that the cardinal's posi-tion was correct, and considering the tremendous tragedy that the Jew-ish people had suffered in the Nazi persecution. After some difficulty, the document was finally released by the Council, although it was not limited to Judaism, but was extended to all non-Christian religions. It was entitled *Nostra Aetate* (In Our Time) and met with widespread agreement among the Council fathers, who approved it on October 28, 1965, with 2,221 votes out of a total of 2,312.

After Vatican II ended, Karol and I saw each other frequently, every time he came to Rome. He was making frequent visits to the Holy See because he was a member of a number of Vatican congregations, and he never failed to contact me when he arrived in the city. Once we went together to the town of Eboli, which the Italian writer Carlo Levi said was as far as Christ went, because the train tracks ended there, and civilization with them. We were there for the first communion of the daughter of an old classmate, Zdzisław Bernas, who had been living there for a number of years.

On that trip, I began to understand how difficult the situation was for the Church in Poland. The communists wanted to create a country without any religion. Karol told me about Nowa Huta, the industrial neighborhood built at the end of the 1950s in the western part of Kraków, where there were no churches, but only a little chapel. The inhabitants of Nowa Huta had protested by raising a tall iron cross, creating their own open-air church, but also bringing down the wrath of the government, which saw it as an affront against the regime. They were ordered to take down the cross, and when it fell to the ground a loud sound rang out, like the ringing of a huge bell. Clashes followed between the police and the Catholics, many of whom were killed or wounded, and many others arrested. Lolek had to wage a long battle to obtain permission to build a church there, because opposition to the clergy was tenacious. To block the formation of young priests, the com-munists had also closed the theology faculty at the Jagiellonian University.

Every time he returned to Rome, Karol spoke of a country that was less and less free. I continued to hear about my homeland only from a distance; although this distance sometimes seemed immense, it really wasn't at all. Karol discovered this for himself when he went with me to the train station, and I told him that my granddaughter was asking me to tell her some Polish fairy tales, but I had forgotten them.

Smiling, Lolek said, "You have to make little Tesia happy." (My granddaughter had been named Stefania, after my sister.)

The train left for Kraków. A few days later, a package was delivered from Poland to our home.

"What is it?" Stefania asked as I opened it.

"They're Polish fairy tales, for you," I answered, "sent as a gift from Cardinal Wojtyła."

Stefania clapped her hands, with an expression of joy and wonder.

"Read me one, read me one," she said. I did, choosing one of my favorites from my own childhood, about Pan Twardowski, a Polish nobleman who sold his soul to the devil to be made into a sorcerer and was able to cheat the devil in the end. In their agreement, the nobleman had a clause inserted which said that the demon could take his soul only if he went to Rome. So Pan became a powerful sorcerer, and soon became so famous that the king of Poland summoned him to his court. He wanted Pan Twardowski to raise his wife from the dead. The wizard brought her back to life, earning a great fortune, which he began to waste on vodka, making the rounds of the taverns every night. One night, the devil caught him in one of these taverns and told him, "Ta karczma Rzym się nazywa" (This tavern is called Rome), and seized his soul, carrying it off to hell. But while they were on the way, his victim sang a prayer to the Virgin Mary, and when the demon heard it he immediately let go of the soul of Pan Twardowski, which fell and landed on the moon. And there it remains to this day, thinking about what a bad idea it is to make a pact with the devil.

The papal conclave came in 1978. Pope Paul VI had been very sick for some time, and after he died all of the cardinals came to meet in Rome and began exchanging their observations. They had a lot of talking to do—behind closed doors at the Vatican, of course, because electing the next successor of Peter is always done in private. Because divine providence is at work in selecting a pontiff, the decision was not long in coming. The announcement was soon made that the new pope would be the patriarch of Venice, Albino Luciani, who out of respect for his two predecessors used both of their names, taking the name John Paul I.

During the conclave, Cardinal Wojtyła stayed at a Polish college near Piazza Remuria, where he also got to know the patriarch before he was elected, when he came to have lunch with him one day. When Karol returned to Poland a few days after the white smoke announced the election of the pope, he had no idea how soon he would have to return to Rome.

"The pope is dead, the pope is dead!" the people were shouting in Saint Peter's Square.

The reign of John Paul I ended after only thirty-three days. His sudden passing led to some speculation that the Holy Father had been killed, a theory that many found convincing. A disturbing shadow fell over his death.

I listened skeptically to the newspaper articles that Kurt Rosenberg read aloud.

"Of course, soon there will be another conclave."

"Who's in the running?" I asked.

"The newspapers are presenting some of the possibilities. All Italians, just to stir things up," Kurt noted sarcastically. "One is this guy named Giuseppe Siri, the archbishop of Genoa, while another is Giovanni Benelli, the archbishop of Florence. It looks like Siri has the support of the conservative wing of the Roman curia." He pondered for a moment before finishing his thought.

"By the way," he asked, "do you have any idea how your friend the cardinal will vote?"

"A-ha!" I said. "You see, you always say you know everything, but you don't know that anything that happens in a conclave is kept secret, and the cardinals have to swear an oath."

Kurt pretended that he knew it. "Of course, of course, but maybe he mentioned some name to you in confidence."

"No, he never mentioned any names," I said. Then I added, "But I don't think he would ever vote for a cardinal who would want to block the path that the Church began undertaking with the last Council."

"Well, then, if the candidates really are the ones I have in mind," Kurt mused aloud, "he'll definitely support the archbishop of Florence, Giovanni Benelli, because the papers say that he's telling the other men of doctrine to remain faithful to the Council's decisions."

Kurt then closed his newspaper, as if there were little more to say about the election of the new pontiff.

The conclave began on October 14, 1978, and the faithful humbly awaited the decision of the cardinals of the revelation of the Holy Spirit, after the *extra omnes* was pronounced and the doors of the Sistine Chapel were locked. A large crowd gathered in the square outside, but at the end of the first day of balloting the smoke from the chimney was black, indicating no pope had yet been chosen. It was black again the following day, so all of the faithful had to keep praying that the sacred moment would come in which the Church would have its shepherd again.

On the third day the smoke was white, and a great cheer went up from the crowd. At that point, everyone in Rome was eager to find out who the new pope was. When the name was announced from the balcony, it was fairly clear that it was not an Italian. Then the pontiff himself came out to impart his blessing.

I was listening to all this at the dentist's office. After the years I had spent as a young man in the prison camp of Maryjskaja, in Russia, and the serious gum infection I had contracted because of malnutrition, my teeth had never stopped bothering me.

The nurse came in saying, "They did it, they did it, they selected a new pope, he's speaking now!" and turned up the volume on the radio. We could hear the noise from the crowd in the square, and then we heard the Holy Father: "Praised be Jesus Christ."

The voices all responded together, "Now and forever."

After this, the pope continued, "I don't know if I can express myself well in your"—he immediately rephrased this—"in *our* Italian language. If I make a mistake, if I make a mistake, you will correct me!" At this there was a loud peal of laughter, followed by long applause, and then the crowd continued shouting joyfully and cheering him on.

"What accent is that? He's not Italian," Dr. Ranieri observed, and the nurse agreed as well. When they turned to look at me, they saw I was weeping.

"It's true," I said, tears running down my face. "This pope isn't Italian, he's Polish! He's from Wadowice."

My boyhood friend Karol Wojtyła, Lolek, was the new successor to Peter. Lolek chose to name himself John Paul II, in honor of his predecessor. The date was October 16, 1978.

Rome became Karol's city, and he its bishop, so he had to leave Poland. An official farewell ceremony was organized a few days after his election, in the hall that Paul VI had built for papal audiences, between the basilica sacristy and the square. The many people invited had to include his old friends from school. Lolek had remained in touch with them, and had even seen them all together at their *spotkania koleżeńskie*, their class reunions. The first of these had been organized in 1948, ten years after our graduation, and even Mr. Krolikiewicz, our former principal, came. He brought the class register with him and called attendance, to remember the classmates no longer among them. Many of them had died during the war. Sheets of paper with their names written on them were placed on the seats. At that time, Lolek, who had just recently become a priest, believed I had also died during the war.

Other reunions followed. One of them took place in January 1968 in Kraków, after Lolek, already a cardinal, had become reacquainted with me in Rome. The gathering that time was held in the archbishop's residence, on Franciszkanska Street near Kazimierz, the Jewish neighborhood. There was snow outside, and although Christmas had already gone by, they sang the *kolenda*, the traditional Christian songs. I didn't attend that reunion either, although I had been invited. Part of what bound me to Poland was the sad memory of my family, which made going back too painful. As an apology for not going, I sent a letter to my friends together with a case of good Italian wine for toasting.

Halina Krolikiewicz, Zbyszek Siłkiowski, and Gienek Mróz came from Poland for the farewell celebration, while Janek Kus, who wanted to come, could not get permission from the communists to leave the country. Kogler came to Rome from Canada, where he was living. Naturally, my family and I were also invited. One evening, I found an envelope with the pontifical insignia in the mailbox. The invitation noted that after the celebration, the Holy Father would receive me personally in another room, one that I knew was just down a corridor from the Paul VI hall.

Once inside the hall itself, I found an atmosphere of celebration.

The architect's design seemed rather austere at first. Looking up, I saw an all-encompassing parabolic ceiling, the structure mostly cement, but seeming tough and light at the same time because of its fine lattice-work. Because of its contemporary architecture, the room had little of the opulence of the other Vatican buildings, even on the inside, where the most noticeable difference was the lack of decorations that characterized the other spaces. But the sense of the sacred was not missing; it was simply expressed differently, in the alternating light and dark tones of the ceiling, the large oval windows, and the backdrop, a bronze sculpture symbolizing the resurrection of Christ.

Even though I arrived early for the ceremony, the hall was already crowded. Still, I was able to get one of the front seats. While sitting there, I felt a hand on my shoulder, and I turned around to see my dear friend Halina Krolikiewicz and Zbyszek Siłkowski next to her. It was a tremendous joy to see them again after all those years. A few moments later, we were joined by Gienek Mróz, who had lived in Wadowice with his family, in a house that had belonged to Grandma Huppert. Halina, the daughter of the principal of Marcin Wadowita, had become an actress, just as she had always dreamed of as a child. I recalled a play that she had acted in with Lolek, which they had taken on tour to the neighboring villages. Lolek played a character named Gustaw, while she portrayed a woman named Aniela.

The last time Halina and I had seen each other was at the graduation dance in 1938. I hadn't seen Siłkowski, who was a few years older and in a different class, since then either. After graduating (thanks in part to help from Lolek, who during his last two years at school had often tutored him at home), Siłkowski and Tadek Czupryński had gone to the officers' academy in Torun, on the Vistula, about sixty miles south of Gdańsk. After this, he had been sent to a light artillery regiment in Bielsko. During the war, Siłkowski had been wounded by a grenade, but he had healed well, unlike many of their friends. Siłkowski had married the daughter of Dr. Home, the pharmacist, one of the few people in Wadowice who already owned cars in the 1920s. Mróz, who had been born in Limanova, about thirty miles northwest of Wadowice, had joined our class in the fifth year, and during the occupation he had become a member of the Polish resistance. Afterward, he had obtained a law degree. He was married now, living with his family in Opole in Slesia, where he worked as an attorney.

"Here comes the pope, here comes the pope!" someone suddenly shouted, and the people who had just sat down had to bounce to their feet again. John Paul II entered with slow, solemn steps, his vestments a brilliant white, followed by a clerical entourage among whom I recognized the primate of Poland, Cardinal Wyszyński. The pontiff slowly made the rounds of the hall, imparting his blessing. The people were reaching out to touch him, calling out, looking for a sign of acknowledgment. All over the room, people were waving little red and white Polish flags. It didn't take long for the confused noise of the crowd to turn into a Polish song that echoed through that space, heartbreakingly bittersweet. It was a good-bye to Wojtyła's homeland. And hearing all of those voices singing together made me nostalgic for that heaven, that hell, from which I'd long stayed away. Lolek passed just a few feet in front of me, but he didn't notice me, and continued forward without pausing. Everyone else passed by me, too, until one of them stopped and stared at me, as if some memory had pulled him up short. It was a monsignor.

"What's your name?" he asked me.

"Jerzy Kluger," I replied, a little surprised.

The monsignor switched to Polish. "Syn doktora Klugera" (the son of Dr. Kluger)?

"Tak" (Yes), I answered in Polish.

"Tego co grał na skrzypcach" (The one who played the violin well)?

"Tak," I said again.

A big smile broke out on the monsignor's face, and he introduced himself. He was Kuczkowski, one of the apprentices who had worked at my father's office in Wadowice before the war—and had also been the one who turned the pages for Father when he played the violin at the concerts at our home. I remembered that every time he turned a page, he threw back a shot of vodka. Monsignor Kuczkowski gestured to me that we would speak later, because he had fallen behind the others who were following the pontiff, who had already finished making the rounds and had mounted the stage at the foot of a bronze sculpture.

It was time for the speeches, and quiet returned to the hall.

The first to speak was the primate of Poland, Stefan Wyszyński. I remembered the first time I had met him, at the Polish college on Via Pietro Cavallini, when I saw Lolek again after so many years. I observed again the great solemnity I had noticed the first time we had met—but now, for the first time, I also noticed that the cardinal was getting old. Lolek had spoken about him often. When he was made a cardinal in 1952, there were arrests of priests in Poland, and Wyszyński was also imprisoned a few years later, when the police burst into his residence and took him away. He had just recently given a speech in which he had recalled the figure of Saint Władisław, the bishop of Kraków who had been killed in 1079 for daring to stand up to tyranny. The communist regime was convinced that this had been a metaphor, a reference to a bishop whom the communists had imprisoned together with some priests and one sister, under the accusation that they were all rebels. Wyszyński was imprisoned for more than three years, and even when he was set free, his adversaries continued to block him in any way they could. Wyszyński's mother had died when he was young, and, like Wojtyła, he had been raised by his father. Like Wojtyła, Wyszyński had a sincere devotion to the Virgin Mary and profound respect for other religions. When he met a group of Jewish students who, after the 1968 uprisings, were forced to leave Poland, Wyszyński told them emotionally that he would pray every day for their return to the country.

In spite of all this, many believed that there was bad blood between him and Lolek. Even the regime thought this and tried to pit the two against each other. Their main intention was to isolate Wyszyński, because they thought he was more anticommunist than Wojtyła. So when Wojtyła was made archbishop of Kraków, party leaders were happy about the news, because Wyszyński must certainly not have supported his promotion. But rumor had it that the cardinal had intentionally refrained from supporting him, because if he had done so, Wojtyła would probably not have been chosen. If this was true, then the primate must have been happy all the same to see Wojtyła put on the golden chasuble that Queen Jiagiello had given many centuries before to the Church of Poland, and afterward the miter and pectoral cross. And Wyszyński was certainly happy after Wojtyła was made a cardinal, and even more so to see him now, as the new shepherd of the Universal Church.

When Wyszyński finished speaking, he went to where the pope was sitting and knelt before him almost as a sign of solemn submission, but as he did so, John Paul II seemed embarrassed, stood up with open arms, whispered something into the cardinal's ear, and embraced him. It was truly a scene of great humility.

When it was the Holy Father's turn to give his speech, the crowd began singing in Polish again, representing many of their fellow citizens. The song mingled with weeping, though, because while communism remained in the country, Karol Wojtyła was gone.

As I already knew, and as my friends confirmed for me that day, religious persecution persisted in Poland. And although this was not the kind of persecution seen in the times of the martyrs, when Christians were not even allowed to exist, they were now being forbidden to pray, and there were constant attempts to make them submit to the communist system. Wojtyła had been one of the most courageous spiritual leaders of the country, together with Cardinal Wyszyński. But now the cardinal would have to fight communism in Poland alone, and without the strength he had once had. Many Poles were concerned. Yet from the way in which the Holy Father spoke, many who shared this fear were convinced that the pope would never abandon them, and that the Church and the Christians of Poland would continue on their journey as they had for more than a thousand years.

After John Paul II finished his speech and thanked the crowd who had come to listen to him, the clergymen who had accompanied his entrance gathered around him again. Many of the people stood up and moved toward him, and I also tried to reach him, but the security guards were keeping everyone away from the pope. Then Monsignor Kuczkowski approached me again, and we greeted each other warmly. I had last seen him in Wadowice as a law school graduate, and my father had considered him one of the most brilliant lawyers in his office. And now here he was, a monsignor in Rome, in the pope's entourage. There was so much I wanted to tell him, but again our meeting was cut short, because a young priest came up to tell Kuczkowski that the Holy Father was ready to receive visitors in another room down a hall to the left side of the stage. Kuczkowski said good-bye to my family and me for the moment, but told us it would soon be our turn to greet the pope.

When we entered the room a few minutes later, we found a long line of people waiting patiently. My granddaughter Stefania was holding two carnations, one white and one red, the colors of Poland. When the master of ceremonies came out to announce who would be the first to meet the Holy Father, it came as a genuine surprise.

"Engineer Jerzy Kluger and his family," he said.

For a moment, I thought I hadn't heard correctly, because it seemed absurd that I would be the first called. Then I saw Kuczkowski, smiling and motioning for me to come forward. Kuczkowski must have been the one to grant my family and me this honor. I felt my legs trembling as I approached Lolek.

"Świętobliwość" (Your Holiness), I said. At that point, my granddaughter held out the flowers for the pope, and he took them and gently kissed her head.

"Mała Tesia" (Little Stefania), he said. Then Irene and Linda curtsied and kissed his ring. After a photo, we had to leave, because there were so many people for the pope to receive.

For me, the moment was so intimate that I didn't even notice all of the journalists in the room who immediately set about learning about the family who had received the privilege of being the first to greet the Holy Father.

The next day, the headline in some of the newspapers read something like this: "The Polish pope grants his first audience to a Jew."

CHAPTER 10

TWO THOUSAND YEARS
OF HOSTILITY

A few days after Wojtyła became pope, I was contacted by a man named Józef Lichten, a Polish Jew from Warsaw who had moved to Rome, where he was the representative of the Anti-Defamation League, an important international Jewish organization. Just a few days earlier, Kurt Rosenberg had talked with an old friend from Bielsko, Hugo Schlesinger, who was a member of the same organization, but in South America. Hugo had asked Kurt if he knew this pope, born in Wadowice, who was all over the newspapers.

"Not personally," Kurt said, "but my business partner, Jerzy Kluger, knows him very well." Because of this connection, Lichten was asked to get in touch with me. Whether out of a spirit of collaboration or simple curiosity—during our telephone conversations Lichten had shown that he was a passionate student of Jewish history—I accepted Lichten's invitation to have dinner together. We agreed to meet one evening early in the fall at a restaurant in the old Roman ghetto.

I glanced at my watch and noticed I was a few minutes late. I wasn't far from the restaurant, but I didn't want to make a bad impression and started walking more quickly. I passed an exquisite fountain by Bernini, depicting four young men on the backs of dolphins, reaching above them to where four turtles were climbing up to drink from the upper basin. I turned down a short street, so narrow that the people in one house could look out the window and easily see what their neighbors were doing. Ahead and to the left was the Via del Portico d'Ottavia. Lichten had said that he would be waiting in front of the restaurant, holding a newspaper so that I would be able to pick him out from the crowd. A lot of people were out walking down the street, but the one who caught my eye was a man who was just standing there, not very tall, with white hair. He had a newspaper, but it was stuffed into his jacket pocket, and he was smoking—a detail that hadn't been mentioned. Still, I thought it must be him.

"Mr. Józef Lichten?"

The man tossed his cigarette to the pavement and extended his hand.

"In person," he said, and almost as if to prove it, he pulled the newspaper out of his pocket. "There, you see?" he said, smiling.

"I'm Jerzy Kluger," I said, shaking his hand. "I apologize for making you wait, but unfortunately I had urgent business that kept me late at the office."

Lichten looked at his watch, and then smiled reassuringly.

"Let me tell you, I've had to wait much longer than this before."

We went into the restaurant and were immediately met by a waiter who seated us at a table toward the back that had just been cleared. Lichten told me that he had worked as a lawyer while he was still living in Warsaw, so I immediately started telling him about my uncle Wiktor Huppert, who had been one of the city's most famous lawyers. Lichten said that he had certainly heard about him and had even met him on more than one occasion. Lichten was deeply saddened when I told him how Wiktor had taken his own life following the Nazi invasion, and how his girlfriend had also gone to her end after she found out. But those memories were grim, and we quickly changed the subject. Lichten was about twenty years older than me, and from time to time he reminded me of my father. Maybe it was just a habit common to all Polish lawyers, but like my father, Lichten also frequently recited Latin proverbs, even giving the impression that he knew the language fairly well, and certainly better than Italian, which he did not speak very well. In any case, he was a good conversationalist.

"Thank you for accepting my invitation," he said when we were seated at the table. "You'll see, here one eats excellent Jewish cooking, and then this is full of memories—do you know why they call this place this name?"

"Do you mean the ghetto?" I asked.

"Yeah, the ghetto," Lichten continued. "Do you know where that word comes from?"

"From Hebrew, if I'm not mistaken."

"That's true, that's what they say, but there's another version. When Venice was in its heyday, the Jews lived in a neighborhood near the foundry, which the inhabitants called the *geto*, because of the way they threw [Ital.: *gettare*] the metal into the furnace. But then the Jews started using the German pronunciation *gheto*, because so many of them were coming from Germany."

We were interrupted by a young waiter, different from the one who had seated us, who asked us (with a touch of local dialect) if we were ready to order. We immediately ordered a carafe of the house red wine, and then the dishes recommended to us, including the Jewish-style artichokes, a specialty of the house.

"Now that you remind me, I have heard that explanation before," I said, referring to our previous etymological discussion.

"That's what happened," Lichten said, "and this was a few decades before the pope had the Jews confined to this neighborhood in Rome, but it was after the book burnings, the ones they held right near here, in Campo de' Fiori." He was referring to an old Roman piazza not far from the place where we were eating.

"I know that they even burned copies of the Talmud," I said.

Lichten nodded. "That's right, toward the end of the 1500s. But can you imagine? Entire libraries destroyed. What a waste."

He continued talking about those events until the wine was brought to the table, together with the artichokes, just out of the fryer and very aromatic. Lichten immediately offered them to me, urging me to eat them while they were still piping hot. I did, and they were very good, even though they almost burned my mouth.

Now Lichten was ready to get to the real reason for the meeting.

"So, you're close to the new pope, John Paul II, Karol Wojtyła."

"Yes, as I told you on the phone the first time we talked, he and I were classmates, from elementary school until the end of high school."

"Then help me to understand something. Do you think this pope might be in favor of the Jews?"

I held back a chuckle.

"Do you think I would've been friends all these years with someone who was against the Jews?"

That made Lichten smile, too.

"Of course, of course," he said. "I hope I haven't been too forward."

"Not at all. But why did you ask? I mean, do you doubt that it's possible?"

Lichten took from his jacket a packet of cigarettes and a lighter and put them on the table.

"I realize that I was a bit indelicate," Lichten apologized, "but you see, this new pope is Polish, and you know how it is. If you look over the history of our country during this century you'll even find members of the Church who weren't exactly on the side of the Jews."

One name in particular came to mind.

"Are you alluding to Hlond?"

"Oh, the former primate of Poland certainly used harsh language against the Jews before the war, but I wasn't referring only to him. There were others, and who's to say no one else thinks that way anymore? It's better to find out fast, at this point, don't you think?"

This was Lichten's way of approaching certain issues. Besides, I understood that his organization's purpose was to oppose the defamation of Jews all over the world, so much of which had been seen in the past, and especially over the last century. The conversation on the topic took an interesting turn.

"Just for starters," Lichten began, "some people over the centuries have been able to foster hatred toward our people just from the reading of the Gospels. Think of John, for example, that says Jews are children of the devil."

"That may have been true before," I observed, "but it isn't anymore, at least since the Church has accepted Isaac's claim that such an interpretation of the sacred scriptures is profoundly anti-Christian."

"Yeah," Lichten admitted, pleased with the reference, "you're right. Isaac carefully reads the Gospels, and what's his conclusion? That they do not in any way instigate hatred toward the Jewish people."

He rolled a cigarette between his fingers.

"But look, it's also a question of timing. The work by Isaac that you mentioned came only in 1948, and the Church incorporated the spirit of it into a document of the last Council, *Nostra Aetate*, but you know this yourself—it was about ten years ago. The Church reconsiders certain things after the immense tragedy of this century has already taken place, while in previous centuries a Christian literature flourished and spread that, for some, was anti-Jewish."

The waiter returned with a plate of anchovies and endive.

"Exquisite," he commented.

I poured some wine into Lichten's glass and returned to the subject.

"What is this literature that you mentioned?"

"Well, think about the letter to the Romans by Paul of Tarsus, just for starters. There he talks about the Jews as enemies in respect to the gospel, but as beloved in respect to election, because of the patriarchs—meaning that they also descend from Abraham, Isaac, and Jacob."

Lichten popped some of the appetizer into his mouth and washed it down with a little wine.

"If you read that letter carefully," he continued, "you'll see that it really doesn't encourage disdain toward the Jewish people, although some of the exegetes over the centuries have been bewitched by that passage."

"You mean the one that says that the Jews are enemies in respect to the gospel?"

"Exactly," Lichten said. "And consider that this description would weigh against our people for a long time."

Fried zucchini and roasted tomatoes came to the table. Lichten continued talking as they were served.

"Toward the end of the first century, another letter appeared, this time addressed to the Hebrews themselves. Maybe it was for those who had converted to Christianity and were tempted to go back to their former religion. Some think it was also written by Saint Paul, but it probably wasn't. Anyway, that's not really important. What counts is that it explains how there is a new covenant, and because of this, the old one between God and the people of Israel is about to disappear."

He offered me some zucchini.

"Then there is another letter where it's written that God does not like the Jews and they are enemies of everybody, and the Revelation, which even mentions a synagogue of Satan. Chilling descriptions, don't you think?"

I realized from the start that I enjoyed listening to Lichten talk. He really seemed to know the history of his people well, and at one point that evening he reviewed this history, beginning with the destruction of the Temple of Jerusalem by the Romans in the year 70, and then again in 135, which began the diaspora of the Jews from Jerusalem and from Judea, the territory that would take the name of Syria-Palestine. The children of Israel began to leave the area, almost all of them moving toward the West. One group of them reached Spain, which is called *Sefarad* in Hebrew, while another arrived in Germany, called *Askenaz*. This led to the distinction between the Sephardic and Ashkenazi Jews.

Lichten picked at the platter of zucchini while he told this story. I did the same, learning in the meantime how the Jews in Spain had suffered during the reign of the Visigoths, but had lived much better under the Muslims, around the seventh century. The *moros* treated them so kindly that the Christians took offense and accused the Jews of helping the Muslims conquer Spain.

"But as you know," Lichten said, "regimes don't last forever. And after the Christian Reconquista, things turned really bad for the Jews."

"Are you talking about the expulsion of the Jews from Spain in 1492?" I asked.

"Oh, that was just the final act. There were more than three centuries of harassment before, with copies of the Talmud confiscated by order of the pope, forced baptisms and conversions, many conversions."

Lichten lit a Muratti after offering one to me, which I turned down. But he only took time for a couple of puffs, as he could see that I was so interested in the stories he was telling me.

"There are many anti-Jewish writings from this period," he said, "not to mention that during that same time a folk tale began circulating all over Europe about how Crusaders returning from the Holy Land had met a Jew—and not just any Jew, but the one who had struck Jesus during his passion. According to the story, that old man, his beard reaching down to his toes, had been condemned to roam around the world until the second coming of the Messiah."

"I've heard about that legend," I said. "If I'm not mistaken, it's that one about the Wandering Jew."

"Yeah. that's the one. And he really must've done a lot of walking, because they started seeing him all over the place. The *judío errante* in Spain, the *juif errant* in France, the *ewige jude* in Germany—there was even an astronomer in Italy who said he had met him!" Lichten laughed. "Excuse me, but that story about the wandering Jew and the astronomer always amused me. What if he found him one night when he was watching the stars?"

While we were waiting for the pasta course—fettuccine with beef stew sauce—and while we finished the appetizers, we continued talking about the situation of the Jews in Spain. They had been forced to convert to Christianity, and to keep them from observing the Jewish precepts in secret, Queen Isabella of Castille and her husband, Ferdinand of Aragon, decided to introduce the Inquisition. This was entrusted to Tomás de Torquemada, a Dominican who was very close to the queen, since she went to him for confession. So if it was discovered that a convert was fasting at Yom Kippur, or eating unleavened bread, or praying from the Torah, it meant the death penalty. The inquisitors sowed terror everywhere, until one of the cruelest, Pedro de Arbues, was killed in the cathedral of Zaragoza. By order of the king and queen, and of the reverend prior of Santa Cruz (the inquisitor general of the entire realm), the Jews who did not convert were expelled from Spain in 1492, and all of their property was confiscated. Many of the exiles went to Portugal seeking hospitality and freedom, but instead they were forcibly baptized, and were again exiled. They then made their way by sea to North Africa and the more tolerant Muslims in Turkey and Egypt, while others went to Italy, to the coastal cities of Ancona and Livorno.

"So, no more Jews in Spain or Portugal," I said, twisting some fettuccine around my fork.

"More or less," Lichten replied, "and things weren't any better in the rest of Europe. There were rumors that the Jews poisoned the wells at night or practiced usury. Unfounded accusations, and it was easy to charge them with usury, because almost everywhere the law prohibited Christians from lending money, so it was up to the Jews. Besides, they didn't have any other ways of making money, because they were prohibited from owning land."

"Those are hateful accusations," I noted.

"Yeah, and as if they weren't enough, a much more horrifying one began circulating. They started saying that the Jews kidnapped children in order to sacrifice them, and used their blood in their unleavened bread. The chronicles had already reported a few charges of infanticide, mostly in France and Spain, but in the following centuries they started coming by the hundreds, especially in Russia, where these trials would continue for a long time."

Lichten stopped for a moment to twirl his fettuccine. After washing down a forkful with a sip of wine, he continued. "Besides, do you know that there were a few fairly famous charges of ritual homicide here in Italy?"

I shook my head no.

"They date back to the second half of the fifteenth century, and they're fairly well known. One of them has to do with a boy called Simonino, who lived in Trent. Bernardino da Feltre, a Discalced Carmelite friar, had just recently left the city after preaching there during Lent. He had put the people on their guard against the Jews, warning them about an outrage that promptly surfaced when the boy mysteriously disappeared. A few days later, a Jew found his body in a pool of water in his cellar. He told the others about it—there were three Jewish families in the city—and the head of the community recommended that they should tell the authorities about it. They did, but then the men of the community were arrested and tortured."

"They confessed, I suppose."

"Of course they confessed, and they were sentenced to be burned alive at the stake, except for two of them who converted. They were allowed to be burned after their heads were cut off."

Lichten finished his wine.

"So at least their death wasn't all that painful," he commented ironically.

"They shouldn't have said anything in the first place," I observed. "But tell me about the other case."

"It involves a certain Lorenzino from Marostica, near Vicenza," Lichten said. "And listen closely to this one, because it's really incredible. When the boy was born, his father began saying that he wasn't his child, threatening to kill both him and his mother. But the infant—just ten days old, mind you—stood up and told his father to stop, because his mother was telling the truth, and he really was his son."

I laughed. "You're making this up."

"I'm telling you, I'm not. That's just how the story goes. Anyway, the father didn't go through with the slaughter, but on Good Friday five years later, while the boy was outside playing, he was assaulted by Jews who stripped off his clothing, crucified him on a tree, and collected his blood. When the body was buried, that's when the miracle began."

"What miracle?"

"Every night, a ray of light comes from his grave, and the little boy's hand pokes out from the ground."

"Come on," I said incredulously. "You've got to be kidding me."

"It's an absurd story, but in the latter half of the nineteenth century Pius IX authorized devotion to Lorenzino. His feast day is on the second Sunday after Easter." Lichten twirled some more fettuccine.

My mood passed from incredulity to seriousness.

"Think how absurd that is," I said. "They accuse the Jews of consuming Christian blood in their rituals, when both the Torah and the Talmud prohibit them from consuming blood of any kind!"

The dinner continued with cod and mixed vegetables and chicory with garlic and mullet's roe. We had dessert as well, biscotti made with cinnamon. After we had finished eating, Lichten insisted on picking up the check. We went for a walk in the ghetto, passing in front of the old Portico d'Ottavia (Emperor Augustus had dedicated it to his sister), and then went by the synagogue to the road beside the Tiber, where we walked along the embankment next to the river, where it splits into two around the island of Tiberina. We were still talking about the terrible accusation against the Jews, that they killed children. It was such a heinous charge, Lichten observed, that kings and popes had never concealed the suspicion that it was untrue.

"To be honest," he added, "in the case of the little Simonino who drowned, there was a great deal of hesitation at the Vatican, so much so that before the last executions of the Jews, the prince bishop of Trent found out that a delegation was coming to the city from Rome, including a bishop charged by the pope to find out what had happened."

"And how did that go?" I asked.

"The bishop concluded that the accused had been coerced into their confession through torture, and that it was quite possible that someone else had killed the boy and had put his body in the Jewish man's cellar. But it didn't make any difference. The rest of the murderous cabal was burned at the stake, and Simonino was beatified as a martyr."

"It's terrible," I said. "My father told me once that there were also Jews in Poland in the past who were accused of ritual homicide, and that there were a lot of trials over this. Did they end up the same way?"

"It's easy to imagine a few hot pokers being used there, too," Lichten said, "only when you consider the numerous accusations of ritual murders which were everywhere from Bielsko to Brańsk, from Lublin to Sandomierz, where there were three of these processes in less than a century. Although at a certain point the chronicles say that one of the pope's administrators was strenuous in his defense of the Jews. Lorenzo Ganganelli. Does the name mean anything to you?"

I again shook my head no, and this time with some disappointment that I didn't know as much as Lichten.

"In the second half of the eighteenth century he would become pope, under the name of Clement XIV."

"Well, based on what you've said so far," I observed, "it seems to me that often the popes rejected these kinds of slanderous accusations against the Jews."

"I don't disagree," Lichten replied, "and in addition to the ones mentioned so far, we could also add Innocent IV and Gregory X, who cleared the Jews of that calumny, because it was contrary to Jewish principles. Still, there were also popes who didn't think like this, and the myth was handed down over the centuries, sometimes spread in bad faith from the pulpit, other times spread by the press, up to quite recent times."

"What amazes me is that all this could been written without any kind of proof," I observed.

"In fact," Lichten confirmed, "there is no proof of any kind. Despite this, however, at the end of the nineteenth century the Catholic press also erupted with reports of other terrible events and other trials."

He lit another cigarette. "As you know, also in those years, it was not only this kind of accusation against Jews, but another very serious one was made. It was that Jews were planning to dominate the world. When the *Protocols of the Elders of Zion* started to circulate, there were many who became convinced that the thesis of the plot 'Free Mason Jews' had finally found an indisputable proof!"

I remembered how that document had been banned at the middle school in Wadowice, when it started to circulate in Poland.

"They could certainly have looked for better evidence of his plot theory, since everyone knows that handbook of anti-Semitism is a complete fraud!" I commented.

"You're exactly right," Lichten remarked, "but amazingly, the bluff worked, and hundreds of thousands of copies were printed in Europe. Although it was maybe a falsehood of the secret Tsarist police, many people believed it was authentic proof against the Jews."

"That's disturbing."

Lichten continued. "The message is clear. And the rest just follows. There's no need to bring it up again."

I lapsed into a long silence. Then I asked, "But what was the opinion of the Church at that time?"

"It didn't recognize any one race as being better than another. Still, there were many who believed in the Jewish conspiracy—that the Jews wanted power, and already had a lot of it, they were plotting against states, operating in secrecy, controlling sectors of the economy and commerce, in the judiciary and in medicine, in the media and in politics. So, for those who believed this, something had to be done to stop it. But no violence, heaven forbid, so instead there was the boycott."

"You mean what Cardinal Hlond was calling for in Poland?"

Lichten nodded, saying that the primate of Poland issued these kinds of appeals in his homilies.

"He said it was better to favor people of your own race when making purchases, and not to buy anything from a Jew, but also not to destroy their shops, damage their merchandise, break their windows, or throw anything at their homes. Many Catholic magazines in Poland diffused the thoughts of the primate, and among these there was also the *Rycerz Niepokalanej* (The Knight of the Immaculate), a magazine founded by a Franciscan, Fr. Maximilian Kolbe. Do you know about him?"

"Of course, I know all about him," I said. "He often published very anti-Semitic articles. At high school, I remember, we had a discussion in class with our teacher of history. There were some pupils who supported the idea of a Jewish Free Masonry in Poland. They were from the *narodowcy*, the extreme right-wing nationalists. The leader of these was a certain Dmowski."

Lichten didn't ask me anything, but it was obvious that he was curious about what I had said.

"But don't worry," I hastened to assure him, "certainly, Wojtyła was not one of those—for him, a Jew and a Catholic were just Poles. Also, he was firmly convinced that Dmowski's movement would bring no good to Poland."

"I understand," he replied calmly.

"Moreover," I continued, "I remember in those years not only that magazine published anti-Semitic articles in Poland. There were others."

"In fact it's true," Lichten confirmed, "also other magazines wrote to be on guard of the Jewish menace in Poland, like *Mały Dziennik* (the Little Daily) or also *Przegląd Powszechny* (the Universal Review), just to name the most famous."

"And were these also Catholic magazines?"

"Yes," replied Lichten. "They proposed to keep Jews separate from Christians, because Jews were harmful for the country, but they didn't encourage violence against the Jewish population."

I reflected for a moment and then responded.

"They didn't instigate violence, but they didn't want a single Jew near them. In any case, that's a pretty strange way to demonstrate charity!"

"So you see," Lichten said, "a certain mistrust remained. Taking into consideration that this was the position taken by many other members of the Church in Poland, from priests to university professors, one can understand the preoccupation of the Jewish community for the election of a Polish pope. I mean to say, your friend Wojtyła became a priest immediately after the war, and also in those years there were still ecclesiastics who had not changed their negative opinions of Jews notwithstanding the Shoah."

"I can well understand your preoccupation," I said, "but don't worry. Karol and I didn't see each other for many years. After the war, when I got to know what had happened to my family, I decided never to return to Wadowice. I re-met Karol here in Rome only in 1965. He thought that I had been killed fighting during the war like many of our old friends. I can tell you, Lichten, that I found him a friend as we always were, perhaps even more so. The extermination of millions of Jews had shocked and saddened him very deeply."

As we sat there beside the river glittering beneath the moon, the humidity started sinking into our bones, while on the shore thin streams of smoke went up from the torches of the fishermen. We had talked for hours, and it was getting late. We said goodnight, agreeing that we would talk again soon. So, you'll tell me more about yourself and about your friend Karol Wojtyła next time. Agreed?" Lichten asked me, shaking my hand.

"Of course, absolutely," I replied. "I'll tell you about him, and you'll see that he has profound respect for our people."

Lichten looked at me tenderly. He said good-bye and walked away along the wall to the left of the river, toward where his car was parked nearby. I had parked on the other side of the Jewish neighborhood, so I had to walk through it once again, passing in front of the remains of the ancient Porticus Octaviae, leaving the synagogue behind, walking past the restaurant again, its shutters now closed, and the large crowds all disappeared. Lichten was right: it really was a place full of memories and terribly sad. I imagined how it once was, when at sundown all the massive gates were closed and locked to keep in all the Jews. They all had to wear a sign on their sleeve to distinguish them from Christians. It was a pope who ordered this, not even five centuries ago, and it was like this for a long time. Then, in the darkness of that night, I seemed to hear the shouts and screams of the men, women, and children captured by the Nazis. It was October 16, 1943. After that night there remained nobody in those little streets and in those houses—only the terrifying silence of the ghetto.

CHAPTER II

SHTETL

There were no *shtetlekh* in Wadowice. When I was a boy, I heard my father speak only a few times about villages in which Jews lived apart from the other Poles, especially in the east. They had everything that the Jewish community needed, from synagogues to ritual baths, from schools to hospices. There was also a cemetery in the *shtetlekh*, and it was said that when the first body was buried in it, someone would have to sleep next to the grave until another body had been buried, because according to Jewish law the dead could not be left alone. People married early, and teenage girls became wives and mothers. The villages had doctors and lawyers, innkeepers and painters, cobblers and merchants, and there were some who went to the Christian villages selling everything, from needles to shoes and even carriage wheels. The language of the *shtetlekh* was Yiddish, but it wasn't spoken in my house.

"We're Polish," my father would always say, "so we speak Polish."

Schooling also began early in the Jewish villages, and the poorer students went to a public school, where it was said that the teachers really were strict, even beating the students who didn't want to learn. So it was better to have enough money to go to the *cheder*, because the teachers there were less strict. The schools looked the same. Both had straw roofs, a stove inside, and a cot for the rabbi. They had dirt floors, which were covered with yellow sand on *shabbat* and on feast days.

In Wadowice, at the Marcin Wadowita school, the Jews studied side by side with the Catholics, although I also had a Jewish teacher who came to our house to give me lessons. But on these days, I would usually bribe the teacher with some of the money given to me by my father or my rich Haberfeld uncle, asking the teacher to put off until another day the lesson on the precepts of the Jewish law.

But the east, and a remnant of the past, was not so far away after all.

During the past century of partitions of Poland, the Russians had harassed the Jews, restricting their rights and limiting their movements to such an extent that at one point each community had to have two rabbis, one chosen according to the will of God, the other chosen according to the will of the tsar. In addition to this, some Polish Christians thought that all Jews were spies for the tsar, and it was not easy to convince them otherwise. In the first November uprising against the Russians, some Christians even refused at first to fight alongside the Jews.

One story had it that a *chazzan*, one of the cantors who went from village to village singing the *shabbat* prayers, was stopped on the street by some of the rebels and accused of being a spy. Because the *chazzan* was unable to make the rebels understand his occupation, he finally told them he was a tailor, and they decided to put him to the test. "If what you're saying is true, then sew a garment," one of them said. But because the man was unable even to thread a needle, the rebels were convinced that he had lied, and that he really was a spy in the service of the tsar. The man was hung. This event occurred during the time when there were dreams of the rebirth of Poland, and after so many centuries of coexistence, there were efforts now to understand if the Jews felt themselves to be Polish at heart.

Of course, in the past the coexistence of Jews and Christians in Poland had been extremely successful.

The Jews arrived in the tenth century among the *polanie* (the people of the fields) looking for new markets. They mainly came from Germany and from the Saxon lands, speaking Yiddish, and because they were good at business and commerce, the Polish princes were generous toward them. At one point, a statute was even established to protect them—the initiative of Prince Bolesław the Pious, in 1264—and it protected Jewish property, synagogues, and cemeteries, and guaranteed their right to practice any profession. Even the courts had to respect the statute, which allowed Jews to swear on the Torah. The wise prince also said that it was not true that Jews killed children and drank their blood, since their own law forbade the drinking of blood. Anyone who unjustly accused a Jew of practicing certain foul rituals would be put to death.

Over their long centuries of exile, the Jews had been people of the Book, so they all knew how to read and write and were the most educated of the people they lived among. The nobles often asked them to administer their property, and the princes even had them oversee the production of coins. It remained this way for a long time, even after Poland converted to Christianity in the year 966, when King Mieszko I was baptized in Gniezno. The clergy of the country were seen as being very generous toward the Jews, so much so that the Church of Rome criticized them for being too permissive.

During the reign of Casimir the Great (who was said to have found a Poland made of wood, and left one made of stone), Jews were still loved and respected, possibly more so than ever. The king even had a beautiful Jewish concubine named Esterka, who gave him four children, two boys and two girls, and while the boys were raised according to the religion of their father, the girls were brought up in their mother's faith.

But eventually the Church solidly established its presence throughout Europe, so that Poland also became a fiefdom and the clergy became less indulgent than they had been in the past. In their homilies, they revived the old accusations against the Jewish people, sparking popular uprisings. In 1407 the Jewish neighborhood in Kraków was set on fire, and violence and looting took place in many other villages. But even this didn't stop the Jews from coming to Poland when they were expelled from other countries, becoming doctors, scholars, and counselors at the court or for the *szlachta*, the Polish nobility. And they never stopped their business activities: managing the property of the nobility, and operating mills and inns. The practice was so common that it was even given its own name, *arenda*, meaning the appointment of bright Jewish administrators.

"But why them instead of us?" Non-Jewish farmers and merchants soon became jealous and complained that they were excluded from the most important activities. In retaliation, it was said that those Jews had been born blind, and that they had become able to see only after drinking the blood of Christians. They were accused of exploiting the poor when they collected taxes and rents. Jews were looked at as being different, but these accusations were based only on rumors, nothing more. And since the Polish king was not believed to rule by divine right, and the *szlachta* had become so powerful that they even had private armies, it was the noblemen who defended the Jews, even allowing some of their Jewish vassals to carry swords, so that eventually no one dared to insult them. All in all, it could be said that the Jews lived peacefully in Poland—and not only them, because all faiths were permitted—as early as around the year 1500, while in the rest of Europe people were killing each other in the name of religion. So the members of dissident religious groups began coming to Poland for refuge, because while they risked being burned at the stake anywhere else, no one ever went up in flames in Poland.

For more than two centuries, the Jews lived in prosperity and happiness. But about halfway through the seventeenth century came a time of horrible suffering. The hetman Bogdan Chmielnicki began marauding through the country and soon became the most infamous figure in Polish history. He was accompanied by Tartar horsemen, Cossack warriors, and Ukrainian riffraff, and all together they seemed like creatures from hell—sowing terror through cities and villages, raping the women, slaughtering the men, butchering the children, and leaving nothing but ashes in their wake. The Jews were also brutally murdered (many were trapped in the synagogues and burned alive), and since the clergy and nobles also died at the hands of those demons, they all had to unite to combat their common enemy.

Then the Swedes came down from the north, the Turks came up from the south, the Russians came from the east, and every one of those wars was terrible. The country was further devastated by tremendous epidemics, until it became easy prey for its powerful neighbors. When Catherine was empress of Russia, she reached an agreement with the empires of Austria and Prussia, so that each of them could take its piece of Poland.

During that century of partitions, many Poles stopped trusting even the Jews. The divisions were especially pronounced in the east, where the Jews were isolated in the *shtetlekh*—the men with their long beards and black caftans, speaking Yiddish, eating *kasher*, and chanting the *shabbat* prayers, without even counting the many who were also Zionists and wanted to return to Palestine, the land that God had promised to Abraham. So because they were not rooted in a single place, shared few of the common customs, and were not even permitted by their Law to eat at the same table as Christians, people began to think that they were not Polish, and never would be.

This was more or less the story as I knew it, as my father had told it so many times, and the tale I had often heard from Captain Wojtyła, Lolek's father.

My own father felt himself to be Polish down to his bones, and many other Jews in Poland were just like him. But during that long century of divisions and insurrections, many thought that in their neighborhoods and villages the Jews were plotting to betray the Polish people, even though evidence existed to the contrary. For example, when the campaigns against the Russians began, the Jews went to fight as Poles, and there was even one rabbi who had the synagogues closed as a sign of protest over the profanation of the Catholic churches in Warsaw. Also during those years, there were authors who reinforced the long-standing connection between Polish Jews and Polish Christians, not only Adam Mickiewicz, but also Juliusz Słowacki, Ignacy Krasicki, and Juliusz Kraszewski.

As for me, I was unable even to imagine a Polish Jew who did not love his country. During the First World War, my father had fought in Piłsudski's legions, and Piłsudski had even been nicknamed "the uncle of the Jews," because of his great consideration for them. After Piłsudski's death in 1935, there were many changes. He was succeeded as marshal of Poland by Edward Rydz Śmigły, an officer who was said to love painting and writing poetry, and although he himself was not an anti-Semite, many other officers were, and they began to act accordingly. It became rather difficult for a Jew to become an officer. "If your son really wants to become one," my father was told at military headquarters, "he should get a university degree first." I knew very well that my Catholic peers could enter officers' training with nothing more than a high school diploma.

Late one evening, a man in one of the taverns was commenting on some of the restrictions against the Jews, maintaining that the Polish officers were all politically to the right, while the Jews were on the left.

"Look, it's just not true that they're all like Trotsky," someone replied to him (Trotsky was born in Janovka, Ukraine, to a family of Jewish farmers). And this was really true: Jews were not all communists, but some of them were socialists, like my father, yet many were on the right. I had seen an example of this in my own family, because my uncle Ignacy Huppert, my mother's brother, was a member of the revolutionary party of Vladimir Jabotinskij. Jabotinskij had wanted the Jews to be armed, and during the First World War he had founded an entirely Jewish legion. I loved to tell the story of one of my Uncle Ignacy's political foibles, although Grandma Huppert did everything she could it to keep it quiet at home. It was said that Ignacy had been very handsome as a young man (and if proof was needed, there was the photo on the piano, showing him in his officer's uniform, cocky and sitting upright in his saddle), and the rumor in Wadowice was that it was his good looks, not his skills as a speaker, that brought so many women to his rallies. One Tuesday afternoon, a meeting was held in the city at the Ludowy House, which as usual was heavily attended by women. To avoid disappointing them, Ignacy got all spiffed up, with his jacket and slacks nicely ironed, his boots shined to a polish, and a beret with the brim pulled all the way down to his nose. He dismounted his horse with the confident air of a god, and leaving a thick odor of cologne in his wake, he mounted the stage. But when he began speaking, a group of men standing near the door started whistling at him, and then throwing rotten eggs, until all of those women hurled themselves against Ignacy like lovers diving into the marriage bed, protecting him with their enormous bosoms. Poor Uncle Ignacy. But if he was not a great politician, he was certainly a brave soldier, demonstrating this at a high price when the Red Army entered Poland, and he was arrested because he had refused to get rid of his captain's uniform. He died in Katyn, killed by the Soviets together with other courageous officers like himself.

The revisionist Zionists were still around in Poland even after the war and were significant enough that at a certain point the communists wanted to undermine them. So they tried to get rid of the Zionists by accusing them of inciting the student uprisings of 1968. But this time as well the harmful effects were substantial, with a revival of anti-Semitism all over, so that many Jews were again forced to leave the country, including those who had nothing to do with the revisionist party.

This time I started thinking again about what my father had repeatedly told me when I was a boy, that the animosity against the Jews had been sown everywhere and was always ready to sprout up again. But I also remembered something Lolek had done during those months of fresh hostility and turbulence. I reminded Lichten about it when we saw each other again.

"Wojtyła went to the synagogue of Kraków," I told him, "to express his support for the Jews of Poland under those terrible circumstances." And after this, I added, "At least now are you convinced that he is not an anti-Semite?"

CHAPTER 12

MEDINAT YSRA'EL

It wasn't only Lichten who contacted me when Lolek was elected pope and the news of our friendship got around. During these months I was inundated with letters and telephone calls from journalists, rabbis, and members of various international Jewish organizations and asked to meet some representatives of the Israel Embassy in Rome: "What's this pope like?" "Is he an anti-Semite?" "Will he do something to help Jews and Israel?" They asked me such questions and many others from all over the world. I reassured them, declaring that Wojtyła was certainly not an anti-Semite, but I also told them that I had no idea of what he would do for Jews and Israel.

Apart from all this, the one who pestered me more than anybody was my collaborator Kurt Rosenberg here in Rome—he never lost the chance to ask me questions.

"Jurek," he would say, "do you think with Wojtyła things will be better between Jews and Catholics?"

When Kurt started his discussions, I distracted myself by telling him that things were already better and had been for a few years.

"We are not called wicked or *deicidi* (God-killers) anymore. Isn't that something good?"

I also had other meetings with Lichten during that period. I could understand from what he said that there were still many controversial points in the relationship between the two religions, beginning with the appeal of many Jews at the last Council, where it was asked that all the fathers then united in the Vatican confront the two thousand years' problem of the Church and Jews. Also, to consider their position on the extermination of millions of Jews during the last war. At the end, this was addressed in the document named *Nostra Aetate* (In Our Time), which said that the Jews were not damned and rejected by God, because this was never written in the Holy Scriptures. They deplored anti-Semitism, the hatred and persecutions of Jews at all times and places. Actually, many Jews had expected that many other crimes would be recognized and regretted. The Church said nothing about the ritual murder of Jews, and although the bishop of Trent abolished the cult of Simonino in 1965, nothing else was said to exculpate completely all Jews of the absurd and infamous processes made against them. Moreover, these terrible deeds occurred not so long ago either. Lichten told me that following the end of World War II in Poland, there were some horrible pogroms against Jews accused of killing Christian children. The last one, at Kielce, had cost the lives of forty-two people who had survived the Shoah. It was also expected that there would be an explicit condemnation of the Holocaust in *Nostra Aetate*, but there was nothing. After the war finished, voices began to be heard accusing Pope Pius XII of not saying or doing anything against the Nazi atrocities, some of which were committed under his very eyes. Some said that he was jointly responsible for the massacre. The Church resented these attacks very much, of course. They were even more resentful when, in the early 1960s, there appeared a play called *The Deputy*, written by a German named Rolf Hochhuth, who again presented the pope as a silent supporter of Nazism. This play was shown widely—Berlin, London, New York. Even in Rome a theatrical company presented it at the time of the Vatican Council II. I asked Lichten about all this, and he gave me a very positive answer.

"I think they are all lies," he said. "There are, in reality, testimonials of Jews he saved from being deported. He ordered that the doors of churches, convents, and the Vatican be opened to give refuge to these poor people."

I knew about this. I'd heard it from a dear friend of mine, Marquis Ferrante Cavriani. He escaped the search for Jews in the Eternal City—his wife was Jewish. He was from a noble Italian family, and they both found refuge in the Vatican together with a few others invited there by the pope. They were there quite a long time, until the Nazi menace went away. Ferrante told me that to pass the time he played tennis on the Vatican court, together with various bishops and a monsignor. When he knew of my friendship with the new pope, he said, "You know, Jurek, I'd love to play again on that court."

One of the things that obsessed Kurt was that the Vatican had not yet officially recognized Israel following its establishment in 1948. In fact, there was a well-known anecdote according to which when Pope Paul VI visited Israel and met President Shazar at Megiddo, he said that he had come there only to pray, and he called Shazar simply "Your Excellency," so as not to create any diplomatic misunderstanding. How could he say "President" if according to him Israel as a state did not exist? But there were people, like Rosenberg, who hoped that this would finally happen, that John Paul II would do what his predecessors had failed to do—that is, to recognize once and for all the Jewish state of Israel in the Holy Land.

"What do you think? Will he?" Kurt asked me.

"I don't know," I replied, "I know nothing about international politics. But I think it would be difficult."

"Why?"

"There's an ancient and dangerous creature down there called hatred among the peoples," I commented ironically.

"Yes, but look at it from a more positive point of view: there were the agreements of Camp David."

He referred to the peace agreement between Israel and Egypt that was brokered by the United States after some difficult years of war. The conflict had erupted because the Egyptians, just like the other Arab Muslims, had taken the uncompromising stance that the Jews simply could not have their own state in the Middle East, so when the creation of the state of Israel was proclaimed in 1948, it was immediately the target of hatred and war. Masses of Arab soldiers had attempted to destroy the nation. In addition to the Egyptian army, there were also the armies of Syria, Lebanon, Iraq, and Transjordan. But the Arabs were defeated and many Palestinian villages were swept away. Only Egypt was able to take any territory from Israel, the area called the Gaza Strip. After almost two decades had gone by, in 1967, another conflict broke out. Syria, Egypt, and Jordan amassed their armies on the Israeli border, and this time the Jews won the war in less than a week, so that afterward it was called the Six-Day War. Israel's territorial gains included the Sinai Peninsula, which it took from the Egyptians. Egypt tried to regain its territory in 1973, in what was called the Yom Kippur War, because the attack was launched on that Jewish holiday. Again, the Israeli army stopped the attack, as soon as it crossed the Suez Canal. A few years later came the astonishing events of the Camp David Accords. The Egyptian president Muhammad Anwar al Sadat arrived in the Jewish state. He shook the hand of Israeli prime minister Menachem Begin. They exchanged gifts. Sadat spoke before the Knesset in Jerusalem, and then the two of them flew to Maryland to sign the peace treaty in the presence of Jimmy Carter, Israel committing to give back its conquered territory, Egypt recognizing Israel and distancing itself from the PLO.

"Of course, of course," I admitted. "It was an extremely important historical event."

"If a Muslim country like Egypt was able to recognize Israel, then the Vatican should do so as well, and this would reinforce the peace process in the Middle East, in addition to improving relations between Jews and Christians."

"And do you expect the Syrians, the Lebanese, or the Jordanians would take it easy on Israel just because the Vatican recognizes it?"

"Oh, come on, I'm not saying that, or at least it's not so simple as that. But I still think it's the way to go. You see, many of the Arab and Islamic countries don't recognize Israel. In addition to the ones that you mentioned, there are others in western Asia, like Iraq, Kuwait, or Saudi Arabia. Then if you add the countries on other continents, from Cuba to Brunei, from Somalia to Afghanistan, from Libya to Pakistan, the list fills up quickly, because there are dozens of countries all over the world that have no diplomatic relations with the Jewish state. So it's important for these countries to recognize it as well. Egypt has already done so, the largest Muslim military power, at war with Israel until just recently. And I'm sure that the Vatican will too, especially since it is from that land that relentless accusations of Christians against the Jews have come for centuries. It would be an equally important gesture, and hopefully other countries could do the same."

"Yeah," I said, "but you have to remember that the fundamentalists in Egypt harshly condemned the decision of President Anwar al-Sadat."

Kurt brushed it off. "Oh, if that's all, he was running into condemnation from the extreme wing of Islam even before he made peace with Israel. They've always blasted him for the *Intifah*—"

"Inti— what?" I interrupted him.

"*Intifah*. Bringing foreign capital into the country, so much that he was called an imperialist at the service of the West, and for all this they had already tried to kill him once. And take note, that was when he was still fighting Zionism!"

"That may be true, but what about the Palestinians?" I responded. "What do you have to say about the Palestinians? And the *fedayeen*? Their leader has announced that the war in Israel could last for fifty years, that the territory taken by the Zionists will be won back, and when the journalists interview him he quotes the Qur'an, where it is written that God helps those who have been unjustly driven out of their country. Don't you think that if the Vatican recognized Israel, those warmongers could become even more exasperated?"

Kurt hesitated for a moment.

"Sure, that's a risk, but you'll see that this is the right time to take it." He then said that if Israel were to remain isolated at the international level, the Palestinians, who already believed firmly that the Jews had no right to be in that land, would be further strengthened in their idea. He finished by saying: "The Vatican must recognize Israel!"

I knew that was just the way Kurt was. He had been raised in a family of Zionists, and his father had been a member of the revisionist movement founded in Paris in 1925 by Ze'ev Jabotinskij. Jabotinskij not only called for the creation of a Jewish state in Palestine; he also wanted it to be as big as it had been before the English had given a large part of the territory to one of the sons of the sultan Hussein. It was a complicated history. I discovered this once through a conversation in my living room between my uncle Ignacy Huppert—who, like Kurt's father, was a staunch revisionist—and my own father, who was nothing of the sort. Lolek had also been there.

"The Jewish state must rise between both banks of the Jordan!" my uncle had said, with a fervor that showed he had no intention of backing down. Grandma Huppert was generally annoyed by her son's demonstrations of political passion and waved him off impatiently.

"Oh, you listen to him!" she said before heading off as usual to attend to her duties.

Just after this, Uncle Ignacy had another outburst.

"We want a revision of the British mandate. For one thing, Churchill just made up Transjordan! He did it to avoid another war with France. He was afraid of Abdallah and his Bedouins, but the price was Israel's land!"

I still didn't understand anything of what was being said, so I asked for an explanation.

"Sit down and listen," my father told me. And I heard the entire story, from the end of the First World War, when the conference was held in Versailles to decide the fate of a few provinces that had once belonged to the Ottoman empire. This meant Syria, Palestine, Iraq, and Lebanon. They were recognized as independent nations, but on the condition that they accept the oversight and help of one of the Western powers. France was given the mandate of Syria and Lebanon, while England was put over Iraq and Palestine. The son of the sultan Hussein, Faisal, who was already the ruler of Syria, was forced to accept the French mandate—but when they found out about this in Damascus, the Syrians began violent protests, demanding absolute independence for the country and insisting that the Jews not be allowed to live there. So France gave Faisal one last chance, warning him to respect his commitments, but since he did not he was overthrown. Faisal took refuge in Iraq. Shortly after this, when his brother Abdallah, backed by a Bedouin army, pressed all the way to the arid lands of Palestine, some were afraid that a revolt would take place in Syria. The danger of the incursion also distressed the English, who had the mandate over Palestine, and to avoid friction with France, they decided to appease Abdallah by giving him an emirate: the territory called Transjordan. It was taken from Palestine, from the arid land east of the Jordan River.

"But if that's desert land, why are the revisionists [the extreme-right Zionists] claiming it?" I asked Uncle Ignacy.

My uncle leaned in close, with an insinuating smile.

"Remember what I'm telling you, sonny. The Jews even know how to farm in sand!"

I saw the rest of the story unfold on my own. After the end of the Second World War, the dream of the Zionists at a certain point became reality, and the state of Israel was created. But the emir of Transjordan at the time was no longer satisfied with the land he had been given east of the river and wanted to take the territory on the other side of the Jordan as well. He got as far as occupying the old city of Jerusalem and changed the name of his emirate to Jordan. It was still called that even after the Haganah, the powerful Israeli army made up of both men and women, drove the Jordanians back across the river to their original borders, the ones established by the English.

It was dinnertime, but before leaving the office Kurt asked me if I had talked to the Holy Father about the question.

"Let's not get carried away," I said. "It's not like I'm a diplomat!"

"Yeah, that's true," Kurt replied, "not by a long shot. But it's not so often that a circumcised guest crosses the threshold of the papal residence."

CHAPTER 13

LUNCH WITH THE POPE

Some of the comments my friend made could be explained by invitations that I had received in the months following the election of John Paul II to go to the Vatican for lunch. The careful scheduling of these meetings had always been the job of Fr. Stanisław Dziwisz, who had been Karol Wojtyła's personal secretary for more than a decade, and who was confirmed in his post after Wojtyła became pope. The first time I received a telephone call informing me that the pope wanted me to be his guest at lunch the following day, I was far from indifferent.

"Please tell His Holiness that it is an honor for me to sit at his table," I had said, embarrassed but glowing. I was told how to get to the pope's residence in the old palace of Sixtus V, at the Vatican.

"Of course, of course, I'll be there," I said quickly, not feeling the need to get directions. The Vatican is a state, I thought, but it's not all that big, so it should be enough just to ask at the entrance.

The following day, a few minutes before noon, I headed up the Via della Conciliazione, the wide roadway leading from the Tiber to Saint Peter's, the imposing basilica that makes an impressive sight for any onlooker. When I reached the square, I drove down the left side of the colonnade, following the route I had taken to go to Poland's farewell ceremony for the pope in the Paul VI hall. When I arrived at the Ingresso del Petriano, the Swiss Guards crossed their halberds in front of me. I introduced myself enthusiastically.

"I'm the engineer Jerzy Kluger. I'm here to have lunch with the pope. Could you please tell me which way I need to go?"

They looked at me with disbelief and suspicion from beneath their black berets. After asking me for identification, one of them disappeared into the booth. A few minutes passed, and I looked at my watch. I was going to be late. Finally, the guard returned.

"You've come the wrong way. You need to go through the Porta Sant'Anna. That's where your name was left."

"And where is the Porta Sant'Anna?" I asked.

"It's on the other side of the colonnade, after the Passetto di Borgo, on Via di Porta Angelica. You need to go back."

"But I'm going to be late!" I'm sure my distress was written on my face.

The guard gave my identification back to me, then gestured for me to wait a moment. He went back into the booth and came out almost immediately with a man who must have been another Swiss Guard, but his uniform was all blue, instead of the typical blue, red, and orange. He told me that he would go with me to the Holy Father's residence without making me turn around. I thanked him profusely as he got into the car, then followed his directions.

We passed the Piazza del Sant'Uffizio, taking a street with the Paul VI hall on the left and the Collegio and Camposanto Teutonico on the right. Just before the Domus Sanctae Marthae, he told me to take the street that went around behind the basilica. We crossed a few more little squares, and then came to one where the guard gestured to me to park the car, next to the IOR—the Istituto per le Opere Religiose, the Vatican bank. The building was just across from the palace of Sixtus V, where the pope's residence was. My guide told me that I could take the stairs or the elevator to the fourth floor, but no more special instructions were needed because Fr. Stanisław was already waiting for me outside.

I thanked him warmly for going with me and then walked over to Fr. Stanisław, who greeted me and shook my hand. We took the pope's private elevator together to a little entrance hall, a heavy damask curtain half covering a window on the right, letting just a little light fall through. On the other side was a door opening onto a long hallway, mostly decorated with typical furnishings—a cabinet with a mirror, a few couches, some paintings. The echo made it seem a bit gloomy. A few steps to our right, and we were in a modest-sized dining room. The Holy Father was sitting at the table, next to another person. He stood up to greet me, embracing me, and then introduced me to the other guest, Monsignor John Magee, who had been the personal secretary of John Paul I. He was Irish and didn't know Polish, so we mostly spoke in Italian during the meal.

The dish was a Polish specialty, *zurek po Krakówsku*, a soup from Kraków. We talked about the first trip outside of his city for the new bishop of Rome, to Assisi, where the remains of Saint Francis were still kept in the old basilica, the lower one. The pope explained that the journey had tremendous spiritual significance for him.

While the coffee was being served, the conversation turned to another topic, when I was unable to resist the temptation to comment on how dim the drapery and wall hangings in the papal rooms looked. John Paul II was unable to hold back a laugh.

"I confess," he said, "even I don't like the color of some of those fabrics." He turned to his secretary. "But we've told them to brighten them up, isn't that right, Stasiu?"

"That's right," he replied, "and our engineer will see that the next time he comes, he'll find these rooms much more welcoming."

But I had to take their word for it, because the next time I was invited to the Vatican for lunch, I was told to go to a different place. I would be going to the old Torre di San Giovanni, and I was assured that someone would be waiting at the Porta Sant'Anna to take me there. When I arrived, a member of the pontifical guard was waiting for me on a motorcycle, and saluted me. We had to go farther this time, heading straight down the street from the Porta Sant'Anna, with the tower to the left. To the right were the printing operation, the grocery store, and the Vatican post office, as well as a small garden. After this, we went through a tunnel beneath a Renaissance-era palace. On the other side was a large courtyard. I could see a fountain in the middle and a deep niche on the left-hand side. Then came a second tunnel, passing through the adjoining building and leading to beautiful gardens with fountains, shrines, little houses, and chapels. I was able to admire the view from the street that passed us, at certain points running almost parallel to the remains of the ancient wall, probably the old boundaries set up by Pope Leo IV, now surrounded by the more recent walls enclosing the pontifical state. The walls made a nearly ninety-degree turn before continuing forward, and immediately we came upon a sturdy tower: the Torre di San Giovanni.

As before, my guide left me in the hands of Fr. Stanisław. We took the elevator nearly to the top of the building, where the Holy Father came to welcome me with an embrace. Behind him was another man, elegantly dressed, short, and with white hair. It took me a moment to recognize him. It was Tomas Romański, who I'd not seen in a long time. Lolek had wanted it to be a surprise, and what a surprise it was. The last time we had met was in Kirkuk, in Iraq, during the war, when Tomas had come to visit me in my tent together with Czupryński, Kogler, Gajczak, and Bernas. That was when I had learned that a ghetto had been set up in Wadowice. After the war, Romański had spent several years in England, just like me, before returning to Poland. In Wiśnicz, he had married and had three children and later had moved with his family to Kraków.

Another guest joined us, introduced by the Holy Father as another of his personal secretaries, Fr. Emery Kabongo Kanundowy, originally from Zaire. I was surprised at how well he spoke Polish, although he had studied it for only three months. They all sat down at the table. The sisters had prepared *barszcz*, a soup made with red beets, one of my favorites. I spent a wonderful afternoon with my friends. It was May 17, 1979. The following day was the pope's fifty-ninth birthday. The next day was also important because it was the thirty-fifth anniversary of the victory at Monte Cassino, which had cost so many young Polish lives. Tomas proudly pulled two medals out of his pocket—the Virtuti Militari and the Cross of Bravery, which he had earned for his resistance against the Germans during the invasion.

We were served a poppy seed cake for dessert, and at that point Romański couldn't restrain his curiosity any longer.

"Your Holiness," he asked, "when will you return to Poland?"

Wojtyła smiled at him and told him that the moment would be coming soon. A trip had already been scheduled for the beginning of the following month. He explained that he was going back to his country for the nine hundredth anniversary of the martyrdom of Saint Stanisław, patron of Poland. In 1079 King Bolesław II had ordered his emissaries to assassinate Stanisław. After killing him, they had mutilated his body and fed it to the dogs.

What an event that visit would be, I thought. After almost five hundred years, a pope had been chosen who was not Italian, but Slavic, a Polish pope. The last time he had left the country, it had been as Cardinal Wojtyła, to go to Rome to participate in the conclave. The communist authorities had confiscated his diplomatic passport and had given him one for tourists. They would certainly have blocked the cardinal from going to Rome if they had known that he was going to become that city's bishop for good. Caught up in his enthusiasm, Romański stood up and, trembling with emotion, recited from memory the verses of a Polish poet, Juliusz Słowacki, who more than a century before had predicted that one day there would be a Slavic pope, one who would bring peace among the peoples.

After lunch, while Fr. Emery and Fr. Stanisław remained behind in the dining room, the others went out for a walk, but not before the Holy Father showed us the view of Rome from above. It was spectacular. Wojtyła told us that we were nearly at the westernmost point of Vatican territory. Back on the ground, we walked along the wall to the northeast. Tactfully, I asked the pontiff whether, when he returned to Poland as pope, he would use one of his speeches to condemn the terrible tragedy of the Holocaust. Lolek smiled at me faintly, and told me that it was the duty of a pope to remember the extermination of millions of Jews by the hand of man, so that nothing like it would ever happen again. And what had happened in Poland especially was an indelible wound in his heart. Romański felt just as passionately about the matter.

"It's never discussed the way it should be," he said, "and the Jews have almost entirely disappeared from the country."

It was my turn to ask another question. "Your Holiness, will you also visit the camp?"

At that point, the pope confessed that he hoped that the regime would allow him to visit Auschwitz, and he trusted that if they did, they would not prevent him from kneeling on that ground and praying for the many innocent victims. Tomas bowed his head, not daring to ask any more questions. Since he was still living in Poland, Tomas already had an idea of the difficulties that this pope would encounter in returning there. Aside from the pope himself being Polish, no pope had ever set foot in a communist country.

We chatted a little while longer, occasionally letting our eyes wander through the exquisitely manicured gardens. At the end of the wall, we came upon a little courtyard with a shrine, a reproduction of the one in Lourdes, which the French had had built there at the beginning of the century. Behind a gate, to the left of a kneeler at an altar with a cross and six candlesticks, there was a little statue of the Virgin Mary in prayer, her robe white, a blue sash around her waist. John Paul II stopped to pray there for a moment before going back to the tower. He may have been praying about his return to his country. Careful not to disturb him, I approached the gate to get a better view of the shrine. There was something in the expression of that statue. It was compassion.

The Kremlin's reaction to the news of the visit was one of unconcerned arrogance.

"The pope's a clever man. Tell him to say he's come down with something," Soviet leader Leonid Brezhnev told party leaders in Warsaw to get them to convince Wojtyła not to come. The iron curtain was still dividing East and West, and the threat of a nuclear war persisted. But the Polish officials didn't want to tell a Polish pope not to come back to his country, out of fear that they would set the entire country against them, so instead they dictated the conditions of his return. It couldn't take place around May 8, the nine hundredth anniversary of the martyrdom of Saint Stanisław, because he had opposed a tyrant in order to defend his people, which for the regime was a symbol of anticommunism. So while Moscow continued to repeat that this pontiff would bring nothing but trouble, negotiations began between the government of Warsaw and the Vatican, making an apostolic voyage to Poland seem likely.

And that's just what happened next.

A high school graduation photo from 1938. Both Karol "Lolek" Wojtyła (the future pope) and Jerzy "Jurek" Kluger are standing in the second row—Lolek at the far left and Jurek three places over.

Jurek with his father in Palestine, 1943.

Jerzy Kluger and his family
are the first to receive a private
audience with the pope on
October 23, 1978.

Lunch with the pope in his
Vatican apartment in 1980.

A kiss for Stefania,
Jurek's granddaughter,
January 5, 1984.

The pope and
Jurek in 1986
and in 1988.

Jurek reads a letter from the pope at the 1989 dedication of a plaque commemorating the 50th anniversary of the destruction of the synagogue of Wadowice.

February 27, 1990, Jurek meets with Lech Wałęsa, leader of Solidarity, the Polish trade-union movement, who was elected president of Poland in the first post-communist government.

The pope admires a copy of a book about his friendship with Jurek in 1993. (Credit: AP Images)

The pope receives Shmuel Hadas, the first Ambassador of Israel to the Holy See, in 1994.

At the wedding of Stefania and her husband Edward in 1997.

The pope comforts Jurek after the visit to Yad Vashem, the Holocaust memorial in Jerusalem, in 2000. (Credit: AP Images)

A last lunch with the pope, December 22, 2004.

Overleaf: Pope John Paul II standing at the Wailing Wall in Jerusalem in 2000.
(Credit: Grzegorz Galazka)

Overleaf, Inset: A prayer, left by the Pope at the Wall:
"God of our fathers, you chose Abraham and his descendents to bring your Name to the Nations; we are deeply saddened by the behavior of those who in the course of history, have caused these children of yours to suffer, and asking your forgiveness, we wish to commit ourselves to genuine brotherhood with the people of the Covenant. Jerusalem, 26 March 2000, Johannes Paulus II." (Credit: Grzegorz Galazka)

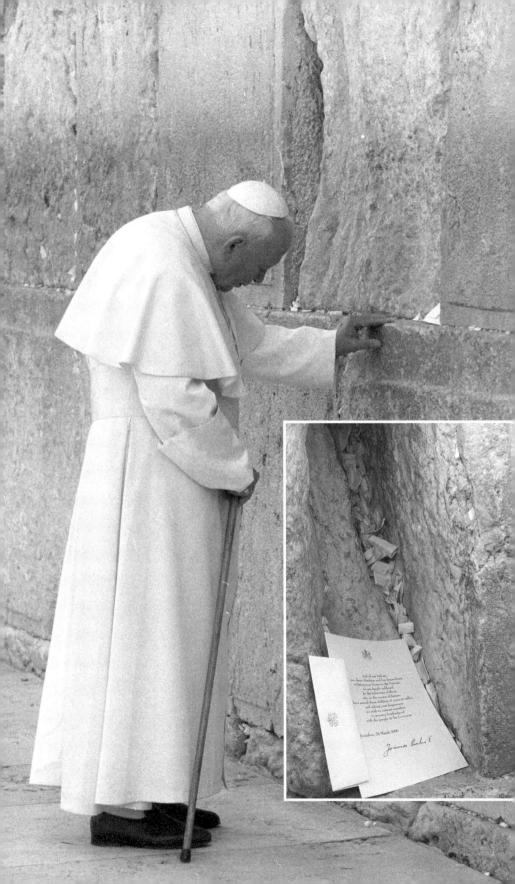

CHAPTER 14

IN THE SILENCE OF
AUSCHWITZ

It was the spring of 1979, June 2, the vigil of Pentecost. It was also the anniversary of the day on which Poland had become Christian, when the king had been baptized more than a thousand years before. The pope celebrated the first Mass in Warsaw, in Victory Square, the one used for communist festivities. There were great numbers of people there, but they couldn't be seen on Polish television, because the regime had ordered that no wide shots should be taken. So all they showed on camera were the sisters and priests, plus the disabled and elderly. The Politburo insisted that young people were not to be shown. But they were there, in force, and there were even more of them the following day, when John Paul II met with the university students, reminding them in the words of the Psalmist that the fear of God is the beginning of wisdom and that each of them had a cross to bear.

After this, the pope went to Gniezno, which at one time had been the capital of Poland, and to the Jasna Góra shrine in Częstochowa. Many laborers from Slesia and Zaglebie Dabrowskie were there to greet him. The Slavic pope explained that God had ordered man to subject the earth and have dominion over it through labor, so that he might be its master, and not its slave, and that in the same way man must not be the slave of labor, but its master. It was a clear reference to the exploitation of workers in Poland. "Szczęść Boze" (May God help you), he cried out.

On the sixth day of his visit to Poland, John Paul II went to Auschwitz. When I found out, a chill went down my spine, as harrowing as the squeal of the overloaded trains on the tracks. And I was well aware that Auschwitz hadn't been the only camp of its kind.

Following the German invasion of Poland, all of the prisons in the country were quickly filled, so other places were needed for internment—especially for the Jews. The decision was to build them in the area of Oświęcim, about forty miles west of Kraków. The *Stammlager* was the main concentration camp, and the first to be opened. The Germans used it mostly for Polish intellectuals and Soviet prisoners of war. The *Vernichtungslager*, a true extermination camp, was in Brzezinka, a town that the Germans called by a different name. Since it was within the administrative boundaries of Oświęcim, the camp soon acquired the name Auschwitz-Birkenau. That was where my mother and sister as well as other relatives had been taken to be killed. A third camp was built in the same district, but in a different town, Monowice, near a factory that used to make synthetic rubber. The factory was owned by IG Farben, a German chemical company that produced paints and dyes, but during the war it had begun to make a pesticide called Zyklon B. In a cruel twist of fate, it had been invented a few decades earlier by a Jew—and would be one of the methods for carrying out the exterminations of the Holocaust.

When the pope arrived at Auschwitz, it was morning. The train tracks that the Germans had laid inside the camp remained, leading to a platform with three bays, called the *bahnrampe*, where the prisoners were taken off the trains. The Germans also used other places to remove the prisoners—the tracks of the main concentration camp or the loading dock of the train station in Oświęcim. The men were then separated from the women and children, forming two different rows. The Nazi doctors came to evaluate them, sending the ones unable to work to the gas chamber, where they joined the other *muselmann*, the "Muslims," as the Germans called those prisoners exhausted by labor and hunger. There were four of these chambers of death at the Auschwitz-Birkenau camp, disguised as shower facilities. Just a few milligrams of the acid produced at the IG Farben factory was enough to kill a man, but the Germans would drop fourteen or fifteen pounds of it through an opening in the ceiling, into a room stuffed with more than a thousand prisoners. The gas quickly caused convulsions and filled the room with corpses.

The prisoners approved by the doctors as able to work were taken to the bathrooms, where they were completely stripped (the men were allowed to keep a handkerchief or belt) and their entire bodies were shaved. They were then washed in the showers, and given their new clothes: smock, trousers, and a pair of wooden clogs. Instead of their names, they had numbers tattooed on their left arms. The number was also sewn into a patch of cloth on the left sleeve of the smock, and there was another on the right pants leg. The Jewish prisoners also had to wear a yellow Star of David.

The camp's inmates slept on straw mattresses, more than one to a bed. They worked in facilities owned by German companies—mostly for Metal Union, Siemens, and IG Farben. IG Farben also used the prisoners as guinea pigs for testing new medicines or conducting experiments.

Above the entry gate were the words *Arbeit macht frei* (Work makes [one] free). The idea of displaying the slogan was said to have been that of Major Rudolf Hess, the head of Auschwitz-Birkenau, although it became the standard motto at many other camps, including those of Terezin, Flossenbürg, and Dachau. The prisoners had to walk beneath the slogan on their way to work and when they returned in the evening, while an orchestra made up of other prisoners played a march.

John Paul II called that place the Golgotha of the modern age. He knelt there, in front of the headstones with inscriptions in so many languages—Polish and Russian, Yiddish and Bulgarian, Spanish and Flemish, Romanian and Hungarian, Italian, and many others. Many of the graves were unmarked. He began to walk among them and stopped next to one with Hebrew lettering.

"This people has its origin from Abraham, who is our father in faith," he said. "And this very people, which received from God the commandment not to kill, has itself felt in a particular way what it means to kill. No one may pass this stone with indifference."

He stopped at other tombstones, one in Russian, the other in Polish. He selected only three, but added that he should have stopped in front of every one of the grave markers in that camp. It was necessary to visit each of those who had died.

John Paul II had one more victim to visit. He went to the cell of a friar, Maximilian Maria Kolbe, to leave a bouquet of red and white roses, the colors of his country. The story of that Polish Franciscan was truly incredible.

Fr. Kolbe was arrested by the SS in May 1941. At first, he was locked up in the Pawiak prison in Warsaw; at the end of the month he was deported to the Auschwitz-Birkenau camp, where he was chosen for forced labor. At the end of July, one of the prisoners of Block 14 had escaped, and in retaliation the Nazis had selected ten of the other prisoners from his barracks to be starved to death in a bunker. The commandant of the camp, Lagerführer Karl Fritsch, came to select from among the rows of prisoners those who would be sentenced to this fate. One man chosen was Francis Gajowniczek, who had a wife and children. He broke down and began weeping. Then Fr. Kolbe came forward, removing his hat in the presence of the commandant.

"Was will dieser polke schwein?" (What does this Polish swine want?) Fritsch asked.

"I am a Catholic priest," Kolbe said. "I am old, and I would like to take the place of this condemned man, who has a wife and children."

The commandant burst out laughing, and after considering that in essence this was a *pfaffe*, just a nobody priest, he agreed to the exchange.

The condemned men were led to the basement of Block 13, where they were locked in by the guards, who before leaving told them that they would wither like tulips in those cells. After two weeks, about half of the prisoners were dead. Each day, the guards came to check on them, ordering other prisoners to remove the dead bodies of their companions. At nighttime, the prayers of the survivors could be heard. By the third week, only four of them were left, including Fr. Kolbe. Because the cell was needed for other victims, it was decided that the remaining men should be killed more quickly. A German named Boch was sent to inject them with phenol. Fr. Kolbe died at 12:50 p.m. on August 14, 1941. His body was cremated, and his ashes were scattered on the following day, the feast of the Assumption of Mary. It was the same feast day on which I used to see so many of the faithful from the villages around Wadowice walking through the streets of the city, going on pilgrimage to the shrine of Kalwaria Zebrzidowska.

After Fr. Kolbe's death, his mother told the story of what had happened to Kolbe when he was a boy. One day the Virgin Mary had appeared to him, holding two crowns in her hand, one white and the other red. She told him that the first crown represented purity, while the second represented martyrdom. She asked him which of the crowns he wanted, and he said that he accepted both of them, after which she looked at him tenderly and then went away.

After this, Kolbe had decided to become a friar and had added the name Maria to his own. He founded the Militia Immaculata on October 16, 1917. This religious community was made up at first of about twenty friars and a few priests, most of them missionary, whose goal was to spread the gospel in Poland and abroad. He also founded Niepokalanów, the City of the Immaculate, in Poland, and decided to create other places like it all over the world. One of them was even set up in Japan, in a poor neighborhood of Nagasaki, Hongochi, at the foot of Mount Hiko-san. It was called Mugenzai no Sono, the Garden of the Immaculate. A statue of Mary was placed atop its highest building, and at nighttime a crown of lamps illuminated it so that it could be seen from anywhere in the neighborhood.

At the end of the war, when the atomic bomb was dropped on Naga-saki, although everything else was destroyed, that building and that statute were spared from the explosion.

The Polish Jews knew Fr. Kolbe well for another reason. He had numerous seminaries and novitiates in the country, attended by thousands of aspiring missionaries. His order also had printing presses that published everything from books to newspapers, from sacred texts to lives of the saints, from monastic writings to periodicals. Every one of those mon-asteries was stuffed with printing machinery—even in the kitchens and dining rooms—and the magazines had many subscribers. *Rycerz Niepo-kalanej* (The Knight of the Immaculate) quickly reached a circulation of seven hundred thousand, and a million for the special edition. These were startling numbers for Poland. One of their publications was a Catholic newspaper called *Mały Dziennik* (Little Daily), first published in 1935. During the period before the outbreak of the war, it published numerous articles against the Jews, to the point that at home I often heard my father criticizing the newspaper.

When Fr. Kolbe was beatified in Rome on October 17, 1971, many representatives of the Jewish community protested. Cardinal Karol Wojtyła was at the solemn ceremony. Pope Paul VI delivered the homily, speaking of the friar's life and also of his work, although making no reference to Kolbe's anti-Semitic writings.

Of course, in Auschwitz, which had brought death to 4 million people of various nations, Fr. Kolbe had been one of many victims, offering himself voluntarily to die of hunger in the bunker in order to save another person, and that's how John Paul II wanted to remember him.

The following day, the pope returned to Kraków, the city where he had been bishop. He gave his homily in Wawel Cathedral, where the mon-archs of Poland had been crowned for more than five centuries. A Polish legend said that a cruel dragon had once lived there, who killed men and devoured their harvest, until one day a farmer named Dratewka gave him a lamb full of sulfur to eat, after which he was so thirsty that he drank

the entire river, until he exploded. Then the church bells rang out in celebration, just as the pope heard them at his arrival that day, ringing out in
loud peals, because the bell of Sigismund was ringing—the largest in all
of Poland.

A pilgrim, like Peter, the pope then continued his journey to Nowy
Targ, to the south near the Tatra mountains, the highest range in the
Carpathians. After this, he went to Mogila, where there was an ancient
Cistercian abbey and what was said to be a miracle-working relic of the
Holy Cross. Wherever he went, the people followed. On the last day of his
pilgrimage, almost 2 million people came to say good-bye to him on the
Błonia plain.

When he departed, everyone thought he had left something behind
for that country.

CHAPTER 15

YEARS OF TENSION

That hot summer when he returned from Poland, Lolek granted the wish of my friend Marquis Cavriani to play again on the Vatican tennis court. We had a nice game with two monsignors whom we beat in two sets. The pope came to the court and enjoyed watching us. At the end of the match, he said to me, "Well done, Jurek, you still play very well—but your sister Tesia was better!"

About that time I also saw some of our old school friends who had come to see Lolek in the city of which he was now bishop.

I went to meet them at the airport, together with Kurt Rosenberg, who also knew them well. We were accompanied by Fr. Przydatek and Fr. Sokołowski, selected by the pope to escort all of them to an old pensione where they were booked near Saint Peter's.

Stanisław Niziołek, Tadeusz Bryzek, Wiktor Gancarczyk, and Wilhelm Mosurski were the first off the airplane. All of them had been in our class because they had been held back. Stanisław Jura and Tadeusz Luty followed. Luty was the oldest of all of them, and at one time had been in love with Wanda Huppert, my cousin, who had lived on the same floor as my home was. She and the rest of her family had been killed in Auschwitz. Teofil Bojes was also part of the group, which turned out to be fairly large; although they were all students from Marcin Wadowita, they hadn't all been in our class.

The following day was a Wednesday, and we all went to the Vatican for the general audience held in Saint Peter's Square and attended by thousands of faithful. The Holy Father arrived in an open car, which slowly rolled past the barriers that had been set up. Suddenly the pope noticed his friends pressed against the barricade, shouting out to him, so he told the driver to stop. The pope stepped out of the car to greet them and told them he would see them again that Sunday, when they could have a private audience and take their time. For now, he had to continue on his way.

The pope's old school chums had a lot to do before that visit to the Vatican. They took a tour of the city, went to Monte Cassino, took a lot of pictures—and there was the obligatory morning visit to the Vatican museums, where I also joined them.

A clause in the Lateran Pacts of 1929, by which the kingdom of Italy recognized the independence and sovereignty of the Holy See, stipulated that everyone had to be granted access to the museums. In fact everyone was, with one glaring exception. When Hitler came to Rome in May 1938, as a guest of the king and of the Duce, Pope Pius XI refused to receive him. It was said that Hitler's visit was the reason that Pius went to spend a few days at his other residence, in Castel Gandolfo, and ordered that the basilica and the galleries should remain closed as long as the Führer was there.

My friends and I saw one exhibit after another, before we finally came to the Sistine Chapel. In a room designed like a Greek cross, we passed the sarcophagi of Constantina and Helena (respectively, the daughter and mother of the emperor Constantine, who, according to a pious legend, dreamed of Christ before a battle and defeated his enemy beneath the sign of the cross). In another rotunda, we saw a gilded bronze statue of Hercules, and—as if they were living flesh and blood—Ariadne asleep, Laocoon struggling with the sea serpents, Eros in thought, Niobe in flight, Alexander awaiting his blushing bride, and Antinous, his head crowned with flowers. These were objects of pure beauty. Next came a large and sumptuous room richly decorated with old tapestries, and after this a wide courtyard with a huge bronze pine cone to the rear (beside two bronze peacocks, and with two lions in basalt crouching at the bottom). Past the courtyard was a building with four more rooms, all frescoed by Raphael. The third, called the Stanza della Segnatura, was where the tribunal of the Holy See, headed by the pope, used to meet. During this period—in the middle of the sixteenth century—the pope had the Jews confined in a ghetto. Behind the Stanza della Segnatura was a chapel with a great number of paintings, and then another apartment, where the Borgia pope Alexander VI had lived. It now accommodated works by modern artists. Our last stop was the room that Sixtus IV had commissioned, and it was said that its proportions were the same as those of the Temple of Jerusalem. The papal court had gathered in that room—the Sistine Chapel—cardinals, members of religious orders, nobles, laity, cantors, and a great number of servants of God. But since its construction, it had become more than anything else the place where the pope was chosen. *Just think,* I pondered, Lolek was elected here.

That evening, I had them all over to our house for dinner and to talk about events of the time that had passed. For example, I hadn't seen Bojes since our graduation. I talked with him about our country, which after so many centuries was again fighting for its freedom. The Church was defending the rights of the Polish people, and the regime could not stand this, obstructing it in whatever way possible. The opportunities for obstruction had not been lacking, even going back to the period of the Second Vatican Council. At that time, the Polish bishops decided to write a letter to the bishops of Germany, forgiving the German people. The communist regime in Poland attacked the bishops, saying that they wanted to absolve the Nazis of their crimes, stirring up the people against the Church. The protesters made it all the way to Wojtyła's window. Most of them were laborers from the Solvay factory, where Lolek himself had worked during the years of occupation. A letter was also written in opposition to Wojtyła, and published in one of Kraków's leading newspapers. But when the archbishop wrote to defend himself from the unjust accusations, no newspaper would publish it.

Bojes told me that silence and censorship were among the means the Polish communists used to preserve their power—when they did not resort to more extreme methods. A few years before, a student had been found dead at the Jagiellonian University. His name was Stanisław Pyjas, and he was a member of the Kor, a workers' rights organization. His body showed signs of foul play, but the police report said that the young man had gotten drunk and fallen down the stairs, striking his head. No one believed this, of course, and instead the police themselves were thought to be behind the murder, because Pyjas had been one of the main opponents of the Polish communist system. Wojtyła was also convinced of police involvement, although he did everything he could to calm down the students who were ready to retaliate. Too much blood had been spilled already. But Wojtyła did defy the regime in his own way, holding an open-air Mass and having the phrase "Your labor is not in vain" displayed over the altar. Because it was taken from the first Letter to the Corinthians (Polish: *Koryntian*), the abbreviation "KOR" appeared after the quotation, and the connection to the workers' rights group was lost on no one. It was especially because of this intellectual way of attracting the people that the regime was so afraid of Karol, so much so that they had him followed and bugged his rooms.

Irene came to serve the coffee. Bojes drank his, and then finished his story.

"You know," he said to me, "times are still hard in Poland. The workers are striking and demanding their rights, but they're being fired or even imprisoned. So then comes the Kor to defend them, but even so, they kill one of its members, and then, as if that weren't enough, at the funeral they arrest more of its leaders. So the ones who are still free organize an eight-day hunger strike to call for their release, barricading themselves inside the old Church of Saint Martin, but when a newspaper takes their side, the regime tells the police to shut it down. That's how things work in Poland, you get it?"

He pointed to Bryzek, on the other side of the table.

"Do you know that he used to be a communist, too? Once I was even afraid of what might happen to him."

"Why?" I asked.

"Once Wojtyła saw him on the street and went to embrace him."

"What's so bad about that?"

Bojes started to laugh. "Well, with all the spies around Karol, they might have sent Bryzek to Siberia for that hug!"

On Sunday, I went with them to their audience at the Vatican. Karol's old friends brought the Holy Father a gift: a collection of *świątki*—prized wooden sculptures made by Polish craftsmen. I remembered the times I had seen the same kinds of statues displayed all in a row on the *stragan*, on the Thursdays when the market was open in Wadowice. Mostly they were depictions of farmers and shepherds, and the best were made by the woodworkers of Jaroszowice, Zawadka, and Ponikwia. The pope thanked them a great deal for the gifts and spent more than an hour with them before returning to his duties. That evening, as they all boarded the airplane for Poland, Bojes turned toward me one last time.

"You know," he said, "I always knew that the snacks your mother put in that basket were meant for me, too. I never got a chance to thank her. May God bless her."

That summer, on July 30, 1980, the Israeli Knesset approved the Basic Law, confirming Jerusalem as the capital of the country. It didn't do much good to say that the holy places there would remain open to the faithful of all religions; the move sparked international outrage anyway.

About twenty years later, a resolution of the UN Security Council censured the declaration. It was an old question. Following the creation of the state of Israel, the UN General Assembly on May 15, 1948, had called for a Jewish state and an Arab state in the land of Palestine, while specifying that Jerusalem should not belong to either one, because out of respect for all of the communities there (mostly Muslims, Jews, and Christians), Jerusalem should be administered by the United Nations.

A few years later, after Britain had withdrawn its troops from the area and the Arab countries had attacked Israel, Transjordan had conquered the land on the other side of the river, the West Bank, as well as the old city of Jerusalem, after which it took the name of Jordan.

But in 1950, Israel had again claimed Jerusalem as its capital. Not even two decades later, there was another war with the Arab countries—the one that lasted six days—and Israel was able to conquer the part of the city under Jordanian control, together with some other territories that it occupied. In addition to Jerusalem and the West Bank, these were the Sinai Peninsula, the Gaza Strip, and the Golan Heights.

The UN General Assembly had immediately condemned the Jewish state for taking the eastern part of the city, and now that the Knesset had proclaimed Jerusalem the united and indivisible capital of Israel, it also faced the hostility of the Arabs, especially those who lived in the holy city.

This situation sowed the seeds for another fiery debate between Kurt Rosenberg and me. Kurt maintained that Jerusalem, all of it, was the one true capital of Israel—so he was against the Security Council resolution.

He had been grousing for a while, as if I weren't even in the room.

"This time, they'll just have to get used to it. Jerusalem belongs to Israel. Anyone who wants to can enter the city, there's room for everyone—Jews, Muslims, Christians, Armenians—but Jerusalem was and still is the capital of Israel."

I wanted to prod him a little. "So what do you have to say about the resolution of the Security Council?"

"Who cares? They've been slapping resolutions on us since the 1950s. And not just over the question of Jerusalem. There was also that one about Syria, remember? And then Lebanon, and Jordan, and the settlements in the occupied territories. But even there, what is it that we've occupied, really?"

I made a list. "The old city of Jerusalem—that's what the international community says—and then Gaza, the Golan Heights, and don't forget the West Bank."

"Come on, not that!" Kurt objected.

"Why? Isn't the West Bank occupied territory?"

"Let's call it 'disputed.' Not 'occupied.' And they've come up with all sorts of names for it—Cisjordan, West Bank, Diffa al-gharbī—but they always forget its real name."

"What's that?" I asked.

"Judea and Samaria," Kurt replied. "That's what it's really called, and it was Jewish land. And I'm not the one who says so; it's in the Torah." He was referring to the two regions that were once part of the kingdom of Israel. Judea had been given to the tribe of Judah, the fourth son of Jacob and Leah. Samaria got its name because King Omri of Israel had bought it from Shemer for two talents, and had then built a city there, which he made his residence. After the death of King Solomon in 931 B.C., the kingdom of Israel was divided into two parts. The northern section was still called Israel, while the southern part was called the kingdom of Judea.

While he was telling the story, Kurt added, "Those regions belonged to two different kingdoms, that's true, but they were still Jewish kingdoms. So you see, Jurek, we haven't occupied that land. It's always been ours."

In reality, the question was more complicated.

Even among the countries with diplomatic relations with Israel, many did not recognize Jerusalem as Israel's capital, so their embassies were outside of the city, in Tel Aviv. Then there were the territories that Israel had occupied after the Six-Day War. Just after the end of that conflict, the UN Security Council had asked for the withdrawal of Israeli troops from the area. After the Camp David Accords between Israeli prime minister Begin and Egyptian president Sadat, the Sinai Peninsula had been returned to Egypt. That still left the West Bank and the Gaza Strip. And recently, another resolution had denied the legal standing of the Israeli settlements in those areas.

Then there was the question of the Palestinian refugees. Already after the Arab-Israeli war in 1948, the United Nations had estimated that more than seven hundred thousand Palestinians had emigrated or had been forced to leave the territory where they lived, about half of the Arab population of Palestine at the time. In December of that year, the UN General Assembly had approved Resolution 194, according to which the Israelis would have to allow the refugees who wished to do so to return in peace to their homes, while the others would be given compensation. The resolution was never observed. And after the Palestinians had been scattered to Lebanon, Syria, Jordan, Kuwait, Yemen, Iraq, and other Arab countries, they became convinced that Arab armies would never be able to defeat the Israeli enemy. Instead, their only chance was guerrilla warfare.

This circumstance was one of the reasons for the creation of the PLO, the Palestinian Liberation Organization. Various movements developed within the PLO, including the one called al-Fatah, which means "victory" in Arabic. It had been created in Kuwait City in 1958, by Yasser Arafat, a Palestinian of the al-Husaynī family, who was working as an engineer in the city. After Nasser's ruinous defeat in the Six-Day War, the organization had secretly moved to Jordan, where it began rigorous training of guerrillas. These soldiers had sworn to dedicate themselves entirely to the aim of liberating Palestine from the invader, so they were called *fedayeen* (from *fida'iyyin*, meaning "dedicated"). They often conducted their attacks at the Israeli border. But on March 21, 1969, Israeli special forces entered Karāmeh, where the Palestinian fighters were hiding, and many of them had to flee and find shelter elsewhere. Many went to southern Lebanon, almost on the Israeli border, and from there continued their artillery attacks on the Jewish villages. A few years earlier, the Israeli army had invaded Lebanon. The operation had been code named "Litani," from the Arab name for the river that the Greeks called Leontes, which had once marked the border between the Egyptian empire and the Hittite kingdom, running from the ancient city of Ba'labakk to the Mediterranean, north of Tyre. At that time, the UN Security Council had passed two resolutions calling for a complete withdrawal of Israeli forces from southern Lebanon. But it had not succeeded.

The situation in the Middle East, then, was a difficult one.

During those months in 1980, I had continued to visit Wojtyła, who was very concerned about what was happening in the Mideast. But he was also worried about events in Poland.

The workers were demanding the right to strike, but the regime continued to imprison them for this. Many factories fired the workers who protested against their exploitation, Obviously, the firings were politically motivated. One of them took place at the Lenin shipyard in Gdańsk. Anna Walentynowicz was a crane operator who had dared to ask for hot meals for the employees and for places where they could warm themselves. After she was thrown out, a note was attached to the clock at the work site entrance, asking that she be rehired. There had already been strikes that year, against rising prices. One had been in Warsaw, at the Ursus office. But there had been a genuine workers' revolt on the Baltic Sea. An electrician who worked in the shipyards had jumped on top of a wall to lead it. His name was Lech Wałęsa. What the world saw were thousands of workers in blue overalls, kneeling to pray in the shipyards. On the gates were an image of the Black Madonna of Częstochowa and a photo of John Paul II.

CHAPTER 16

"THEY'VE SHOT THE POPE!"

T he time and place were the Wednesday general audience, Saint
Peter's Square at the Vatican, May 13, 1981. When the Holy Father
arrived, there was nothing but an ocean of faithful as far as the eye
could see. The sweet spring air was full of joyful cheering. When the pope
came to just a few steps away from the bronze gate in front of the colonnade on the right-hand side, a father held up his young daughter. John
Paul II took her and lifted her up into the air, kissed her, and gave her back
to her parents. Then came the beating of pigeons' wings, together with a
loud and disturbing noise. And after this, another.

Vatican City—*Two shots were fired at the pope at 5:21 p.m., as he
entered Saint Peter's Square for the general audience, in an open car.*
                    —Bulletin from the Ansa news agency, 5:33

*According to initial reports, the pope has been wounded and was imme-
diately taken away by ambulance.*
                    —Bulletin from the Ansa news agency, 5:34

I went to visit Lolek at the Policlinico Gemelli a few days later. He
was in a great deal of pain, but at least he was alive. I didn't want to tire
him, so I didn't speak. Fr. Stanisław Dziwisz said that the pope had spoken
just a few words after the shooting, saying that he had been hit in the chest
and that he was in pain. After this, during the race to the hospital, there
had only been the certainty that this pope was human just like everybody
else. He had lost a great deal of blood and seemed close enough to death
that he was given the anointing of the sick. Then the surgeon had come
to operate, and the procedure had lasted many hours. It wasn't completed
until the next morning, when the doctors gave word that the pope had
been saved.

A few days after that visit, and only five days after the shooting, the
pope recited the Angelus from the hospital window. "Pray for the brother
who shot me," he said, "whom I have sincerely forgiven."

135

John Paul II was released from the hospital at the beginning of the following month, but while recovering back at the Vatican he had to be hospitalized again because of an infection. A second operation was required, after which he stayed in the hospital for another month. It was a hot summer day when he left, the vigil of the feast of the Assumption, and after a few days at the Vatican he went to Castel Gandolfo, the pope's summer residence about twenty miles south of Rome.

Toward the end of September 1981, I was invited to dinner at Castel Gandolfo. I was told that the Holy Father had important things to tell me, so I should arrive a little bit early to leave plenty of time to talk.

On the day of my visit, I took the road up to the top of the hill, to the old wall of the castle that had belonged to the noble Gandolfo family, and then to the Savellis. But when the Savelli family was unable to pay a debt of 150,000 scudi, the property had passed into the hands of the Church. The papal residence had been built on the ruins of the ancient fortress, atop those high walls with their parapets, overlooking Lake Albano. There was a profoundly spiritual feel to the place.

Fr. Stanisław Dziwisz took me to the Holy Father, and I was happy to discover that Lolek was in good health. The atmosphere was very relaxing. Lolek showed me the view of the lake, and told me that he was getting his energy back.

Back inside it felt almost like evening, the way the light filtered through the window in that exquisitely appointed room with its antique paintings and furniture. The bookshelves were full of volumes that appeared to be very old, although they were perfectly intact. We were left alone, and the conversation began.

The pope said that he was very concerned about what was happening in the Middle East between Israel and the Arab countries. A few months earlier, eight Israeli F-16 fighter planes had appeared from the west over Iraq, and in a few minutes had dropped thirteen bombs on the Osiraq nuclear reactor near al-Tuwaitha, wiping it out. The code name for the operation had been "Babylon." The attack had brought forceful condemnation from the UN Security Council. Fighting also continued along the area between southern Lebanon and northern Israel. There had been many civilian victims in July.

I saw Lolek wince while he explained what was happening, but I couldn't tell whether it was from the pain of his injuries or distress over what was happening in the Middle East. But it soon became clear that it wasn't his body that was troubling the pope.

"That occupation and those attacks," he said, "couldn't be any more serious than they already are. They mean the threat of another war. But the way to go is dialogue and peace, just like Egypt and Israel courageously did with the Camp David Accords. But if those border clashes continue, then that effort will be in vain."

"But Egypt recognized Israel, something the other Arab countries don't want to do. Instead, they reject the Jewish state—like the Palestinians do, for instance." Then I added, "To tell you the truth, many Jews are asking why the Holy See doesn't recognize Israel. . . ."

I was about to say something else, but I stopped when the Holy Father's secretary returned to the room. Dinner was ready.

The dinner table was set with crystal glasses, fine silver, and china. I was enjoying the first course too much to start chatting, so the pontiff was the one to resume the conversation. He reiterated the importance of Jerusalem for Judaism, Christianity, and Islam, and then said that since the believers of these religions all have Abraham as their father, they should live in peace instead of warring with each other.

After the simple but succulent meal, while the sisters were clearing the table, the Holy Father asked me if I could wait a little longer to continue the conversation. I replied that I also wanted to keep talking, so we went outside to the gardens, which were exquisite.

In the beginning there had been only one garden at Castel Gandolfo, called the Moro Garden, its paths bounded by myrtle shrubs. But it had been thought too small to stroll in, so eighteen thousand scudi had been spent to purchase a nearby villa that had belonged to a cardinal, together with its park full of beautiful statues and fountains. After this, the Villa Barberini was purchased, and the Belvedere Gardens were planted there. This plot of land was connected to the other villa first by a walkway and then by a gallery that led directly to the palace above the public road, on the arch of the ancient Porta Romana.

In private again now, I told Lolek about my recent conversation with Nathan Ben Horin, who worked at the Israeli embassy in Rome and was in contact with the Holy See. He had spoken with me about certain developments, because the Israeli government wanted to know if I might be able to bring a few matters to the pontiff's attention, especially the recognition of Israel, since I was Jewish and a friend of the pope. My role was to remain secret, because I was not an Israeli citizen. The pope did not reject the idea, but simply restated what he had said at dinner: that if the Jewish people had the right to return to the land of their ancestors, the Palestinians also had the right to remain there and have a state of their own.

At that point, I remembered that in a few days it would be Rosh Hashanah, the Jewish new year. The midrashic literature told about God seated on his throne during Rosh Hashanah, with all of the books of human history in front of him, in order to decide who deserved forgiveness. It was an extremely important feast for the Jewish people, and Lolek himself was well aware of this. On the afternoon before the feast, in order to free themselves from their sins, the Jews in Wadowice would perform the *tashlich*, throwing their old objects into a fountain, after which they went to the synagogue in the morning. There, before the prayers, the shofar, the ram's horn, was sounded to remind everyone that the day of judgment was coming. That evening, they ate apples mixed with honey and pomegranate seeds, to symbolize sweetness and prosperity. The last year of the Jewish calendar that I had celebrated in this way together with my family had been 5698 (in 1939). Then the war came. I asked Lolek if he might send his greetings to Israel that year, and Lolek told me that he would do so, since it was a religious matter.

While we were walking in the open air that evening, we found ourselves on a terrace facing the lake. The shore was perhaps less than a mile away. I gazed at that calm surface in the darkness and saw that it reflected the lights from the surrounding countryside. The air was cool and pleasant. Lolek turned to me again.

"The Church also expects to have diplomatic relations with Israel, so that one day peace may reign among the peoples there. I'll have you talk with Janusz Bolonek, a leading expert in international diplomacy, at the Vatican. He'll tell you what the best course of action is. At any moment, there is the risk of compromising the progress that's been made in the Middle East so far." He was referring to the Camp David Accords.

I agreed eagerly to the proposal, and on the strength of Lolek's confidence in Bolonek, I said I was willing to meet with him as soon as he was available.

As we were turning to head back, Lolek had one more thing to get off his chest.

"I have a strong desire to return to the Holy Land. The last time I was there I was a bishop, and it's been many years." He paused for a moment. "There were so many Polish Jews there. It was like being home."

CHAPTER 17

WAR IN
THE MIDDLE EAST

Just a few days after that meeting, the tensions that had been building in recent months in Egypt abruptly came to a climax. During a military parade on October 6, 1981, in Cairo, President Anwar al-Sadat was assassinated.

His killers were two officers and a sergeant, although a theologian was also involved in the plot. Abdel Salam Farag had written a book condemning Egypt's corrupt government—stating that Sadat's administration was at the service of atheistic imperialism and that the enemy close at hand should be defeated before the enemy farther away. Some people maintained that Sadat's internal policies were the reason those fanatics had killed the president, not because he had negotiated with the hated Zionists.

At the end of October, I saw Józef Lichten again. He had a different interpretation of what happened to Sadat, and at that point Lichten was concerned about the fate of the agreement between Egypt and Israel. In fact, an article had appeared recently in *Afrique Asie* that contained an interview with Yasser Arafat. The head of the PLO had said that the Egyptian people had judged Sadat because of his refusal to understand that 500 million Arabs did not want that peace at all, and that Sadat was the only one who did.

I met Lichten again a few months later and again perceived that my friend was concerned about what was happening in the Middle East. Israel had annexed the Golan Heights, the territory that had previously belonged to Syria but was occupied by the Israelis during the Six-Day War. Because of this, there was a constant danger that there would be more fighting on the border with Lebanon and that the ancient rancor of the Syrian people could now erupt in war.

The UN Security Council had tried to prevent the undesirable effects of this annexation, asking Israel to reverse its decision. But the request went unheeded, and any hope of realizing peace vanished. At the end of the year, there was the sense that Israel's prosperity was increasingly rooted in lands that were not its own. People all over the world began criticizing the Jewish state.

At the time, Syria was ruled by a dictator named Hafiz al-Hasad, an air force general and a member of the Ba'ath Party (which means "resurrection" in Arabic, symbolizing the rebirth of the Syrian people). He discriminated against anyone who was not Arab. Because he had formed an alliance with the Soviet Union, which had invaded Afghanistan a few years earlier, many Muslims had condemned al-Hasad as an enemy of Allah. Partly for this reason, there was an uprising in the city of Hamah in February 1982. Al-Hasad conducted a violent repression against the rebels, and in order to prevent any more revolts in the future, he instituted mass executions. As the *norias* (water wheels) on the Orontes River turned, along with the water those enormous wheels lifted up the blood of more than twenty-five thousand victims. Al-Hasad's hatred was not limited to the rebels he had killed but also extended to Israel. Although Syria had stopped firing on the Golan Heights at the order of the United Nations, it continued to use Palestinian guerrillas to fight the Israelis, and now there was the danger of another war, less than ten years after the previous one.

And yet another war was about to begin, in Lebanon, a country already devastated by conflict. Since the Palestinians had taken refuge there, they had joined the Lebanese who were fighting the Maronites, whose powerful militias were led by a man named Bachir Gemayel. The Maronite Christians had long been the majority in Lebanon, at least until the refugees came from Palestine and tipped the balance to the side of the Muslims. The two religious groups had been fighting in the country since the mid-1970s.

Various Arab states, including Syria, had intervened to put an end to the war, which struck hard against the Palestinian fighters and their allies. At the refugee camp in Tell el-Za'tar there was a massacre of men, women, and children, and even the Maronites understood that the appearance of restoring peace to their country concealed Syria's dream of returning to its former regional glory. Syria's troops even invaded Lebanon, and soon afterward the armies of other nations followed. There was civil war in June 1982 when the Israeli army entered Baadba, the Christian neighborhood of Beirut where the presidential palace was located. The soldiers were met with the joyful shouting of members of the Kataeb Party (Phalangists), who had called for the assistance of Israel. Israel called the military operation "Peace in Galilee," but it cost the lives of thousands of Palestinians.

Beirut was also the home of the PLO's headquarters and thousands of its militant members. They barricaded themselves inside the city out of fear of reprisal from the Israeli soldiers and their Maronite allies. At the end of August, the guerrillas and their leader, Yasser Arafat, were able to escape, taking refuge in Tunis. After this, the Phalangist Christians arrived in the neighborhood of Bir Hassan, near the refugee camps of Sabra and Shatila. Gemayel, their leader, had been elected president of Lebanon. Israel had asked him to sign a peace agreement, but he was opposed. After the Syrians assassinated Gemayel, the Maronites went looking for revenge and found it in the camps where the Muslim Palestinians were staying. The massacre went on for two days, leaving the torn and mutilated bodies of several hundred refugees, including women and children, under the burning sun.

Israel was held to be an accomplice to the slaughter because its soldiers had been assigned to Sabra and Shatila to protect the refugees—but Israel didn't do so.

These were the events taking place while I was preparing to go to the Vatican to meet Janusz Bolonek, a handsome, blond Pole working at the Vatican secretariat of state who had known Wojtyła when he had been archbishop of Kraków. The monsignor told me a story about an event that had taken place in the archdiocese back then. An image had been placed on a wall of the Kalwaria Zebrzydowska shrine, a depiction of Jews drinking the blood of Christians they had killed. Wojtyła had ordered that the image be taken down and then brought to the damp basement where the rats could eat it once and for all. He was convinced that the contrived scenario might induce some to hate the Jews.

At the meeting, Bolonek and I talked about Israel. Bolonek was very forthright, telling me that many in the curia would be opposed to Vatican recognition of the Jewish state, essentially for the same reasons that the pontiff had presented that evening at dinner in Castel Gandolfo. In fact, as long as the border dispute persisted and the question of the Palestinian refugees was unresolved, these elements alone would be an insurmountable obstacle for normal diplomatic relations between the Holy See and Israel.

But I knew that these weren't the only reasons that the Church had refused to send apostolic nuncios to the Holy Land. Lichten had pointed this out to me during a previous conversation.

"Think about it, Kluger," Lichten had said. "Before 1967, there was no question of occupied territories, and the exodus of the Palestinian refugees wasn't like it was after the Six-Day War. And there are still millions of Christians in the Middle East."

"So what?" I had asked.

"At the time, diplomatic relations with Israel could have meant putting all of those people in danger. There was the risk of retaliation. And there still is."

I had also talked the matter over with Kurt Rosenberg, who seemed much more blunt on this point than anyone else.

"It's simple. They haven't recognized Israel because it's the state of the Jews, the perfidious deicides. Otherwise, how do you explain the refusal of Pius X? I mean, when Theodor Herzl went to talk about it with the pope, asking him to support the Zionist movement, what did he say? 'Forget about it! Your people rejected Christ as the Messiah, you've lost your Temple and your state once already, and now you're not going to get our help to return to that land. Instead, convert!' "

Who knows? Maybe both sides were right.

At Vatican Council II, the bishops of the Arab countries had opposed the idea of absolving the Jews from the accusation of deicide. These were the Syrian patriarch Tappouni, Melkite patriarch Maximos IV, and Coptic patriarch Stéphanos I. They were afraid that talking only about the Jewish people, and in that way, might provoke the anger of the Muslims. Some of the bishops listened to them, because the Council's *Nostra Aetate* did not concern only the Jews and their faith, but non-Christian religions in general. It made reference to Islam, and mentioned Buddhism and Hinduism as well. Another question then arose, because during those same years a play was released, *The Vicar*, written by a German Protestant author who harshly accused Pius XII of remaining silent during the extermination of the Jews. There was a great deal of controversy over the text, and at the time the Palestinians maintained that the Jews had used all of those heated discussions to exert pressure on the Council fathers to get them to remove permanently the accusation of deicide. The Organisation for the Liberation of Palestine (OLP) had written about it in a volume published in Beirut titled *We, the Vatican, and Israel.* It was partly in order to avoid provoking the Arabs that the 1964 text of *Nostra Aetate* was modified. At first, it included terms like "Jewish people" and "nation," but these disappeared in the definitive draft of 1965 in order to avoid any kind of resentment. The only word employed was "Jews."

I was also aware that some in the Vatican had theological prejudices against recognizing Israel. Archbishop Andrzej Maria Deskur explained this to me. He was from Sancygniów in Poland, near Kielce, but his family was of French origin. He had met Karol Wojtyła as a young priest, and the two had remained close. The day after his election as pope, John Paul II had gone to the hospital to visit his friend, because just before the conclave Deskur had suffered a stroke. When the pope arrived at the hospital, the people seemed to lose their minds, they were so taken by surprise by the visit. I had also known Deskur before Lolek was elected and had continued to visit him after his stroke. Although part of his body had been paralyzed, his intellect and his sense of humor were as sharp as ever. He loved to play bridge, hosting games at the Vatican in his free time. I was often invited to play. During one of these games, the bishop had cautioned me about what some members of the curia thought about the Jews. Deskur was very well informed about certain things, having spent a long time in the secretariat of state. So he also had some valuable advice.

"Here's what you should do, Kluger," he said one evening, taking the king of hearts with his trump card. "Do some research on the Arab countries that have diplomatic relations with the Holy See, and see how many of them have constitutions that permit slavery and other horrible violations of human rights. If it were ever known that the Vatican has relations with these countries, then why not with Israel?" It really was an intelligent solution.

In the meantime, I continued to visit Lolek often. Hardly a week went by in which we didn't get together at least once for lunch or dinner, either at the Vatican or at the pope's residence in Castel Gandolfo. April 1982 would be the fortieth anniversary of the ghetto of Warsaw. When the time came, the pope sent a message to all Jews: "How can I not be close to you, to remember in prayer and meditation such a sorrowful anniversary? Be certain of this, you do not bear the pain of this memory alone!" Warsaw before the war was home to many Jews; only New York had more. There were Jews who were born in Poland and also some who had fled from

Russia. Most of them lived in a single neighborhood, so Russian could be heard there in addition to Polish, Hebrew, and Yiddish.

When the Nazis entered Warsaw, the Jewish area was turned into a ghetto, with a wall erected around it. Almost five hundred thousand people were shut up inside—a third of the inhabitants of the entire city. They had to live crammed together in an area of about one and a half square miles, in buildings with no more than five floors. When the deportations to the concentration camps began, about three hundred thousand of the Jews in the Warsaw ghetto were sent to them. Most of them were taken to Treblinka, a little village along the railway line linking Warsaw and Białistok, a city about thirty miles to the northeast. At first it was a work camp, but in 1942 it was turned into an extermination camp for the Jews, as part of the Reinhard Operation, intended to eliminate about 2 million of the Jews present in the area controlled by the General Government. Treblinka had two sister camps, in Belzec and Sobibór.

Inside the ghetto, a few political groups organized themselves into a resistance movement. Some spies for the Nazis were killed; one of them was the head of the Jewish police. Early one morning in January 1943, a German battalion came to the ghetto to round up the Jews to be sent to the concentration camps. A dozen men belonging to the resistance (including their leader, Mordechai Anielewicz), armed with pistols, joined the prisoners being marched toward the Umschlagplatz, where the trains were waiting to take the prisoners to the *lagers*, the concentration camps. When they reached the corner of Zamenhof and Niska streets, the resistance members opened fire on the Nazis. More SS officers came, and some of the members of the resistance were killed in the streets of the ghetto. But many of those destined for the gas chambers were saved.

On the Sunday of the Jewish Passover, April 19, 1943, a full moon shone in the sky. The Germans had surrounded the ghetto, ready to strike. The members of the resistance knew of these plans and had issued an alarm to the other Jews in the neighborhood so that people could take shelter. Dawn arrived, and the Germans invaded the ghetto in two armed columns. A bomb was launched at them, then shots were fired, and grenades and Molotov cocktails were hurled. "Juden haben waffen, juden haben waffen!" (The Jews are armed!), a German shouted. On this Passover morning began the Warsaw Ghetto Uprising, which would last almost a month. Fighting took place in the streets and housing complexes until they were burned by the Germans. Many Jews tried to escape through the labyrinthine sewer system. Games of cat and mouse were played for entire days, until the order came to destroy the Jewish quarter completely. It was now Easter, and that night the ghetto was a sea of flame from one end to the other. Those who came out of their hiding places were apprehended and deported. There were so many Jews that the trains could not hold them all, so more than a thousand of them were sentenced on the spot, stripped, and lined up against the wall. They were singing psalms as they awaited their fate. The rest were in their underground hiding places, and around them were the scalding walls, the smell of mold, silence, darkness. Not even a candle was lit, to avoid consuming what little air there was. Just above their heads were the Nazis, hunting for them with dogs and sound monitoring equipment. One of them must have stumbled upon the spot on Mila Street where the resistance leaders were hiding several floors below the surface, in a bunker equipped with lighting, a kitchen, and food supplies. The final battle took place there, from May 4 to May 8. On the last day, German combat engineers came to launch tear gas into the tunnels leading to the hiding place. Even then, the Jews did not come out. Rather than being taken prisoner by the Nazis, they preferred to die where they were, and those who were not suffocated killed themselves. The head of the resistance shot his girlfriend Mira, after she asked him to do so, and then took his own life. The synagogue fell.

A year after the sacrifice of the Jews in the ghetto, the entire city rose up against the Germans.

So it must have been unsettling to hear again, as back during the war, the sound of those Caterpillar tracks on the ground when the tanks returned to the streets of Warsaw on December 13, 1981. The Poles had not yet gained their freedom. General Wojciech Jaruzelski had instituted martial law in Poland, on instructions from Moscow, to bring order back to the country after the workers' protests and establish the communist version of military dictatorship. The borders were closed, communications were cut off, and news stopped coming out. No information was available anymore about what was happening in the country, except for the fate of Lech Wałęsa and the other labor organizers and intellectuals—internment—and of the mine workers at Wujek coal mine in Katowice who rebelled and were shot dead by the military.

It was a Christmas full of anguish for the Holy Father because of the events taking place in his country. He would have liked to have been there, and in the following months he tried to organize a trip. Częstochowa seemed to be the ideal destination, possibly during the month of Marian celebrations, but the regime blocked the visit. Solidarność (Solidarity, the first noncommunist trade union in Poland) was also suppressed, and with it the dream of millions of Poles.

For Lolek, the state of siege reminded him too much of the Nazi occupation.

CHAPTER 18

A KEFIA AT THE VATICAN

After the Palestinian guerrillas who had fled from Lebanon—together with their leader, Yasser Arafat—had taken refuge in Tunis, an international conference was held in Rome in 1982. About one hundred countries participated, and the leader of the PLO was also invited to attend as an observer.

There was no lack of tension when Arafat arrived in the Eternal City. Some of the Italian political authorities, like the president of the Council of Ministers, Giovanni Spadolini, refused to have anything to do with him. So the welcome had to be extended by others, primarily Minister Giulio Andreotti, who had invited Arafat in the first place. Once the ice had been broken, the Palestinian leader was also received kindly by Nilde Iotti, president of the Chamber of Deputies, and Foreign Minister Beniamino Andreatta. Even President Sandro Pertini welcomed him with open arms at his office in the Quirinale. There was nothing surprising about this; the Italian president had been the one who, in the traditional year-end message to his people, had commented on the difficult situation in the Middle East with the remark, "What is it that these Jews want, really?" The truly shocking development had come a few days before Arafat arrived in Rome, with an official announcement from the Vatican that the pope would grant him a private audience on September 15, a Wednesday, after the general audience that was routinely held on that day. The news was announced by Fr. Romeo Panciroli, and when the time came, the Muslim militant appeared before the Holy Father wearing his characteristic black-and-white checkered *kefia* on his head. The pope laid his hand on Arafat's head in a gesture of blessing. A few moments earlier, John Paul II had reminded everyone of the death of Bachir Gemayel, a Maronite and a devoted son of the Church, the president-elect of Lebanon. Gemayel had been put in charge of guiding a country ravaged by conflict, but a few hours before the audience he was assassinated in an attack by the Syrians that had taken the lives of others as well. Such a short time after the siege had been lifted in Beirut, more blood had already been spilled. So the pope had again prayed for peace, although afterward he said that in order to achieve this there needed to be respect among the different peoples and reconciliations between the Israelis and the Palestinians. He may have been thinking already about the meeting that followed his homily for the faithful—a private conversation with the leader of the Palestinian people.

I opposed my friend Lolek's decision to meet with Arafat. In the days following the historic encounter, I had a chance to talk about it briefly over the phone with Archbishop Deskur, who did not conceal his own perplexity. Deskur explained that although he considered the pope's gesture as a purely Christian one, he was concerned about the political reactions it might unleash in the world—especially in Israel, where the head of the PLO was believed to be nothing more than a common terrorist. At that point, I became concerned that the secret negotiations to establish diplomatic relations between the Jewish state and the Vatican might be called off, and the pope's meeting with Arafat wasn't the only threat to the talks. I felt that I should tell Deskur about some of my concerns, in order to get his advice, but the subject matter was too delicate to discuss over the phone. So I asked for a meeting in the next few days at the archbishop's apartment in the Vatican—to be scheduled with his personal secretary, of course.

It wasn't long before the archbishop's concerns were justified. Controversy broke out over the audience with Arafat at the Vatican, and some people accused the pontiff of siding with the Palestinian militants and opposing the existence of a Jewish state in Palestine.

The last time that I had heard these kinds of accusations was during the pontificate of Paul VI. The Israeli secret service had arrested Hilarion Capucci, auxiliary bishop of Antioch of the Melkites and archbishop of Caesarea in Palestine. The police caught him transporting dynamite, machine guns, grenades, and munitions. It was later discovered that these were being supplied to the combatants of al-Fatah, Arafat's political faction. An Israeli court sentenced him to twelve years in prison, reduced to three after the pope asked for his release. He was set free, but on the condition that he leave the Middle East and never return. Many Jews then claimed that there was a deep-rooted opposition to Judaism in the Middle Eastern Church, supported by the Vatican.

A short time later, after lunch with Lolek at his apartment in the Vatican, I asked my friend if he was bothered by the insistent claims that he was against Israel and in favor of the Palestinians. I was surprised when I saw an expression of amusement instead of distress on the pope's face.

"Look, Jurek," he said, smiling, "sometimes these silly things are like ocean waves. They swell, they swell, but then they scatter."

But ominous signs were emerging for the Jews and their state.

The military campaign in Lebanon had received practically no international support. Even some in the Knesset were opposed to the conflict, accusing the government of wanting to drag Israel into the abyss, although their loyalty was questioned for their opposition. Then came the news of the massacre in Sabra and Shatila, which the Israeli army had failed to prevent. Four hundred thousand Israelis protested in Tel Aviv over the scandal.

Despite the many resolutions of the UN Security Council against the deployment of troops in Lebanon, Israel maintained that the military operation was necessary in order to prevent the border raids by Palestinian militants and their constant artillery attacks.

Besides, the border towns weren't the only place where Jews were being killed. Israel could count its victims everywhere. An Israeli airplane had been attacked in Athens in 1968. At the Munich Olympics, in 1972, eleven Israeli athletes had been slain. In Antwerp, in 1980, a bus full of Jewish children going camping was bombed, killing one of them and seriously injuring many others. Then there had been the attacks on the *kasher* restaurants in West Berlin in 1981, and then in Paris the following year, with eight dead in all and almost fifty injured. Of course, synagogues were popular targets for terrorists. In 1980 four people were killed and eleven wounded at the synagogue on Rue Copernic in Paris. The following year, a similar attack at the synagogue of Vienna killed two and injured nineteen. In Antwerp, terror was unleashed when a car loaded with TNT crashed into a synagogue.

The atmosphere was heavy with tension in Rome as well, and I began to notice it more and more. At the end of June 1982, during a demonstration by the labor unions, a coffin was dropped off in front of the synagogue, like a dark prophecy.

About four months later came the Shemini Atzeret, the eighth day of the feast of Sukkoth, commemorating the time that the Hebrews spent living in huts in the desert before they reached the promised land, Israel. It was October 9, 1982, a Saturday. The children had just received the blessing that is given on that day and were leaving the synagogue of Rome with their families when four grenades were thrown at the people outside, followed by automatic weapons fire. Thirty people were seriously injured, and a two-year-old boy was killed.

The attack was attributed to Palestinian terrorists. And because not even a month had passed since John Paul II had received the head of the PLO at the Vatican, he was even more harshly criticized in Jewish circles all over the world.

On the following Sunday, Fr. Maximilian Maria Kolbe was canonized in Saint Peter's Square. The Church had beatified him in 1971, and that Sunday, he was proclaimed a saint. Also at the ceremony was Franciszek Gajowniczek, the man whose life the friar had saved by sacrificing his own at Auschwitz. The pontiff called him a martyr and cited the psalm that says how precious in the eyes of the Lord is the death of his faithful ones.

A few days later, the funeral was held for the little Jewish boy killed in the attack on the synagogue. Thousands of people went to the Rome synagogue and not only Jews. Many Italian politicians were there, and even President Sandro Pertini decided to go, although the chief rabbi of the Roman Jewish community sent word to him that it would be better if he didn't attend. He had received Palestinian leader Arafat at the Quirinale not even a month before the assault. But when Pertini stepped out of his car, instead of protests, he was met only with a heavy silence. The local Jewish community had raised its voice the day before, accusing the Italian government of sending Italian soldiers to protect the Palestinians in Lebanon while failing to protect its own Jewish citizens in Italy. After the recent terrorist attacks at the synagogues in Paris, Berlin, and Antwerp, the chief rabbi had in fact asked the interior minister to protect the synagogue of Rome, especially during the Jewish holidays, but it was no use. So, on the day on which the Church was canonizing an innocent martyr, the Jewish people had just been given another of their own. And then there was the fact that for the Church Fr. Maximilian Kolbe was a saint, but for many of the Jews he was not.

As if all of this were not enough to make relations between Jews and Catholics difficult during the early years of John Paul II's pontificate, I received a telephone call one evening from Lichten, who told me that he had some very urgent things to say to me, and could he see me that same day, if possible? Since it was almost eight o'clock, we agreed to meet immediately after dinner at Lichten's apartment.

Lichten and his wife lived in an elegant building in Rome, just outside the Aurelian walls marking the border of the historic city center on the Via Salaria. The road derived its name from the Sabines, who had used it to transport the salt produced from the shore of the Adriatic Sea. I climbed two flights of stairs to Lichten's apartment, and when I arrived there, Lichten was already waiting for me inside the open door.

Lichten had certainly been mysterious over the phone. I had tried to press him for an idea of what he wanted to talk about, but Lichten had insisted on waiting until we met in person. As he ushered me into his home, he seemed to have more clichés than words of welcome for me: "Sometimes, old friend, it's better to learn certain things sooner rather than later." His entire demeanor was vague and cryptic.

Lichten's wife, Carol, was also at the door to greet me. She was a truly lovely woman in appearance and manners, and her English was so refined that although I understood the language fairly well, I apologized for my own speech.

Carol left the two of us alone, and we walked together down the long hallway. I glanced at the exquisite furniture along the wall until we reached a room on the left that Lichten had made into his study. It was the stereotypical intellectual's den—large and open, with books, pamphlets, and magazines everywhere, even on the chairs. Lichten was an expert on the Kabbalah, and there was a shelf full of books on that subject against one wall. Lichten cleared a chair in front of a desk for me, and gestured for me to sit down. He left the room for a moment and returned with two heavy crystal glasses and a bottle of bourbon, explaining that it had been aged for twenty years.

"So then, my good friend," he continued, "do you know who Wiesenthal is?"

"No," I replied.

"Oh, come on, Simon Wiesenthal, the Nazi hunter."

"Now that I think about it, I've heard his name a few times, but I don't know much about him."

"Well, then," Lichten said, "if you don't mind, I'll tell you more. He's a Ukrainian Jew, who was living in Lviv when the Russians came." He paused. "You were also living in Lviv then, with your father, if I'm not mistaken?"

I nodded. "Yes, but does that have anything to do with the person you're telling me about?"

"No, no, I was just reminded of the stories you've told me."

Lichten uncorked the bottle and asked me if I wanted ice.

"Neat, please," I answered.

Lichten poured the bourbon and then continued, "So, when the Soviets entered the city, Simon's stepfather and stepbrother were killed by members of the NKVD. Simon himself was sent to work in a factory in Russia, until the Nazis invaded the country and he was deported to the concentration camp in Mauthausen. He was able to avoid execution a number of times, until the Americans came and freed the prisoners in May 1945. Just think, that poor fellow weighed barely ninety pounds. As soon as he regained his strength, Wiesenthal began collecting information for the United States government, for the trials against the Nazi war criminals. He set up his offices in Linz, Austria, with about thirty volunteer researchers. After the U.S. government lost interest in tracking those murderers, the group was forced to disband. But Wiesenthal wouldn't give up and continued hunting the swastika'd persecutors on his own. I don't remember where, but he smoked out Adolf Eichmann, the main architect of the Endlösung, the Final Solution, who was eventually sentenced to death in Israel in 1962. After this, Simon orchestrated the capture of Karl Silberbauer, the Gestapo officer who had arrested Anne Frank. Then came Franz Stangl, the commandant of the concentration camps in Treblinka and Sobibór. There was even a German housewife now living in New York who had assisted in the killing of hundreds of Jewish children. The list goes on, but I don't want to bore you."

"I understand," I said, "but why have you brought me here to tell me these things? Has Wiesenthal found another Nazi?"

"Something like that," Lichten said. "I mean, not an actual criminal, but still it's someone who served the Führer."

"And who would that be?"

"Hermann Josef Abs, a famous German banker, one of the engineers of Germany's postwar economic miracle. Before that, he worked at Deutsche Bank in Berlin, and—as I'm sure you know—this bank financed Hitler and his projects beginning in 1933, when the Jews were first forced to resign from the board. He was also a member of the board of the factory that manufactured the gas used to kill those in the concentration camps,

IG Farben, some of the directors of which were charged and sentenced for war crimes in the Nuremberg trials, as I'm sure you know."

"Was he one of those under investigation?" I asked.

"Not according to the file that was sent to me. But keep in mind that after the war, the German bank sent him to London to discuss, as a representative of West Germany, the question of reparation for damages—and he was the main opponent of compensation for the Jews. Then, in 1960, General Franco decorated him for his service to his dictatorship. So what we have here is an anti-Semite, pure and simple."

"Excuse me," I interrupted. "Was this the sensational thing that you had to tell me about?" I was trying to conceal my growing impatience.

Lichten paused. "Not exactly. The really troubling thing is where he's working now."

My curiosity grew now. "Where's that?"

"At the Institute for Works of Religion. But maybe I should use its better-known name, the IOR. It's the central bank of the Holy See."

I knew about the IOR only because the building in which its offices were located, the Tower of Nicholas V, stood in front of the palace of Sixtus V, where Lolek's apartment was. It could be reached from the Courtyard of Saint Damasus through a passageway that led to the Courtyard of the Marshal.

"As I was saying," Lichten continued, "there would be a scandal if it were known that a banker like Abs, notorious for his connections with the Third Reich—and far from invisible, since Rockefeller called him the greatest banker in the world—had by some strange means become part of the advisory committee that assists the Vatican bank. So, Kluger, the IOR is an unusual bank: no teller windows, but plenty of clients, and I don't mean just priests, bishops, and sisters. In fact, it seems to be highly sought out by people who want to move money while remaining, shall we say, unobserved. There's no name and no photo on its credit cards, and no receipts from its operations. No hard documentation at all. It seems that only the pope and three cardinals have access to its records. So you should be aware that a scandal could erupt if it were known that there's a former Nazi sympathizer at that financial institution."

I didn't have much to add. "Sure," was my only response.

"I mean, it's probably just a coincidence that he's there—but for that very reason, don't you think it's better to avoid controversy?"

"What do you suggest should be done?" I asked.

"The pope should be informed right away. It's possible that he has no idea what's going on. You know what happens. Someone starts the rumors, and then there's the danger that false ideas begin to spread."

My meeting with Archbishop Deskur was the following day, and I brought in my briefcase the documentation that had been gathered about Abs.

When I arrived at the archbishop's apartment on the first floor of the Palazzo San Carlo, behind the Domus Sanctae Marthae, I was graciously welcomed by the young secretary who had scheduled the appointment over the phone. The secretary accompanied me to the archbishop's office, where he was sitting in his wheelchair behind the desk. As always, I greeted him respectfully. The archbishop motioned that I should make myself comfortable, while the secretary left the room and closed the door behind him.

Now that we were alone, I began by telling the archbishop about my meeting the day before with Lichten, and Wiesenthal's dossier on the connections between the IOR and the German banker who had been one of Hitler's trusted men. Finally, I asked the archbishop if he was aware of this, and if in his opinion the pope should be told about it. Deskur asked to look at the file, and I placed it on his desk. The archbishop began leafing through it attentively, and when he had finished he said:

"Do what you suggested, and talk with the Holy Father. You'll see, he'll find the right solution."

I was reassured, but still seriously concerned about how criticism over the Abs connection, together with the criticism already unleashed after the pope met with the head of the Palestinians, could complicate my own efforts to establish informal ties between Israel and the Vatican. During the previous months, I had expressed the pope's regard for Israel to the Israeli embassy in Rome, and I had gained a certain trust at the embassy that I was now afraid of losing. There was also the fact that during those same months, I had met with various curia officials at the Holy See, some of whom appeared in favor of relations with Israel (Deskur was one of these). But it seemed to me that some of these officials were really against the idea, and not always for the same reasons given in the past. This was just an impression, but perhaps it was inevitable. After all, I was Jewish, and the pope's best friend. What usually happened was that the prelates at first expressed appreciation for the Holy Father's intention to establish official relations with Israel, but after this they voiced all of their doubts that such a thing could actually happen. There were so many questions still to be resolved, some of them very delicate, that there was a long journey of reconciliation ahead for Jews and Catholics, they told me.

This was one reason that I had asked to meet with Archbishop Deskur: to get a better idea of the views inside the curia and to find out if there were other reasons that there had never been an Israeli embassy at the Vatican, in addition to the reasons I had already heard. So during our meeting, while I was putting the file on Abs back into my briefcase—given that Deskur had made it clear that he had nothing else to say on the matter—I spoke with him about my impressions of months of consultation with cardinals, bishops, and monsignors, and about their doubts over the success of the mission in which I was involved. From the archbishop's expression, I could tell he was much more interested in this topic than in the previous one.

"What are you most upset about?" the archbishop asked me. "That in addition to the resistance to Israel outside of these walls, there could be some inside them as well?"

"Well, in a certain sense—yes, Your Excellency. I get the feeling that there are other factors keeping the two states from having normal international relations, and not the ones that have been given to me. You know what I mean: the Palestinians, the occupied territories, Jerusalem."

I was hoping that Deskur would tell me that I was mistaken. But he didn't.

"Yes, you're right, there are reasons beyond the ones you just referred to."

The archbishop was very perceptive, and he could tell immediately that I was discouraged by this confirmation. Deskur tried to reassure me.

"Diplomatic relations are hard to establish. They take a lot of time and a lot of work, so it's best to continue moving forward, as far as we can. And actually, there's one idea I haven't been able to get out of my head for weeks."

"What's that?" I asked.

"A letter by which Israel would declare itself officially willing to institute diplomatic missions in the respective states, just as a start. And considering the trust that you've established at the Israeli embassy in Rome and in Vatican circles, you could even act as mediator."

CHAPTER 19

MEETING SHAMIR

After my meeting at the Vatican with Archbishop Deskur, I had scheduled two other meetings the very next day. One of them was in the morning with the pope, to give him an update on Wiesenthal's dossier on the German banker who worked at the IOR. The pope appeared concerned when he learned certain facts for the first time and thanked me for informing him immediately. The other meeting was in the afternoon, with Nathan Ben Horin, at the Israeli embassy in Rome. I wanted to tell him about the idea that had come to the archbishop.

"He suggests that a letter should be sent from Israel to the Vatican, stating the government's willingness to establish diplomatic missions in the respective states," I said, presenting the archbishop's proposal without embellishment in order to avoid any misunderstanding. At that point, Ben Horin asked what the reward would be for taking on that kind of risk. I politely explained that the Vatican Secretariat of State was in favor of recognizing Israel and would certainly try to promote the issue if such an explicit signal were to arrive from the Jewish state, because even those who were more skeptical about Israel would have a hard time rejecting such an offer of dialogue. Ben Horin agreed to discuss the proposal with the Israeli authorities.

Now all I had to do was wait. I did this in my own way: sleeping very little at night, and in the daytime constantly asking my wife or business partner if anyone had called from the Israeli embassy while I had been out.

One afternoon the telephone on my desk rang. It was the Israeli ambassador, as I had been hoping.

"His Excellency the foreign minister Yitzhak Shamir asks to speak with you personally about the proposal made by the archbishop, and invites you to come to Tel Aviv in the near future."

"If the minister thinks it would be helpful for me to make this trip to discuss the proposals of His Excellency the Most Reverend Archbishop Deskur, then tell him I will indeed come to Tel Aviv, but on the condition that I obtain permission to do this from the Supreme Pontiff." Without question, this was the proper protocol.

I made another appointment to see the pope the following day, to tell him about the Israeli foreign minister's invitation to meet with me, and why it was important for me to go. The pontiff happily gave his permission, saying that Deskur's idea was a good one. While Lolek talked, I was already thinking about what I needed to pack. In fact, all that was left to do was to arrange the details of the meeting with Shamir's secretary, through Ben Horin. The ticket from Rome to Tel Aviv had been reserved at the embassy's expense, together with accommodations at a four-star hotel.

I was cautioned to arrive at check-in at least three hours early, and when I arrived at the El Al terminal, I understood why. The airline had a solid reputation for its antiterrorism measures, evidence of which was all around. There were police officers and soldiers looking for explosives and suspicious faces, and every piece of luggage was inspected by a specialized team. There were even plainclothes officers patrolling the area. It was all intended to prevent attacks and hijackings. The first hijacking that the airline had experienced took place in July 1968. Ten members of the flight crew and thirty-eight passengers were taken hostage by three guerrillas of the Popular Front for the Liberation of Palestine, who diverted the flight path from Lod to Algiers. Negotiations there stretched on for forty days. In the end, the prisoners were set free, but so were the hijackers. After that, strict security measures had been put in place, and apart from a few other attacks carried out in the following months on planes at the airports of Athens and Zürich—in which an Israeli mechanic and an Israeli pilot were killed—no more hijackings had taken place, and in fact a number of attempts had been foiled in the following years. I myself had to undergo an interrogation of sorts by the personnel, and after my ticket and passport were carefully examined, I was finally allowed to board the Boeing 707, its powerful engines already roaring.

Now that the turquoise livery of the airplane mingled with the blue of the sky, and my seat mate had ordered his *glatt* kosher meal (he was Orthodox, and with his beard, his blue blazer, and fighter's physique he could even have been a sky marshal, a police officer disguised as an ordinary passenger), I sipped a fine cognac, with nothing on my mind but a single destination: Israel.

We landed at Ben Gurion Airport about three hours later. It was definitely hotter there than in Italy. The date was January 19, 1983.

I had been in the region before. The first time in 1942, it was still known as Palestine, and I had gone to visit my father near Tel Aviv during the war. Later, I had spent a few days among the dusty dunes south of that city, before my brigade was transferred to Heliopolis, just outside of Cairo. Later still, after the creation of the state of Israel, I had gone back to visit some relatives who lived in the country—the Aleksandrowicz family, whom I had been able to free from the prison camp of Kizyl-Orda while I was staying in Kara-Suu, in the Fergana Valley. The family had gone by sea to the port of Haifa in Palestine. They were Zionists, and before the world wars they had bought land from the powerful Arab property magnates, most of whom lived in Damascus, Cairo, and Beirut. But they weren't allowed to buy the fertile land in Samaria, so they purchased arid plots, which hard Jewish labor had miraculously made arable. They mainly grew *pardes* (oranges) in that soil to the north of Jaffa, and by the time of the British Mandate the Aleksandrowicz family owned a number of these orange groves. My cousin David had died, but his wife, Maria, was still living in Tel Aviv with their three children, Marycha, Richard, and Hugo. I had another cousin in the city, Jerzy Huppert, the son of Ignacy Huppert, who had fulfilled his father's lifelong dream by moving to an entirely Jewish country. Ignacy had died before the creation of the state of Israel.

At least two decades had passed since I was last in the city, and I found it even more bustling than before. There were hundreds of thousands of Jews there now, although occasionally one also came across Muslim and Christian Arabs. More than anywhere else, I saw them in Jaffa, named after the Jewish word for "beautiful." Its history and various rulers had imprinted upon it the distinctive image that I now saw—the old Arab city with its dome-shaped roofs, the tall minarets standing out like obelisks to perpetuate the muezzin's call to prayer, and the bell towers of the churches that also stood against the horizon. The sea was nearby, and over the centuries this access to the water had increased the prosperity of the port that was built in that natural harbor, said to be as old as Noah's flood. Both the Temple of Solomon and the royal palace in Jerusalem had supposedly been built with cedar that had arrived from Lebanon at the port of Jaffa. But it was also at Jaffa that Andromeda had been chained to a rock to be devoured by a sea monster. And Jonah, the Hebrew son of Amittai, departed from there in disobedience to the Lord, who unleashed a tempest against him, so that the storm-tossed sailors threw him overboard. But he didn't drown, because the Lord also sent a huge fish that swallowed him up, and after Jonah had prayed for three days and three nights in the belly of the creature, it spit him out on dry land. In Jaffa, which had become a suburb of Tel Aviv, I also visited the flea market, where the people were bartering over everything displayed in the stalls.

The following morning, I found a car waiting for me outside of the hotel to take me straight to my appointment with the minister.

Yitzhak Shamir's office was just a short distance from the Knesset, and it really was very modest. There was nothing ostentatious about that little room, just a few pieces of essential furniture—a bookshelf, a few chairs, and a desk. Except for a prominent Israeli flag placed on the desktop, everything else there was just the typical office mess: some scattered papers, a telephone equipped with an intercom, a glass ashtray, a letter opener, a bottle of water. There was a portable radio on the cabinet to the left. The light-colored curtains let a beam of light fall onto the floor. In some ways, I thought, the tight quarters in which the minister worked were not simply proportioned to his small frame; they must also reflect his character, which at first glance seemed to be that of a rather simple man, but also a very intelligent one. This was also what the pontiff had told me, after the favorable impression he had received of the minister at a meeting at the Vatican about a year earlier.

I smiled and shook the minister's hand, greeting him as "Your Excellency." But Shamir immediately told me to leave aside the formalities and speak more casually. I nodded, although it was hard for me to imagine any other way of speaking to a minister. But what certainly put me at ease was the fact that I could speak to Shamir in Polish. I had studied Hebrew as a child, but had almost completely forgotten it.

I began to explain the reason for the visit, even though there wasn't much need for me to do so, since it had already been communicated through the embassy. Shamir looked at me from across the desk, his eyes gentle and penetrating at the same time.

"As you know well, Minister," I said, still maintaining a certain respect, "I am here to relate to you the words that were spoken to me by Archbishop Andrzej Maria Deskur, suggesting that the Israeli government send a letter to the Holy See with the request of establishing diplomatic missions in the respective states."

I paused for a moment before continuing.

"It is the Excellency's view—"

The minister interrupted, asking me not to call him that.

"I meant His Excellency Archbishop Deskur," I explained.

"Ah," said Shamir, embarrassed. "I understand. Please continue."

"Yes. As I was saying, the archbishop believes that such a letter could prompt reflection among those in the secretariat of state who still reject the idea that the Vatican should recognize Israel and might even convince them of the opportunity that this would bring."

The minister must have prepared his reply already, because he paused for just a few moments.

"We are honored to learn that his Excellency Archbishop Deskur is so concerned about Vatican recognition for our state, and it is certainly a very interesting proposal, which will be taken very seriously by this government."

Then came a calculated pause.

"Nevertheless, because of my experience in international affairs, I can tell you that these kinds of initiatives require great prudence, because if the Vatican secretariat of state did not agree to this, and if instead the Holy See were to reject our proposal for diplomatic missions, this might compromise Israel's international standing even more."

This was a risk, of course, and I saw this. Also, Shamir's skepticism was understandable, considering his political role.

"What does your government need in order to have more confidence in His Excellency's proposal?" I asked.

"Guarantees," Shamir replied, "that would make it reasonable to think that the letter would have its intended effects. I mean, something that would demonstrate agreement in the Vatican secretariat of state to instituting official relations with Israel." He paused again. "Do you think this would be possible?"

For all I knew, the letter would be enough to break the stalemate between the two states. And this condition had gone on so long, practically since the Jewish state had been proclaimed in 1948, that I thought it would be unlikely for the curia even to consider the issue without such a declaration. This was partly because it was primarily in Israel's interest to have official relations with as many states as possible (since there were many that had not yet recognized it, including the Vatican), so I thought it was up to Israel to take the first step. But I couldn't say all of this to Shamir.

"I admit that I am not capable of providing an answer now. It would be better for me to consult the archbishop about this first."

"Of course, of course," the minister said. "I understand. Although I also believe that your role is important enough to be able to bring this government the confirmation that it is looking for, at the appropriate time. As soon as we receive this, I assure you that Israel will send the letter that it has been suggested that we write."

I smiled. "I thank you for your trust, but I think that more than my word alone will be needed to assure that everyone in the secretariat agrees in accrediting an Israeli delegation at the Vatican."

"Oh, I am sure that the important mediation you are carrying out with the Vatican will allow you to understand certain things."

"There are many different points of view in the secretariat," I confessed, "but I will do what I have told you, if you will permit me. I will explain to His Excellency Deskur your legitimate concerns about writing this letter, and I will also ask his advice on how to resolve this question. He is a wise man. I have seen this many times, and just as important he supports Israel, although he hopes that it can come to an understanding with the Palestinian people as soon as possible. If he believes that this is not the way to establish relations with the Vatican, by which I mean that the guarantees you require cannot be provided, you will see that the archbishop will be able to suggest other avenues, without compromising your country in the eyes of the world."

Shamir nodded emphatically as I spoke, and he responded, "The last thing you just said is especially important, particularly at this time. You read the newspapers, you know what I am referring to."

I was confused for a moment. What was he talking about? Was it that international public opinion had turned against his government after the war in Lebanon and the horrible massacre in Sabra and Shatila a few months earlier? That was the most likely explanation. The UN Security Council had even condemned the massacre, with a resolution in December 1982. The Israeli army itself had been accused for its conduct, for failing in its duty to protect the Palestinian refugees in those camps. Israel's defense minister, Ariel Sharon, had suffered a severe blow to his reputation and with him the military commanders in Lebanon. Although most of the responsibility for the slaughter had been attributed to the Christian Phalangists—because they were so thirsty for revenge after the assassination of their president, Gemayel—it had still been Israeli soldiers on the roofs of the buildings around the camps, with their binoculars focused on that enclosed area. So it was easy to believe that the massacre had taken place right in front of their eyes. A commission of inquiry had been set up to determine Israel's negligence—or even complicity—in the incident, ten days after it had taken place. The investigation was still going on when I visited Shamir. I might have said something about all this, but I refrained, careful to limit myself to conveying the archbishop's proposal and nothing more than this, since I didn't feel qualified to speak on certain matters. Fortunately, I didn't have to answer.

"Please continue to communicate with this government through the Israeli embassy in Rome," the foreign minister continued. "We are very grateful for what you are doing on behalf of our country."

I smiled. I was truly happy, but I remained realistic.

Our conversation lasted about ten more minutes. Shamir reminisced about his meeting with the pope, almost exactly one year before. He had been impressed by the pontiff's personality and by the vigor of his intellect.

"It is incredible that a town as small as Wadowice could produce such a great man," the minister commented.

Shamir then asked about the pope's health. He was happy to learn that a year and a half after the attack, which had almost cost the pope his life, he had fully recovered. Shamir didn't say anything about the audience granted to Arafat, which had brought a storm of protest from Israel. It was better not to talk about it, because the meeting between the pope and the Palestinian leader had taken place one day after the assassination of Gemayel, and one day before the bloody backlash in Sabra and Shatilah. All of these events were intertwined politically, and I wasn't a politician. So we chatted for a moment about the hotel where I was staying, and about how much my Israeli relatives had contributed to Zionism before the war. Then it was time to leave. Shamir rose from his chair, but he wasn't much taller standing up. We shook hands again, and then went to the door.

"You are working for the sake of Israel," the minister said once more, "and for this we are infinitely grateful."

We said good-bye. I hadn't convinced the minister to write the letter, but I had done what I had gone there to do. Even so, diplomacy seemed tremendously complicated to me.

While I was visiting Yitzhak Shamir in Israel, the Holy See was promulgating the new code of canon law, with the apostolic constitution *Sacrae Disciplinae Leges*. The code it was replacing was called "Pio-Benedictine," because Pius X had begun the revision, and then after his death it was continued by his successor, Benedict XV. Pope Benedict was born to a marquis in Genoa and christened Giacomo Della Chiesa ("of the Church")—his future already reflected in his name. He received a law degree in Genoa before studying theology. These two popes entrusted to skilled canonists the difficult task of codifying all of the laws—and only the laws—that govern the Church. It had to be a fair and comprehensive collection of norms. One of these stated that baptism should be administered by force to the children of infidels at the point of death, even against their parents' will, because this was the only way to save their souls. Otherwise, the best that could be hoped for them was limbo. This had actually been the rule for many centuries, and although even Saint Thomas had opposed it, there were cases of children—especially Jewish children—who had been baptized secretly, and then taken from their families to live "properly" as Christians.

The question of forced baptisms was a complicated one.

A few days after my return from Israel, I went to Lichten's apartment, and this was among the topics we discussed.

In the first place, we spoke about the German banker at the IOR during dinner, and then I told him about my last trip to Tel Aviv. After the meal, seated comfortably on the sofa, I thought I would easily fall under the spell that Lichten wove with his words. I was even the one to get him started, asking him what he thought about the promulgation of the new code of canon law. My friend would certainly have a perspective on this, since he was thoroughly informed on anything related to his work representing the Anti-Defamation League, although his expertise was not limited to this. I explained my own position on the decision not to change the canon imposing baptism on the children of infidels, noting the glaring contradiction between this norm and what the Council fathers had written in *Nostra Aetate*. Lichten said that he also had been stunned by the

Meeting Shamir 167

decision to reconfirm that statute, and his remarks did not disappoint my expectation that Lichten would have an excellent command of the subject.

"I'm really not sure what to think," I said. "I mean, *Nostra Aetate* says that although the Church is the new people of God, it can't be said that the Jews have been rejected by the Lord or accursed. But I just don't get the connection there. I mean, if the Jews aren't rejected and condemned, why should they be converted by force at the point of death?" At that point, Lichten thought to add something.

"In this regard, there are also contradictions with another document from the Council, and these are even more fundamental than the ones you have rightly mentioned."

Lichten continued, "From what I have learned about this law of the Church, baptism is imposed on non-Christian children in order to save their souls. And it doesn't matter if the sacrament is administered against the wishes of their parents, because they're infidels anyway, so the children can receive the sacrament validly even if their parents are against it. So whether they like it or not, their children become Christian. In this case, as you see, freedom of religion is sacrificed in the interest of faith.

"The only thing is, it's hard to reconcile all of this with the declaration *Dignitatis Humanae*, which Paul VI and the other Council fathers left as a permanent testimony to religious freedom."

"I'm not familiar with that one," I admitted.

"I can assure you that it's just as famous as the other. In the introduction, it says that the purpose of the Church is the same one that Jesus gave to his apostles: go out and teach all nations, baptizing them in the name of the Father and of the Son and of the Holy Spirit, because those who believe and are baptized will be saved, and those who do not believe will be condemned. But Jesus Christ didn't force anyone to be baptized. And then those Council fathers and the pope tell us that the Church has always taught that no one can be forced to embrace the faith—"

I interrupted him. "And what about the *marranos* in Spain? It seemed that there were more than one hundred thousand of those *conversos*, and I don't think it was a free decision for all of them."

"That's true. Many of them accepted Christianity willingly so that they wouldn't be oppressed as Jews anymore, maybe so that they could get some lucrative position. They even mocked the other Jews who didn't do the same, and told the authorities about those converts who still wanted, in their hearts, to return to their former faith. But many more were forced to become Christian together with their children. And as soon as they were baptized, they went to wash their foreheads where the holy water had been poured. At night, they went in secret to pray in the synagogue, they continued to refuse to eat pork, they celebrated the Jewish Passover, going far up into the mountains or down into the valleys to sound the shofar, so that the sound wouldn't be heard in the cities and villages where they lived. Because they did this, the rabbis, following the Talmud, still considered those sinners to be Jews."

"But if that's true," I asked, "then how can it be claimed that Church teaching rules out forced baptisms?"

"Technically, it was the Jewish parents who brought their children to the baptismal font," Lichten replied, "and in fact, the Holy Office did not admit that those Jewish children received the sacrament without the agreement of their father and mother, although in a certain sense they were given no choice. As you can see, this is where the question gets tricky. Only sick and dying children were baptized by force, and in those cases the Church thought it was permissible to do this, just as it seems to think today."

"But even in those cases," I stated, "it's a matter of coercion. And excuse me, but what's the difference between not baptizing a healthy Jew and baptizing a sick one who recovers? I mean, if that happens, is the sacrament invalid?"

"No, not at all. Even if the child survives, for the Church he has become Christian, and at that point he has to be raised and educated as a Christian. There are even heartbreaking stories about Jewish children who were taken away from their parents after it was reported that they had been baptized, sometimes in secret. There's one story from the Roman ghetto that some guy was able to have three of the young girls of the community baptized, and the little ones were taken away from their families. There's also the story about Prospero di Pultro, whose children were taken away because of an unfortunate remark he made. When he was asked if he would allow his children to be baptized, he laughed and let slip that he would agree to this only if the pope himself conducted the ritual. But unfortunately, that's just what happened. When Pope Urban VII found out about it, he had the children brought to him, and he baptized them. The most famous story also involves a pope, and it's about little Edgardo, the son of Momolo Mortara and his wife, Marianna."

"I don't know that one," I confessed.

"What you need to know is that when this child was about one year old, a maid had him baptized in secret, convinced that he was about to die. But he got better, and the maid revealed what she had done to another servant. Edgardo was seven years old when the news reached the tribunal of the Inquisition in Bologna, which ordered the gendarmes to take him away from his Jewish parents so that he could be raised as a good Christian. The boy was taken to Rome at the behest of the pope, and it was Pius IX himself who cared for him."

"That's really an incredible story," I said earnestly.

"Yeah," said Lichten, "and just think that it became so famous that even at the time it inspired some literary works and even theatrical pieces in Italy, France, and the United States. This was partly because the poor father did not at all resign himself to losing his son and tried to have the baptism annulled, while the Roman Jewish community was moved with compassion and helped him to press his appeal at the Vatican. The Jews in France even pressured Napoleon III to intercede personally with the Holy See. But the pope ultimately decided to keep the boy who decided to become a novice, and to take the name Pio, just like his guardian."

"So then," I remarked, "it's just like you said. Once a Jew was baptized, even if secretly or by mistake, there was no going back. In the story you just told, not even the powerful French emperor was able to convince the pope."

"In this case, no," Lichten said, "but in another case he succeeded. A French Jewish couple, the Montels, moved to Fiumicino, near Rome. Their daughter was baptized just after she was born, without their knowledge, and was taken away from them. But this time, Napoleon III helped them, and Pope Gregory XVI had to order that the girl be given back to her family, because to the French government they were not simply Jews, but also French citizens, and it did not recognize church jurisdiction over the affairs of the empire. The pope tried to convince the emperor at least to educate the girl as a Christian, but the emperor wouldn't listen to him and told her parents that they were free to raise her according to the Jewish religion, without any negative consequences."

"A wise king," I commented, "but to me it seems like an exceptional case."

"I would agree. There are very few other stories with a happy ending like that one. Almost always, the children converted to Christianity were taken from their homes.

"And do you want to know what the upshot of all this is?"

I nodded.

"That on the one hand we have a rule in the code of canon law that says it's not a sin if a Jewish child who seems to be dying is baptized, even against the will of his parents. While on the other, those bishops and cardinals gathered in the sacred council were all panting to write and promulgate *Dignitatis Humanae*. This document says that parents alone are responsible for choosing their children's religion, whatever their faith may be, but canon 868 says the opposite. So now there really is no way to know what the Church thinks the truth really is."

CHAPTER 20

CONVENT OF DISCORD

L ech Wałęsa (the activist who founded Solidarity) had been freed from his prison in Arłamów, in Poland, and there seemed to be no more internment camps in that country, but this was nothing but a façade. There were still the special tribunals, almost no rule of law, and the entire nation was afflicted with misery and violence.

During the days that preceded it, I saw Lolek cling almost desperately to his trip to his beloved country, distilling its meaning in a few words: peace and freedom. Sometimes I even got a glimpse of the pope's fleeting thoughts, at dinner or during walks in the Vatican gardens. It was as if he ardently wished that his presence in that place where so many had died could bring an interruption to that inexorable onslaught of chaos. When he thought about it, Lolek was able to convince himself that this could happen only if the harshness of the regime (hardly inclined to offer anything more than constant and poorly paid labor) could be softened through dialogue.

So when Lolek was finally able to return to Poland in June 1983, he agreed to meet personally with General Jaruzelski, first at the Belweder Palace in Warsaw, and then on a sunny afternoon in Wawel. The pope also asked for permission to talk with Lech Wałęsa and was allowed to meet with him at a cabin near Zakopane, at the foot of the Tatra Mountains, where the pontiff was taken in a helicopter by the security services. During those days back in Poland, Lolek also visited the tomb of Cardinal Wyszyński, who had died a few years earlier. He recalled the agony that the primate of Poland had suffered before he died, while he himself had been suffering in his hospital bed after the assassination attempt. The cardinal had called, about to render his soul to God but happy to hear that the pope was still alive. He would die soon after, sparing himself the tragic events of December 1981. "May God bless you," Wojtyła prayed for him, kneeling.

The pope then went to Częstochowa, to the shrine where his arrival was greeted by throngs of sick people hoping for a miracle. He also celebrated Mass in Niepokalanów, the City of the Immaculate founded by Fr. Maximilian Kolbe, whom the pope had proclaimed a saint. Before he left, in his speeches in Poznan, Katowice, and Wrocław, he talked about Solidarity and defended the rights of workers to form unions. The pope repeatedly shouted "Szczęść Boze" (may God help you). He had prayed to the Lord repeatedly during that trip, that life might return to his country. Then he left. One month later, Poland was not entirely free, but it was no longer under siege, and political prisoners were being released.

The regime had decided that, for now, it was not to its advantage to put too many restrictions on the Polish church, at least not like in the past. One beneficiary of this new approach was a group of Discalced Carmelite nuns. They had long been searching for a location for their community, and they finally found an abandoned building in Auschwitz. It seemed ideal for their mission, so they asked the local authorities for permission to use it. The permission was granted, with a ninety-nine-year lease. So the sisters began the work of setting up their convent there. But what may have been overlooked was that the building (which everyone still called the "Old Theater") had been a warehouse for Zyklon-B, the deadly pesticide used by the Nazis as the poison for the gas chambers, which helped explain why the structure was so close to the site of the Auschwitz-Birkenau concentration camp. Since this place held so many horrific memories, especially for the Jews, they would have preferred that it remain abandoned. But the nuns weren't concerned about any of this and moved in to practice their cloistered life.

As if this weren't enough, a Dutch priest unintentionally complicated the matter even further. Fr. Werenfried van Straaten had learned about the sisters' project, and in the spirit of solidarity he began to raise funds to help them build their convent. He was so zealous that he referred to this as the triumph of the cross over Auschwitz, repeating this over and over to the faithful until they erected a cross more than twenty feet high behind the gate of the camp.

"Be generous, brothers and sisters," he would say. "Help these poor sisters in Auschwitz, because what they are doing is worthy of your compassion and would also make our pope happy." He presumed that the pontiff must have the same view, given his Polish origin. But he had no idea that his remarks would provoke the indignation of many Jews, who were already upset about the raising of a Christian symbol over that spot, which shouldn't belong to anyone, and became even more irate when they came to the conclusion that the Holy Father had ordered it himself. As a cardinal Karol Wojtyła had given an interview to Vatican Radio while he was visiting Rome for the beatification of Fr. Kolbe, saying that an altar and shrine should be built where the friar had been killed, just as in the earliest centuries of Christianity, when churches were erected over the tombs of martyrs, saints, and blesseds. But it was also true that the pontiff knew nothing about the convent being built at the concentration camp, much less about the Dutch priest's initiative to help the Discalced Carmelites. So when I heard about some of the criticisms that Jews were making about the pope and then talked with him about the entire affair, I quickly became convinced that this was another unjust accusation.

While more crosses were planted at that camp, so many that they couldn't be counted anymore, one more than any other may have explained why the convent had been built there. It was a cross placed in memory of Teresa Benedicta of the Cross: Edith Stein. Her remains were elsewhere, just a handful of ashes buried beneath the floor of the Church of Saint Michael next to her family home in Wrocław, where she was born in 1891. But the sister had also died in the gas chambers of that concentration camp, and her body was burned, becoming smoke in the gray vault of the Auschwitz sky. She had gone to her death as a Christian, while the Nazis had eliminated her as a Jew, since she was the daughter of Jewish parents. Even after her conversion, the Germans had come to arrest her at the Carmelite monastery in Echt, in the garden where she and the other Carmelite nuns were contemplating the Virgin Mary.

So even Cardinal Franciszek Macharski, whose diocese included the city of Auschwitz, was struggling to understand what harm the Jews could find in the decision of the sisters to found a convent there, a place for praying and reciting the psalms, as their sister had done before her martyrdom. And while Cardinal Józef Glemp, who had replaced Wyszyński as primate of Poland, was wondering about the reason behind that vehement protest, other cardinals were asking the same thing, including the ones who were appointed by the pope to meet with some members of the international Jewish community to discuss the question. That was when it became clear that this was a purely religious matter. A rabbi from France explained that in Deuteronomy, the Second Law that Moses gave to the people of Israel shortly before he died, it was written that when an entire city had fallen into idolatry, the Hebrews had to destroy it to its foundations, and never let it be rebuilt. It was also written in the Talmud that this passage had never found an application, although after the war there were some who maintained that the idolatrous city cited in the Torah was Auschwitz, where human beings had usurped a right that belonged only to God, the power over life and death. So that place had to remain in ruins, as the Law prescribed, and nothing must be allowed to stand there again—but now the sisters were building a convent.

During that year of controversy over the convent, another event horrified more people than just the Jews. The date was October 8, 1985.

The *Achille Lauro*, an Italian cruise ship, had just pulled up anchor to return to Port Said, where it had to pick up many of its passengers who had disembarked to see the pyramids. After this stop, it would return to Ashdod, in Israel. But after a few hours at sea, a suspicious crew member discovered that some of the passengers who had decided to remain on board had weapons, including Soviet Kalashnikovs, machine guns, grenades, and dynamite. The crew member tried to raise the alarm, but it was no use. They were four Arab guerrillas, and they took a hostage from among those people. His name was Leon Klinghoffer, a Jewish American citizen. He was also paralyzed and in a wheelchair. In tears, his wife pleaded with his captors not to hurt him.

The ship, now in the hands of the terrorists, was looking for a port to dock in, but neither Syria nor Cyprus would grant permission. One of the terrorists, named Omar, who claimed to be the leader of the group, sent a message by radio: "We will sink every ship and we will shoot down every airplane that approaches us," he said, and it was clear that he was not joking. After this, he and the other members of the group went back onto the deck, one of them with blood all over his shoes and pants. When the captain asked where the stains had come from, he was told that the American hostage had been killed, and another, Mildred Hodes, was about to meet the same fate. They showed him her passport. At that point, the captain sent a message to the Syrian authorities in Tartus, telling them not to do anything, that the passengers on board were safe and were about to be set free.

On the morning of the following day, the ship dropped anchor fifteen miles from Port Said. Then Muhammad Zaidan, also known as Abu

Abbas, came from Tunis. He was the head of the Palestine Liberation Front, the group created in the middle of the 1970s to which the terrorists aboard the ship also belonged. By radio, Abbas ordered the hijackers to break off the operation. It appears that the Egyptian government had promised safe conduct for the terrorists in exchange for releasing the ship and all of the hostages. The men followed his orders to the letter. A tugboat came to pick them up, and they disappeared into the bay. They resurfaced a few hours later, on an Egyptian flight taking them to a secure location. The PLF leader who had acted as negotiator was also with them.

It seemed that Abbas had gotten away with his actions, until American fighter planes appeared in the sky, forcing the plane to land in Sicily, at the NATO base in Sigonella. Once it was on the runway, American soldiers surrounded the plane. But then the Italian carabinieri came and surrounded the American troops, pointing their weapons at them. They had been ordered to do so because the terrorists had committed the kidnapping and murder aboard an Italian ship, and now that they were on Italian soil, it was the prerogative of the Italian authorities to take them into custody.

There was the danger that a diplomatic incident would erupt that night. But the embassies of the two countries worked out a solution, and the plane took off again for Rome, where the police put all of the terrorists into handcuffs, except for one. Abu Abbas wasn't with them on the plane. In the meantime, while the politicians in Rome and Washington were frantically trying to reach an agreement, the U.S. State Department ordered its ambassador in Egypt, Nicholas Veliotes, to board the *Achille Lauro* to check personally on the American passengers. The tragic news came shortly afterward: "Leon Klinghoffer is dead. The terrorists killed him outside the port of Tartus."

Many were outraged over the man's death at the hands of those Palestinian guerrillas, and not only the Jews, although in their case sorrow was accompanied by a strong sense of humiliation. The killers belonged to the PLF, but although it had its own separate designation, the group really took its orders from Arafat's PLO. And in fact, it was discovered that Arafat had been the one, from his refuge in Tunisia where he had established himself after the Israeli army had forced him out of Lebanon, who had convinced Abu Abbas to order his men to release their prisoners. After this, it was plausible to maintain that someone had felt constrained to act pragmatically simply to avoid a massacre, bartering safe passage for the terrorists in exchange for the safety of the other passengers, and coming away with just one hostage dead, the Jewish American killed in one of the ship's cabins. And although in the end the prominent international terrorist Abu Abbas had been able to escape (it wasn't clear how this had happened, since two armed squads had surrounded the plane he was on), many thought that the Italian government had covered his tracks. This theory was bolstered by the fact that Abbas was a close associate of Arafat, who had been received with full honors by the Italian authorities (even the pope had granted him an audience, some people maliciously pointed out), in spite of the fact that he called openly for Israel's destruction.

This was believed to be a concession in line with the political context of the day, in which anti-Semitism was coming back dangerously, and together with it, fear in the heart of every Jew.

I also noticed a great deal of tension in Rome at the time, where the Jews did not limit themselves to criticizing the country's institutions only because of the mysterious escape of Abu Abbas. They had also noted that the communists were exclusively on the side of the Arabs, the same ones who had attached a banner to a small Roman synagogue, reading, "We will burn the dens of the Zionists." The president of the republic, as mentioned earlier, had even asked, "What is it that these Jews want, really?" The Catholic associations did not defend the Jews, and even attacked them, and those who remained silent in the face of terrorism lashed out against the Jews in Europe, as they did against the schools and kibbutzim in Galilee. Of course, there were also many leftist Jewish intellectuals who apologized for the decisions of the Israeli government, like those who wrote the appeal "David, Repent!" after the war in Lebanon, and especially after the massacres in Sabra and Shatila. Lichten had defended Israel, at least on the first point: "Israel is still a country, and from the first day it has had to fight for the right to exist."

This is what was happening in Italy and in the world at the time, while many Jews continued to be incensed over the still-unresolved question of the sisters who had decided to found their convent in Auschwitz, demonstrating that they had no concern for the values of Judaism. And there was no letup in the accusations against the pope over this same issue, because of the growing conviction that the pope himself was behind the construction of the convent, especially because it was located in the diocese where he had once been the archbishop. It was not enough for Vatican spokesman Joaquín Navarro-Valls to release statements to the *New York Times*, saying that the pope had not blocked the initiative of the Discalced Carmelites, but had also not encouraged it, and that matters like these were the responsibility of the local bishops.

During those months, Lichten was constantly asking me if I knew anything about any initiative of the Holy See to resolve the controversy. One afternoon, I was able to reveal to Lichten what I had learned a few hours before at lunch in the pope's apartment: that a delegation would soon be going to Geneva, made up of four cardinals. The delegation would be meeting with another, composed of four Jewish representatives, to see if they could work out a compromise. The Catholic delegation was headed by Cardinal Albert Decourtray, the archbishop of Lyons and primate of the Gauls. It also included Cardinal Aron Jean-Marie Lustiger, the archbishop of Paris, who had converted from Judaism in 1940. His mother and some other relatives had died in Auschwitz. In fact, when the pope had named then-Monsignor Lustiger as head of the Diocese of Paris, some had commented ironically on how an Ashkenazi had been installed at Notre Dame, criticizing the decision based on the conviction that the promotion had been a reward for receiving baptism. It seemed as if the only way to be a good and worthy Jew was to convert, and this had been the only reason for including Cardinal Lustiger on the commission. But the pope had put him there, together with Cardinal Godfried Danneels, the archbishop of Brussels, and Cardinal Macharski, who had replaced Wojtyła as archbishop of Kraków. Macharski may have had the keenest interest in the matter, since he had been the one who had authorized the convent. The Jewish delegation was led by French rabbi Théo Klein.

It was a good initiative, but a more significant gesture was needed.

CHAPTER 21

THE OTHER SIDE
OF THE TIBER

After dinner Lolek seemed to lose all interest in his surroundings inside the room. His detachment was fascinating. He stood up and went to the window, parted the curtains, and looked outside. His demeanor changed completely when he was deep in thought like this. He stood in front of the window for a few moments and then invited me to come admire the city from that special point of observation. I went over and saw that the square down below was empty. The vast number of faithful who usually filled the space between the colonnades weren't there. Cars were moving up and down the Via della Conciliazione, probably people on their way home from work. Not far away were the seagulls circling gracefully above the river.

"You see," Lolek said, pointing to where those birds were, "there behind those houses, right where the Tiber flows. There's the synagogue. It's so close, we could walk to it from here."

I wanted to relate a story that Lichten had once told me.

"You know," I said, "when the Jews came here, long before the diaspora, they first settled in the area west of the river, where the Vatican is, and they stayed there for many centuries, building synagogues. Then they decided to move to the other side of the Tiber, and it's said that while they were moving the sacred furnishings across the river, in full stream, a menorah fell in, a candlestick with seven branches symbolizing the seven days of creation. It was never found again."

Then a question came to my mind. "Are you thinking about going to the old ghetto?"

Lolek smiled and said it would be easier to talk about it sitting down, inviting me to sit in one of the armchairs, while he remained standing—a sign that it would be a long conversation. Lolek began telling me about a proposal made to him a few days earlier by the archbishop of Los Angeles, inviting him to visit the city and its synagogue. It seemed like a good idea

179

to him, until one of his colleagues advised him that if the bishop of Rome were to make such an important gesture, he should do so first in his own diocese. He then said that he had sent two of his most trusted advisors, Bishop Clemente Riva and Monsignor Jorge Mejía, to find out if such an event could be arranged with the leading rabbis of the Roman Jewish community. They had to agree to this first, and the pope told me not to say anything about it in the meantime. I assured him that I would say nothing, but meanwhile, I was thinking about what an extraordinary thing it would be for the pope to set foot in a synagogue. None of his predecessors had ever done so, and in fact some of them had made the synagogue off-limits for all good Catholics. Only one other pope was known to have gone near a synagogue: John XXIII, who one Saturday morning had told his driver to stop outside the Roman synagogue. The people were leaving, and the pope had put his right arm out the car window to bless them, thinking there was nothing contrary to the gospel about this. As soon as they realized it, a crowd gathered around to thank him. But as symbolic as this gesture was, the pope had remained outside on the street, so I was sure that my friend's action would be even more solemn. Bishops and cardinals had been inside a Jewish synagogue (and Wojtyła himself had done so before becoming pope), but no successor of Peter had ever gone so far. I was certain that such a religious experience would mark a turning point in relations between Jews and Catholics.

The pontiff sat down next to me. "Do you remember the time my father and I went to the synagogue in Wadowice? That was such a long time ago."

Finally, a few days later, I was able to break the silence with Kurt Rosenberg. Fr. Stanisław Dziwisz had given me permission, after the pope had asked him to tell me the date scheduled for this extraordinary event: the visit of a Supreme Pontiff of the Universal Church to the Great Synagogue of Rome. To get a sense of the excitement that had arisen around this event, one simply needed to hear about the meeting between the representatives of the Holy See and those of the Jewish community (during which Monsignor Jorge Mejía was said to have been especially effective as a papal ambassador). The rabbis had said they were surprised but honored by the idea, and were ready to welcome the pontiff with great respect. Even Kurt was unable to contain his enthusiasm when I told him about it, and contrary to his skeptical nature he flung himself backward in his chair, almost tipping over, and began to sing the *Hatikvah*, the hymn of the Jewish people. I was just as happy as my friend and was even more so a few days later when both of us were invited to the ceremony, scheduled for April 13, 1986. We couldn't wait.

When the moment came, the solid walls of the synagogue on the bank of the Tiber were surrounded by a huge crowd, such as had never been seen before, but there was no reason to be surprised. Newspaper and television reporters had come from all over the world to cover the event. It took a lot of work. The cameramen inside the synagogue were constantly roaming around looking for the best angle, while the photographers jamming the entrance quickly used up their film. Nothing had been overlooked, inside or outside, and the security personnel were keeping close watch. The guests had to display their invitations at the gate on Via Catalana, and then once inside the synagogue they had to separate according to the ritual division—women to the balcony, men to the floor below, although it was explained that this was not a commandment, but an ancient custom. On the street along the river were the carabinieri, equipped as always with their M-12s and bulletproof vests. Leaving the building unprotected had led to tragedy once, when a Jewish boy had been killed. There was a bouquet of flowers marking the spot, and someone was praying in front of it.

But it was springtime, and there was celebration in the air.

After parking the car near the Church of Sant'Angelo in Pescheria (so called because the Jewish women used to collect the garbage from the market, mostly fish heads and bones, for making broth), Kurt and I suddenly found ourselves immersed in a crowd in which it was no longer possible to tell Jew from Christian. Before us was the Great Synagogue of Rome, the largest in Europe, facing Jerusalem. It had been built at the beginning of the twentieth century, on land that gradually sloped downward to the level of the river. It used to flood there when the river was high, turning the ghetto into a huge swamp, which favored the spreading of disease. Part of the ghetto was demolished, and the remainder was divided into four new plots of land where four buildings were constructed, one of them being the synagogue. It was a tall edifice, visible from any elevated spot in the city. To me, it seemed eclectic in design, combining Assyro-Babylonian motifs with art nouveau, making it much different from the synagogue in Wadowice, which was fairly simple in its contours, not to mention much smaller. But it wasn't only architecture that distinguished the two synagogues; they also practiced different rituals inside. The ceremony in Wadowice was Ashkenazi, while in Rome it was Sephardic, because most of the Jews in Rome had originally come from Spain. I had never become accustomed to the Sephardic ways, so I had rarely been to the synagogue since moving with my family to Rome. But what all synagogues had in common was a plain interior, with no images, according to the rule that God is the sole shaper of all bodies, and no one is allowed even to reproduce his creatures.

Kurt and I entered the synagogue and sat just a few steps away from the pulpit—the *Bimah*, as the Ashkenazi called it, while for the Sephardi it was the *Tevah*. On the raised platform in front of them were two chairs, identical in form and color. They were the seats for the pope and the chief rabbi, carefully placed so that they were slightly angled toward each other, but were still facing the assembly. It was happening: Jews and Christians were coming together under the same roof, and a strange thrill seemed to run through everyone there. This feeling became even more pronounced a moment later, when John Paul II entered the synagogue (I just barely turned around in time to witness the moment), his steps solemn and slow, and beside him the chief rabbi Elio Toaff, both followed by an entourage of cardinals and rabbis. The chief rabbi and the others were all wearing white mantles, striped shawls, and yarmulkes. The silence was suddenly replaced with murmuring, until the choir intoned a psalm in Hebrew, and the *hazzanim* sang it in their powerful, pulsating voices. The Torah was read, with the Lord telling Abraham to look up into the sky and count the stars, because such would be his descendants, and the prophet Micah proclaimed that the law would go forth from Zion.

The Holy Father and the chief rabbi sat down in their places. The first to speak was the president of the Jewish community, who talked about the people of Israel and its persecutions, finally recalling the figure of John XXIII, whom he called a righteous man.

Then it was the turn of the chief rabbi Toaff, who admitted that he was happy with the pontiff's gesture, but also felt the need to clarify that the past remained what it was, although now there might be reason to look to the future with confidence. He then quoted Deuteronomy, "You are children of the Lord your God," and said that if all people had one

Father, then they were all brothers and sisters, and there should be no hatred among them. But there was hatred dividing them, and it manifested itself in so many different ways: terrorism, anti-Semitism, the denial of human rights. In his view, then, Jews and Catholics had the same duty to restore peace and brotherhood in the world, because while their religions were different, their roots were the same.

At that point, it was time for the Holy Father to speak. He stood up and began by saying "Todà rabbà" (Thank you), first of all to the Lord (who had spread the sky, founded the earth, and then had chosen Abraham as the father of his many children, as many as the stars or the grains of sand on the seashore), and then to the Divine Providence that had willed that the bishop of Rome should meet with the city's Jewish community in that synagogue. Finally, he thanked the chief rabbi, who had also welcomed him to that place. There was one word burning inside him more than any other: genocide. He said it out loud, and the silence around him became even more hushed. He spoke of the millions of victims of the Holocaust and recalled his visit to Auschwitz, and the stone before which he had stopped one morning, with its inscription in Hebrew: "No one may pass this stone with indifference." He also spoke of the high price that the Roman Jews had paid in their own blood in 1943 and of the substantial work done by the Church in those years, when it decided at its own risk to throw open its doors to the Jews hounded by their persecutors. After this, he addressed the Jews in the synagogue with sincerity: "You are our beloved brothers," he told them, "and in a certain way, our older brothers."

Seated next to Kurt, I certainly did not fail to recognize that expression. I had heard Lolek use it on other occasions, when we were still classmates in Wadowice and there were discussions about anti-Semitism at the meetings organized by the history professor. It was a phrase taken from Adam Mickiewicz, the author of *Pan Tadeusz* and Poland's greatest poet. Hearing it again at the synagogue that day, I was suddenly brought back to those years before the war, and all of those old emotions welled up in me again. When the pope finished speaking, there was again silence and prayer in the synagogue. After the end of the liturgy, John Paul II and Elio Toaff met for a private conversation. It wasn't the first time that the two had met. Five years earlier, the Holy Father had been visiting the Roman parish of San Carlo ai Catinari. It was very close to the old ghetto, and the rabbi went to meet him in the church sacristy. In any case, the day after the pope's visit to the synagogue, the rabbi would send a message to the pontiff that was dense with religious significance: "We Jews are grateful to you Catholics for spreading the idea of the monotheistic God in the world."

Kurt and I left the synagogue and made our way back along the Via del Portico d'Ottavia. Beneath that crumbling colonnade, I looked up and saw that there were still people watching out the windows of their homes. Just moments ago, they had seen the pope and the chief rabbi exchange an embrace. It was like previous gestures of affection between John XXIII and the Anglican archbishop of Canterbury, Michael Ramsey, and between Paul VI and Athenagoras, the patriarch of Constantinople. So this was the journey that the Church was on, I thought, and those few steps that John Paul II had taken into the Roman synagogue went a long way toward reconciliation between the two religions, after the long centuries of hostility that had blocked any form of dialogue—even though they had the same prophets, the same law, and the same God, giving them a solid foundation for communication.

We headed toward the car, parked on the Rione Sant'Angelo, where compulsory preaching had once been held (and it was said that the Jews stuffed wax into their ears to keep from listening to it). On the right side of the church, I saw a stone set in the wall, a little more than three feet wide, with an inscription in Latin. I remembered that my father had translated it for me once when he came to visit me in Rome after the war, and we had visited the city's Jewish neighborhood. The inscription referred to an old rule in the ghetto, because the stone had once been used for measuring fish, and the head and part of the body of the longer ones had to be given to the tax collectors, ". . . *usque ad primas pinnas*" (up to the first fin). Kurt commented on the tax, saying it was better not to catch the bigger fish, and then chuckling over the thought of one Jewish fisherman catching a hundred small fish, while another who was less fortunate might catch just one, half a finger longer than the stone. I was thinking about how happy my father would have been to witness such an unprecedented gesture by the pope—and not just any pope, but a pope named Karol Wojtyła, his beloved Lolek.

I spoke my next thought out loud. "What would he have said?"

"Who?" Kurt asked me. "The unlucky fisherman?"

"What fisherman?" I replied. "I meant my father. Who knows how happy he would be today if he were still alive?"

"Yes," Kurt said. "He would have been happy."

"Although I'm also thinking about what my Grandma Huppert would've done after everything that happened today."

"What's that?"

"Well, without a doubt she would've gone up to Toaff, saying, 'Look here, Rabbi, the first one to get Wojtyła into a synagogue was my grandson!'"

CHAPTER 22

RETURN TO WADOWICE

Six months after Lolek's visit to the synagogue came the meeting in Assisi, the city of Saint Francis, brother of Sister Poverty, detached from all possessions. It was October 27, 1986, the celebration of the first World Day of Prayer for Peace instituted by the pope (and reinforced by the UN proclamation of 1986 as an International Year of Peace). The leaders of many religions came to Assisi for the occasion—Buddhists, Hindus, Jainists, Muslims, Shintoists, Sikhs, practitioners of native African religions, American Indians, and Christians from both the East and the West. There were also the Jews, naturally. Out of respect for the Jewish law, the prayers were not held inside the basilica, where the walls depicted images of living things, but outside of it, in the enclosed lower square. After they recited the *limmùd* (the Mourner's Kaddish) all of the Jews gathered in a separate group, on one of the roads of Assisi next to a building that must have previously been a synagogue. Following this, the Jews joined the others, and Rabbi Toaff mounted the platform decorated with olive branches, sitting to the right of the pope, where the Protestants and Orthodox were also seated. The Buddhists and Muslims were sitting on the pope's left. It was a typical autumn day—cold, the sky full of clouds, the wind whipping the vestments of those ministers of so many different religions. Below the platform, on all four sides, were those attending the ceremony, including Lichten. Many of those present were local residents. When it was time for the rabbi to recite his prayer, the words were from the Psalms and the prophets of Israel.

All of those religious representatives had met there because full peace had not yet been attained in the world. To tell the truth, there wasn't even complete harmony between Jews and Catholics, because the questions that divided them hadn't been resolved.

One of these was still the issue of the Carmelite convent in Auschwitz. The Catholic and Jewish delegations had met in Geneva to discuss the matter, the cardinals reiterating that for the Church there was nothing wrong with the sisters being there, and the rabbis disagreeing, maintaining that although there was no harm in praying, there were places they could do this other than a spot where Jews had been exterminated. The clear impression was that the groups were cordial enough with each other, but completely inflexible in their positions. But because the cardinals had no intention of imposing their own view, and considering that the pope had been extremely friendly toward these Jewish older brothers (and it wasn't a good idea for them to take a different stance), the cardinals graciously agreed to have the nuns move somewhere else. People were hoping that the discussion might be revived at some point, but at the last meeting, in February 1987, the announcement was made that the nuns would move within two years. The extra time would be needed to build another convent. To some it might have seemed like too long a delay, but then again, the nuns could have stayed put instead. Even Kurt said that, all in all, the Church had made a sound decision.

But with that question resolved (or at least so it seemed), others sprang up in that year of controversy.

One of these concerned another Carmelite, Edith Stein, Sister Teresa Benedicta of the Cross. She had come from a Jewish family, and for this reason had been killed by the Nazis in a concentration camp. The pope had beatified her on May 1, 1987, a Friday, during his apostolic visit to the Federal Republic of Germany. The ceremony had been held at the Köln-Müngersdorf stadium, in the presence of thousands of faithful. The Church considered her a Christian martyr and had her own extensive writings as evidence. But for the Jews, she was no such thing; she was one of their martyrs. For them, the proof was something she had said to one of her sisters at the convent in Echt, in Holland, when the Germans had come to take them away.

"Come, sister," she had said. "Let's go to die, today, for our people."

And in fact she had been killed at the camp together with fellow Jews. To the Jews, then, Edith Stein was one of the victims of the Holocaust.

But that wasn't all.

On June 25, 1987, Kurt Waldheim had gone to the Vatican on an official state visit. Waldheim had been secretary-general of the United Nations from 1972 to 1981 (serving consecutive terms), but about a year before his visit to the pope, he had been elected president of his country, Austria. There was fiery controversy over that official visit. The World

Jewish Congress, and especially its representatives in Israel and in the United States, were accusing Waldheim of war crimes as a Nazi. There were widespread rumors that he had participated in killings and round-ups during the Second World War. He had fought for the Wehrmacht in France, and then on the eastern front and in the Balkans. But he also lied about his military record, saying that in 1941 the army had sent him home because of an injury he suffered during fighting in Russia. Many eyewitnesses appeared to refute his claims, most of them Greek and Yugoslavian partisans, who also accused him of participating in the deportation of Jews from Thessaloniki, which was the largest Jewish community in all of Greece. During that period, about eighty thousand Jews lived there—the "Jerusalem of the Balkans," as it was called at the time. From March 15 to August 10, 1943, the Germans cruelly implemented the transfer of Jews to the camp of Auschwitz-Birkenau.

"Here's what's going on," Kurt Rosenberg had said when he found out that the pope had received the Austrian president at the Vatican. "There are people who swear that they saw him command the firing squad for a group of Italian soldiers arrested after the armistice. And then there are the fifty thousand Jews forcibly deported to the concentration camps, with documents coming out saying he was part of that operation, too. The chickens are coming home to roost, and how does he defend himself? 'Oh, terribly sorry, but I was following orders.' What a great excuse, just what all the Nazi leaders have said, ever since Nuremberg. But the secretary-general of the United Nations, of all people, shouldn't be saying it. I mean, all they do is talk about peace at the UN, but if he tries to use the word, he might not pull it off. But no, they elect the guy, twice in a row. And now the pope welcomes him, too."

I kept silent while my friend spoke. Waldheim was the object of serious accusations, that much was true, and because of his past he was persona non grata in the United States, but still he had never been tried. And Simon Wiesenthal was defending him, saying he was not guilty of Nazi crimes.

But while all of this was reigniting the debate between the Jews and the Holy See, it came to light that the other issue was still unresolved: the question of the Carmelite convent in Auschwitz. The two-year deadline for the sisters to move had already passed, but they were still there at the camp and seemed to have no intention of going anywhere. Since the beginning of the controversy, Cardinal Macharski had taken quite a bit of umbrage at the controversy raised by the Jews, and he continued to insist that out of respect for the Church and for Christians, all of the decisions made in Geneva should be scrapped. Even the primate of Poland, Cardinal Glemp, decided to chime in at the height of the controversy by calling for another meeting to start the discussions over from square one. Not only that, but he wanted new delegates to be appointed, because he thought the original ones were completely inadequate. Someone pointed out to him that these were four cardinals to whom the Holy See had entrusted the task of meeting with the rabbis, who for their part were entirely respectful representatives of the Jewish community—but Cardinal Glemp insisted on his own point of view, even complaining about Cardinal Macharski. In Cardinal Glemp's mind, Cardinal Macharski represented only the Diocese of Kraków, while for the primate the question concerned Poland as a whole, if not the entire Church. By now, everyone was waiting for the pope to break his silence, and decide once and for all whether the Carmelites should remain in Auschwitz, or leave (although Cardinal Albert Decourtray still hoped that a solution could be found without inconveniencing the Holy Father).

Meanwhile, I had received a letter sent from Wadowice that stirred up a lot of old memories. The letter said that a kindergarten had been built where the synagogue used to stand, and that fifty years after its destruction, a plaque would be set into the right-hand wall of the new building, in memory of the house of worship and of the city's Jewish Holocaust victims. The committee sponsoring the initiative was inviting me to Wadowice on May 9, 1989, the day on which the plaque would be set. My first thought was to turn down the invitation, because I wanted to keep intact my memory of all those places as they had been before the war. I decided to write a letter thanking all the members of the committee for thinking about me, but saying that I would not attend the ceremony. I also told Lolek about the invitation and my decision not to go.

A few days went by. One evening, I went to the pope's apartment, down in the dumps because that afternoon I had reread the short letter sent to me from Wadowice. When I arrived, Lolek was waiting for me, on his feet. A little bit later, when we sat down for dinner, we returned to the subject of that letter.

"You have to go, Jurek," the pope told me. "This is a ceremony for commemorating all of the Jews of Wadowice who were killed, and that means your mother, your grandmother, and your sister, too. It's a way for you to honor their memory."

"I can't do it. I can't go back, Lolek. Please, just let it go."

We changed the subject and finished our dinner.

A few more days went by. One morning, an envelope was brought to our household, with the papal seal and insignia on it, delivered personally by a chauffeur. It was for me, but since I wasn't at home, Irene accepted it (wondering why it had a stamp, since it had been delivered by hand). When I got home, I broke the red wax seal and found a letter inside. On the top left-hand side, there was another Vatican insignia.

"Drogi Jurku" (Dear Jurek), it began. It had been written by the Holy Father, with his signature at the bottom, and it was his last attempt to convince me to go back to our hometown for such an important occasion. Lolek wrote that he remembered the synagogue very well, there next to the school, and the people going there to pray. He also quoted the words that he had spoken to the Jews in Warsaw during one of his trips to Poland, when he told them that the Church and all people and nations that were part of it shared in their suffering, and that the one speaking to them was indeed a Polish pope, one who had personally experienced the tragedy of that country. At the end, he addressed me directly again, telling me that if I were to decide to return to the place where I had been born and had spent my carefree childhood, I could bring this letter with me, and even read it in public. The letter was dated March 30, 1989. Spring had just begun.

When May came, I went to Poland. I was carrying the letter that the Holy Father had written to me, which more than anything else had convinced me to make the trip. It was like a talisman that I carried, to give me strength.

The airplane landed in Kraków, in a country still in crisis, although Solidarity was still in operation and Jaruzelski had come to an agreement with his opponents, tenacious negotiators who had succeeded in getting the regime to allow one-third of the parliament to be chosen by free elections, although the remaining legislators would still be appointed by the general.

I walked down the steps of the ramp, and when I reached the bottom I realized that my legs were trembling. It had been fifty years since I had set foot on that soil, but I had to move along quickly to keep from holding up the line and started making my way through the airport. It was a pleasure to hear my own language being spoken all around me again.

During the drive to my hotel, I looked out the window and saw that not everything had changed. Much was different, but still familiar. That evening, my friend Jan Kus came to pick me up at the hotel, and even more memories started coming back. Kus took me to Hawełka, one of the two restaurants that my father had usually eaten at when he had to go to Kraków for work.

The ceremony was held the following day. A car came to pick me up and took me to Wadowice. The drive took the same amount of time as it always had, about forty-five minutes. But as the journey got under way, it seemed to me that the road was a hidden pathway of my own heart, although it was leading me toward a world that was no longer mine. At least the spring weather was as pleasant as ever.

We arrived at Wadowice without any delays, and just inside the city we reached the spot where the synagogue once stood, at the end of a street crossing Adama Mickiewicza Street (where I glanced briefly, but emotionally, at the Marcin Wadowita school), turning to the right from the direction of the Rynek. As we crossed the square, it seemed smaller than I remembered it, perhaps because things take on different dimensions when they are measured according to nostalgia. I saw more than one hundred people already in front of the school building where the city's Jewish synagogue had stood.

I stepped out of the car, and although I took a spot a bit off to the side, some people came up to greet me and thank me for coming. One of them was the mayor—not old Mr. Kluk, of course, but another man, elegant and courteous. I recognized a few people, but none of the rabbis among them. I had never seen these rabbis before. There was also the archbishop of Kraków, Cardinal Macharski, and Monsignor Kuczkowski. A few times I thought I recognized someone, but I was just fooled by a physical resemblance. Everyone knew that I had a letter from the pope.

The mayor climbed the steps to the entrance of the school and stood at the cement railing. He said a few words before uncovering the plaque. There was applause, and then a brief moment for silence and personal prayer. I climbed the steps to deliver my own remarks and pulled the Holy Father's letter from the breast pocket of my coat.

I remembered the times on the sabbath and holy days when I had read the prayers in the synagogue, since this was one of the responsibilities of the son of the *rosh ha kohel*, the head of the community. (I had to be careful not to call my father by the Yiddish form, *roshikuel*, because he wanted only the Hebrew terms to be used.) Because the prayers were sung, my father always apologized to the other faithful in the synagogue, reassuring them that the tone-deaf ritual would not last long. I couldn't wait to stop reciting the prayers either. In part, I was ashamed of my singing, but mostly it was because my friends were already playing soccer outside in the courtyard behind the synagogue. These were almost always other Jewish boys. They were allowed to play then, as long as they didn't yell and disrupt the service.

On the day I read the pope's letter to the Jews gathered there I kept my hat on my head out of respect for the sacred edifice that had once stood there, in which men were not allowed without wearing their yarmulkes. It was an ancient Jewish custom for men to keep their heads covered when they prayed to the Lord (and it wasn't only the Jews who respected this tradition; it also explained why the Catholic clergy often wore a *zuchetto*— purple for bishops, red for cardinals, and white in the case of the pope). According to Ashkenazi tradition, the Jewish yarmulke had to be dark in color, and my fedora was dark. A few moments before, Macharski had also supported his decision not to take off his hat. I read the letter that the Holy Father had written to his Jewish friend, convincing me to return to my beloved land. The intimate words that the letter contained, which became public at that moment, earned me the same kind of applause that the mayor had received. When I finished reading it, some of the audience members came up to me with a sort of deference, but that was certainly not what I needed at the moment. Winter may have been gone, but the chill inside me was there all the same.

The people said their good-byes and went on their way. Jura and Kus approached me with another friend of mine who also was present at that ceremony.

"Come on, we'll show you around a little," one of them said, adding that I had been gone from the city for too long.

I could tell that the other two were picking up on the strong emotions that I felt as I walked again down those streets. We soon came to the home that had once belonged to my family. In the square below, I looked up at the window, the same one where my grandmother was always perched. The last time I had stood there, I had seen my sister behind the windowpanes, crying and waving good-bye. That day, I had been disgusted over the beginning of the war, and I had tried to hide my sadness as best I could in front of Tesia. I went to the front gate of the house and found that it was locked. Jura told me that if I wanted to, we could try to get someone in the house to open it for us, but I shook my head no.

We walked on. At the Hagenhuber pastry shop, which used to belong to a man named Lisko, they were still selling *kremówki*, Lolek's favorite. Lisko's son ran it now, and when he recognized me he offered me some pastries, and glasses of vodka for my friends and me.

On the other side of the Rynek was the building where my father's law office had been, but my friends couldn't get me to go inside there either. Besides, all of the property that had once belonged to the Klugers and the Hupperts (and back then, my grandmother alone had owned about a hundred units) now belonged to the state, which had rented them out.

We went to Koscielna Street, where the Bałamuts' building was, and the house where Lolek lived before moving to Kraków after graduation. Across from it was the church, with the Latin inscription on the front about how time flies. To me, the statement had never seemed more true.

We continued our walk to Kluk's tavern. We had almost never gone there as boys, in part because my grandmother would have found out, just like she found out when the other boys went to drink at the tavern outside of Wadowice, next to the pond that froze over in the winter. Jura and Kus bought a bottle of vodka at the tavern, agreeing that they would open it when the time was right. They were going with me to Auschwitz.

It wasn't far, a little more than twenty miles away, and it didn't even take an hour for us to drive there. The site of the German camp was on a wide plain, beneath a sky that was clouded over from time to time. My friends went and talked to the caretaker, and he agreed to accompany us.

As we walked, the place filled me with the kind of anxiety that I had only vaguely imagined until that moment. I walked between the rusty train tracks, entered a barracks that reeked of death, and at one point saw the world disappear from behind the barbed wire fence. I had a moment of panic but wanted to continue. The guide took us to the cremation ovens, and then to an area reserved for the women, and then another where there were piles of hats, prostheses, crutches, eyeglass frames, and other items that had belonged to the prisoners. We came to the twenty-two plaques inscribed with the names of the victims. Scanning these, I did not see the names of my mother and sister. Many of them were written in Hebrew, and others were hardly legible. Once outside, Jura offered me the bottle of vodka, like a potion for relieving the pains I was suffering, but I didn't want it and pushed it away. I wanted to remember every detail of that horror.

CHAPTER 23

ISRAEL EXISTS

I later made other trips back to Wadowice. Lolek had been right when he told me that if I went back there it would become as dear to me as before. I felt less and less of the anxiety I had suffered the first time, and my friends were there to make sure I was never alone. Usually it was Józef Kwiatek or one of the Piotrowski twins (Włodzimjerz and Zdzisław) who went with me to the places I remembered from childhood. There were many of them to revisit.

One summer afternoon, I went to Dzwonek, the hill with the bell on top. I went to Łysa Góra and to the Bliźniaki, the Twin Mountains, continuing all the way to Czumowka, the huge mysterious crater that may have been formed by the impact of an enormous meteorite, where Lolek and I had learned to ski when we were children. I also visited the farm property that had belonged to my grandmother. The farm in Błonie, near the Skawa River, had mainly produced apples and peaches. Its peaches were considered the best in the entire area, and when Lolek, the other boys, and I played soccer on a nearby field, we always stopped to pick the peaches when they were in season. We would gorge ourselves on so many of them that it wasn't unusual, on the way back home, for one of us to have to duck behind a bush.

At sundown I returned to Kraków. I was due to return to Rome the following day. That evening Jura, Kus, and Halina Krolikiewicz took me to eat at Ariel, a Jewish restaurant on Szeroka Street in the old Kazimierz neighborhood. There was a silver-colored menorah stenciled on the window by the entrance. Inside, there were Jewish dishes, vodka, and klezmer music. Later, a violin would accompany me as I sang "My Yiddishe Momme." It was like the violin my father played. I was happy.

In the Middle East, meanwhile, any hope for peace seemed to have disappeared.

The United Nations had been calling—to no effect—for Israel to withdraw from Lebanon, respect the rights of the Palestinians, and put an end to the deportations. The backlash came with the revolt of the Palestinians. They called it *intifada*, which in Arabic signifies shaking something off. Retaliations included children throwing rocks at Israeli tanks; the men screaming with rage, their faces covered with the *keffiyeh*; the women weeping for their slain sons and husbands.

Something historic had happened in December 1988. Yasser Arafat, the head of the PLO—Israel's enemy number one—had recognized Israel's right to exist. The Jews began to speak more loudly of peace. The word "peace" was also spoken in Saint Peter's Square, shortly after another war had broken out in the Gulf. President Saddam Hussein had invaded Kuwait in August 1990, and the United Nations had given him an ultimatum, demanding that he withdraw his troops immediately. Baghdad refused, and U.S. air and ground forces began Operation Desert Storm. It was January 17, 1991. After about ten days, the pope came out onto the balcony to recite the Angelus. He prayed that the fighting would soon come to an end, recited another prayer for the civilian and military victims, asked for respect for prisoners, and condemned the use of terrorism. Finally, he prayed for the Jews, Christians, and Muslims in the Middle East. After this, he saw a banner with the word "Shalom" on it, held by a group of Jewish pilgrims. "Shalom means peace," John Paul II said to them, "and I wish this peace for your people and for the state of Israel."

No previous pope had ever spoken of the state of Israel. They had been afraid that it might be taken as official recognition of the Jewish nation, and the Holy See didn't want that. But John Paul II had already used the term on other occasions. The first time had been not even two years after his election as pope, when he was in the Italian town of Otranto, on October 5, 1980. Some had shrugged it off as the indiscretion of a young pope—until a few months later, in Magonza, when he had spoken with the same kind of solemnity of the land of Israel. And on the day on which he recited the Angelus in Saint Peter's Square, his words about that country and about the Church seemed even more prophetic.

Israel had responded to the Palestinian intifada with curfews, mass arrests, and deportations. The United States had tried to bring peace with a conference in Madrid. The first session was held on October 30, 1991. It was a good idea, but it brought no results, signaling that there was little chance of reaching an agreement. Israeli prime minister Yitzhak Shamir had agreed to participate in the talks, on the condition that the PLO not have its own official delegation, but instead join that of the Jordanians, who had been invited to participate along with the Syrians and Lebanese. So Arafat's men tagged along with Jordan, but even so the Israeli prime minister made it absolutely clear that he had no intention of reaching any agreement—especially not with any of those participants. Shamir also said he would continue sending settlers to the West Bank, conveying the message that there could be no question of creating a Palestinian state there, with so many Jewish inhabitants. And while Shamir was saying this, Ze'ev Jabotinskij appeared in person. Obviously, under these circumstances, the negotiations failed. But one of the Palestinians still managed to make an impression. Haidar Abdel Shafi gave a speech in which he said that the Palestinians were willing to live next to the Israelis, and even spoke of reconciliation between the two peoples.

It was then that Jean-Louis Tauran, head of the Vatican delegation, made a crucial comment: "If the PLO is negotiating with Israel, then why can't we?" From that moment, everything that had been put off for so long came together in a hurry.

Lunch was at one o'clock, and Sister Germana had been cooking Polish food at the apostolic palace. It was a springtime Sunday afternoon. I went there with Irene, who had also accompanied me on my latest trip to Poland. She had finally seen Wadowice and Kraków, and the Holy Father asked her what she had thought of them.

"Wadowice is nice," Irene said, "but Kraków is prettier."

There were some others there for lunch that day, including Deskur. He had an assistant pushing his wheelchair, and he made his entrance singing a Polish song and wearing a gaudy broad-brimmed hat. Even the pope seemed unable to do without his antics. The soup was served, and grace was offered over the food. After the soup came the fish in aspic. When the white wine went around, the pope took just a little, diluting it with water. For dessert, *kremówki* had been specially prepared for the Holy Father, who was crazy about them—but he was hardly the only one.

Deskur sat next to me during the meal.

"Have you noticed, Mr. Engineer?" he asked me at one point. "A lot of things are changing."

I smiled at him, knowing very well what that wise old man was talking about. In October 1991, when the peace conference was being held in Madrid, a meeting of cardinals in the Vatican had voted in favor of establishing official contact with high-level representatives of the Israeli foreign ministry. Before that, there had only been informal relations, often arranged through me. There was a lot to talk about—everyone knew that. The Holy See was willing to recognize Israel, but it wanted some guarantees in exchange. Above all, it wanted to make sure that the faithful could continue to worship in the holy places. So it wanted religious freedom, but it also wanted to find out about what had happened to its many churches in the Holy Land and to the other Catholic institutions. Also, nothing in the city of Jerusalem should be off-limits to Catholics.

Deskur said at lunch that the road would by no means be easy. The PLO may have said that it was no longer staunchly opposed to Israel's existence, but an agreement still had to be reached, and the other Arab countries would continue to oppose peace in the Middle East. I nodded in agreement, and then the archbishop went on to say that relations between Israel and the Vatican were about to improve, because those between the Jews and the Palestinians had also taken a turn for the better.

During those months in 1992, I had often heard rumors in Vatican circles that secret negotiations were in progress between Arafat and Shimon Peres (originally from Vishniev, formerly Wiszniew, a Polish city), who had been appointed as Israel's foreign minister that year. This was one more reason to be optimistic that the Holy See would officially recognize Israel, because if the rumor was true, and if the Palestinians really did succeed in reaching a compromise with the Israelis, there would be no more obstacles to diplomatic missions.

But reconciliation with the Jews was not limited to diplomatic activity. It was also taking place on the religious level.

On December 7, 1992, the Holy Father together with the cardinals had celebrated the promulgation of the new catechism. For six years the experts commissioned by the pope had been hard at work writing it, led by a theologian the pontiff particularly trusted, Cardinal Joseph Ratzinger. It was his special responsibility to incorporate the teachings of Vatican II into the document. A decade after the approval of the code of canon law, which had affirmed the practice of baptizing the children of non-Christians if they were in danger of death, even without their parents' permission, the new catechism revealed that the Church saw this matter in a different light. It reserved the hope that there might be a way of salvation even for those who had died without the sacrament, because God's mercy is infinite.

The question of the Carmelite convent in Auschwitz also seemed close to a resolution. Through Cardinal Johannes Gerardus Maria Willebrands, the pontifical representative for relations with the Jews, John Paul II had asserted that the agreement reached in Geneva would be respected. So in 1990, the archbishop of Kraków, Cardinal Macharski, had done the honors of laying the first stone of the new convent, on a plot of land not too close to the camp. At the end of 1992, the new building was almost complete, and the nuns were expected to move into it soon.

Everything seemed ready for 1993, a truly important year, not only because the nuns were finally leaving Auschwitz and not only because the pope had personally ordered this with a letter dated April 14, 1993 (just a few days before the anniversary of the Warsaw ghetto uprising, and two days after a concert at the Vatican to commemorate the victims of the Holocaust), but also because the rumor from the year before about secret negotiations between Israel and the PLO turned out to be true. The Al Fatah leader and the Israeli foreign minister had met in Oslo, Norway, and had reached an initial agreement. On September 9, 1993, Yasser Arafat signed a letter stating that Israel had the right to exist in peace and security, and that the PLO would renounce all forms of terrorism. After this, on September 10, another letter was signed, this time by Israeli Prime Minister Yitzhak Rabin, recognizing the PLO as a legitimate representative of the Palestinian people.

"You sign first, then I'll sign," Kurt Rosenberg commented ironically that Friday. "Israel is no dummy." But the most important thing was that a few days later, both men signed the agreement that had been reached in Oslo. It established that the Israelis would vacate part of the Gaza Strip and the West Bank, and that the Palestinian Authority would govern there. All of the other questions (mainly concerning Jerusalem, the Jewish settlements, boundaries, and refugees) would be discussed later. Yitzhak Rabin and Yasser Arafat shook hands in Washington in front of President Clinton and the entire world on September 13, 1993.

At that point, my expectations about relations between Israel and the Vatican were soon satisfied. There was already a draft agreement between the two states at the end of October, and the definitive accord was signed two months later in Jerusalem. It was December 30, 1993; for the Jews it was the sixteenth day of the month of Tevet, year 5754.

And then—since one thing leads to another—after peace was made between the sons of Isaac and those of Ishmael (or so it seemed), in the end everyone recognized everyone else. The Vatican recognized both Israel and the Hashemite kingdom of Jordan, which recognized Israel and vice versa. Official contacts were even established between the PLO and the Vatican. The Fundamental Agreement between the Vatican and Israel went into effect on May 10, 1994.

Later, at the end of September, letters of credence were presented by the apostolic nuncio to Israel, Archbishop Andrea Cordero Lanza di Montezemolo, and by the Israeli ambassador to the Holy See, Shmuel Hadas, previously the ambassador to Spain. The pope spoke in French, the traditional language of diplomacy. It was a solemn occasion, held at the papal residence in Castel Gandolfo. The sun was shining, and the heat of summer still hung in the air. There were plenty of cardinals, bishops, and monsignors, but also representatives of the Israeli embassy in Rome, rabbis, and members of international Jewish organizations. There were also quite a few journalists and photographers who occasionally crowded around one of the guests in the reception room, while the Swiss Guards closed ranks to keep order. Other than that, the atmosphere was relatively relaxed. Irene had a very pleasant conversation with Shmuel Hadas, who spoke with a perfect English accent. He was a textbook diplomat: tall, handsome, and elegant. He even bent forward to kiss Irene's hand, as if she were a princess.

"That's very nice, but do you do that with all the ladies?" she asked him.

I was having a drink at one of the buffet tables. It was quite a feast. From some other point of this big hall I noticed a look from Monsignor Stanisław Dziwisz, who gave me a nice smile lifting a glass. He was our beloved Dziwisz. Stasiu (as the pope called him) for many years already had accompanied Lolek wherever he went. They met many years earlier, in 1957; Dziwisz was at the seminary in Kraków, and Wojtyła was there teaching morals. Stasiu was deeply taken by the great natural merits of this professor, the deep humanity he was emitting. Later, after the death of Archbishop Eugeniusz Baziak, Wojtyła was called to take his place and could not teach the young seminarians anymore. Dziwisz had met him again some years later, in 1963, when Wojtyła gave him Holy Orders, and it was not for the last time because in October 1966 the archbishop called him and said, "You will come with me to help me." He accepted this, and from then on they never left one another. That day at Castel Gandolfo we celebrated the beginning of diplomatic relations between the Vatican and the state of Israel. I noticed how happy Stasiu was there. I knew that he loved the Jewish people, because I heard the story of how, during the Nazi invasion of Poland, in Raba Wyzna near the Tatra mountains, Stasiu's family took tremendous risks to give shelter and hide a Jew called "Vilus." At this very moment when all those sad thoughts were in my mind, while I was there I also tried for a moment to imagine all of the refugees who had been sheltered there during the war. Many of them had been Jews, according to the story that Lichten had told the last time I had seen him.

A little group of people had gathered around the Holy Father, talking and laughing. It was natural to have a good time on a day like that, and there was a lot of noise in the room—some people trying the sandwiches, others with crystal goblets full of fruit salad. I was disappointed for a moment that Lichten hadn't been able to see it. I missed him quite a bit, ever since he had died in 1987.

As I finished my coffee, I pondered that Israel's affairs were much more complicated than they seemed. There were still many questions about the future, as Deskur had pointed out in recent days. As incredible as the agreement between the Israelis and Palestinians was, he said, it would be almost a miracle if it actually held up. Time would tell. But as for diplomatic relations between Israel and the Vatican, this was something more than two states recognizing each other. After centuries of prosperity followed by millennia of diaspora and persecution, the Jews had returned to the land of their fathers, which had been promised to them. It would have been another matter for the Vatican to recognize the rights of the Jews to exist somewhere else. Accepting the state that had been created in Palestine seemed to be a sublime gesture of religious understanding.

It was yet one more gesture of its kind under the pontificate of John Paul II.

CHAPTER 24

IN FRONT OF THE WALL

The first time I saw the pope tremble, we were at dinner. Lolek was unable to hold the fork steady in his left hand while he tried to cut his meat. I thought he was probably just tired and that with a little rest the hand would return to normal. Also, he had recently been hospitalized to have a tumor removed from his intestines, so the trembling could just have been a side effect from that. A little later, when I said goodnight, I took my friend aside and told him to get some rest.

But I soon realized that the pope wasn't just neglecting his health, and he wasn't suffering from a former illness. This was something new, and it now seemed that there might be a defect in that apparently indestructible body. Bitter confirmation of this hunch came as a single word: Parkinson's. Lolek told me about it after he had fallen down and injured his shoulder. After the fall, his doctor had told him that the loss of balance might not have been a coincidence, considering the persistent tremor. Tests confirmed the diagnosis of Parkinson's, a disorder of the central nervous system. In a certain sense, the pope's illness didn't concern him. He accepted the news calmly. He told me that he only cared about his ability to continue his mission.

Nonetheless, Lolek used to be able to get through the most exhausting day without fatigue, astonishing everyone around him. But now it took much less to tire him, and he had to be more careful not to overexert himself. A few months later, in April 1994, he fell again. He had just come out of the shower, and he fell hard, breaking his right thigh bone. He had to get a hip joint replacement, which caused him a lot of pain and made him walk with a limp. He didn't let it show, but he also suffered a great deal on the day the diplomatic letters of credence from Israel were presented at Castel Gandolfo, as he told me that day. It was also heartbreaking that he would have to give up skiing, one of the great passions of his life. He had to content himself with reminiscing with me about our childhood, when we would go skiing in Leskowiec, toward Bielsko, where there was always the danger of getting tripped up by the tree trunks concealed beneath the snow. But we also recalled more recent days, when we had gone skiing in the mountains around Rome.

Before long, the pope was walking with a cane. It was his stubborn way of continuing along the Church's path, at least into the new millennium. But his symptoms would progress as well—his once-expressive, actorlike face becoming wooden, his voice becoming more and more faint until he could hardly speak. He continued his travels and his activity all the same.

One question that tormented him was whether the Church was in part to blame for the Holocaust. The possibility that this might be true brought him much more pain than his own illness did. Already in 1991, during the closing ceremony for the synod of European bishops, he had asked God for forgiveness for the passivity shown by so many Christians in the face of Jewish persecution and the Holocaust. Before this, during the summer of 1987, a few months after receiving Austrian President Kurt Waldheim at the Vatican, the Holy Father had written a letter to Archbishop John May, president of the American bishops' conference. It said that the sufferings endured by the Jews were a source of sincere suffering for the Church as well, especially because of the resentment and indifference that have historically divided Jews and Christians. After a few days, it was announced that a Catholic document on the Holocaust and anti-Semitism would be drawn up, ordered by the pope himself. A commission of the Holy See was charged with writing it, and a Jewish committee would participate in the working sessions.

But at the fiftieth anniversary of the liberation of Auschwitz, January 29, 1995, the document had still not seen the light of day. On that occasion, the pope said that many innocent people of various nationalities had died in that camp, and in others, but that the Jews had been the main victims of that horror, because they had been the objects of extermination and had suffered the Holocaust. He had spoken in similar terms during the controversy over the convent that was established in the concentration camp, saying that any trace of humanity had disappeared in that pit of suffering—that of the martyrs first of all, because of the violence against them, but also that of their murderers, because of their reprehensible conduct. And the Jews, who together with the gypsies had been the only group to undergo mass extermination—including women and children—didn't want anything built there, even for a religious purpose. It should remain a place of silence, and the Church could understand this very well, just as it understood that this silence was intended to be a reproach against God, in the same way in which Jesus had said from the cross, "My God, my God, why have you forsaken me?"

In the end, it took more than a decade for the document on the Holocaust to be published. The release date was March 16, 1998, and its title was *We Remember: A Reflection on the Shoah.* The pope wrote the preface, a letter addressed to Cardinal Cassidy, but the rest of the document was not his own work. It was a gesture of repentance from the Church, known as a *teshuva* in Hebrew. After many years, the scholars who drafted the document answered the question of whether the Church had been partly responsible for the extermination of millions of Jews by stating that the Nazi ideology had been anti-Christian, and that many Christians had rebelled against it, although the Holocaust may have been fostered by the prejudices that many of them held against the Jewish people. Having admitted this, the Church expressed profound sadness for the faults of its sons and daughters in every age. A long footnote at the end defended Pius XII.

Nonetheless, the sensibilities of many Jewish leaders were rattled. They were not entirely persuaded by the reasoning of the scholars appointed by the Holy See and their claim that individual actions could not be attributed to the Church as a whole, saying that although the wrongs of Catholics were a source of great affliction, the Church would not ask God for forgiveness because of them. To many, it was a missed opportunity. Also, there were different and even contradictory attitudes to be considered. A few years earlier, the German bishops had admitted that they had turned their backs on the persecuted Jews, including during the sad events of *Kristallnacht*, and not even one year earlier the French bishops had apologized for failing to speak out about the racial laws and saying little in defense of the Jews. All in all, those bishops had stated that the fault had been their own, and that of their churches, not only that of individual Catholics.

Of course, it was not only in those countries that the Jews had been persecuted. I remembered something Lichten had said years before his death, when he had told me that the racial laws had also been promulgated in Italy under fascism during the 1930s. Jewish teachers and students had been required to leave the schools, the armed forces, and public companies, and were prohibited from marrying Christians, while the Church had not opposed these laws as it should have. I asked Lichten why not, and he replied that it might have been because many of the laws had been enacted by the Church in the past. One of the members of the fascist grand council, Roberto Farinacci, had made a game of this, saying that the legislation was in agreement with the councils and papal declarations of times past, and that in regard to the Jews the fascists were simply following the Jesuits, who were even more severe toward the Jewish people. The only protest from Pius XI came when Jewish converts were considered on a par with the others who had remained faithful to Jewish principles, so that they too were prohibited from marrying Christians. Violation of this law was referred to by the deprecating term "concubinage," which was seen as a crime. The Holy See was incensed over the measure and objected that only the Church could decide whether marriage followed the concordat, not the state. The pope even appealed to the king for recognition of this exclusive jurisdiction. But, I now thought, if that was the way it had been, it was easy to understand why so many Jews were disappointed by the contents of a document that had been anticipated for so long.

As weakened as he was, the pope never seemed to tire of traveling. He returned to Poland in June 1999, after the violent confrontations of recent memory had ceased. The last time he had been there, exactly two years earlier, an election campaign was still under way. A new parliament was to be elected in September. The Solidarity party won, and the democratic constitution was approved. It was the second such constitution for the country, after the one it had adopted on May 3, 1791—the first of its kind in all of Europe.

The pope—who to many seemed to be at death's door—in reality showed himself able to draw on inexhaustible reserves. It may have come from the robustness he once had, but it also displayed a form of religious stubbornness, his desire to continue leading his Church, which seemed to make it possible for him to meet the challenges of his illness. Earlier, the question had been raised of whether he should resign if he was unable to bear this cross. He had decided that as long as the Lord would give him the strength to do so, he would continue his pontificate and fulfill his mission. So he went back to Poland—greeting the crowds in Gdańsk, traveling down the Augustowski canal in a little boat, speaking with the villagers in

Leszrewo. Before parliament, he spoke about Solidarity and about the Polish workers' protest in the Lenin shipyards on the Baltic coast, which had brought freedom back not only to Poland, but also to other countries under the yoke of totalitarianism. The Soviet Union was no more, the Warsaw Pact had been disbanded, the Berlin Wall had fallen, and free elections had marked the end of communism in Hungary, Bulgaria, and Czechoslovakia. Such change had also happened elsewhere, but in a violent way.

One Friday afternoon, the pope entered the little enclosure of the Umschlagplatz in Warsaw, where the freight cars had been loaded with the Jews sentenced to forced labor and to the gas chambers. There was a monument there to commemorate them, just four walls of white marble, and on one of them a few hundred first names, the ones most common among the victims, and a phrase from the book of Job: "O earth, do not cover my blood, nor let my cry come to rest!" The pope stopped to pray in front of the plaque and called for respect and love for the Jewish people among those who still did not understand their sufferings, and also among those pained on account of the deep wounds that had been inflicted upon them.

A survivor of the uprising in the Jewish ghetto—the last one still alive—described the tragic sequence of events for him. His name was Marek Edelman. Leading rabbis from various communities around Poland were also there—at least of the communities that had remained in the country after the war. There were not even ten thousand Jews living in Poland in 1999, when before there had been 3.5 million. The dispute over the convent in Auschwitz had been resolved for a few years, but there was still a cross in the camp, twenty-five feet high, placed there in 1979 when John Paul II came for the first time. A rabbi who did not come to the ceremony was asking that this be taken down, just as all the others had been removed. Nothing but suffering should remain in that place of extermination, especially of the Jews.

Yet Jews had not died only in Auschwitz and not only during the war. Not far from the Umschlagplatz there was another monument, a bronze freight car loaded with Jews, Christians, and gypsies in chains, commemorating the victims deported from Poland to Siberia from the time of the tsars until 1953. There were more than a million of these, sent to the forced labor camps at the mines or in the forests, who had died of exhaustion. The pope also prayed for them.

After that apostolic voyage to Poland, I visited the pope at the Vatican. The pontiff apologized for not getting up when I entered the room. This was one of the most visible signs of his illness, and one of the most humiliating for him, that he could no longer move as he wished. The disorder had made his face rigid, but I could still see an expression of sadness there. In addition to this immobility, his doctors had attached themselves to him like a mother with her little boy, and he always had assistants watching over him. He needed them to perform even the simplest task. The pope talked with me as best he could, telling me that the great jubilee was at the doors—the doors of the four Roman basilicas—and that he wanted to be the one to open them. Even though his body continued to deteriorate, he still had one last favor to ask from the Lord: to prolong his life and strength just a little while longer, so that he could lead his Church into the third millennium. I was touched by these words. For a long time, I had been able to see no other destiny for my friend than for him to love and serve God to the end, and he sincerely believed that the pope's mission was not quite finished yet. I approached my friend.

"You'll be the one to celebrate the holy year. You'll see, Lolek. The Lord will give you the strength."

I saw a grimace appear on that inexpressive face, and a gesture of appreciation for my sentiment. Then the pope's arm fell heavily back onto the armrest. Dinner was served, and the food seemed to revive him a little. At the table, he talked about Israel and its children and also about the Palestinians, warning that the work of making peace in that land could not be halted. About one year earlier, the Jewish state had celebrated the fiftieth anniversary of its existence. They had not been easy years. The pope had prayed that there might be happier times to come.

After we finished eating, we went out onto the terrace on the top floor of the pontifical palace, because Lolek had said he wanted to walk around a little. The summer had just begun. We talked about the pope's future travels. He was scheduled to visit Slovenia, then New Delhi and Georgia. But there was another trip closer to his heart than any other, for the holy year that was about to begin. He whispered it to his friend in their own language.

"Podróż do Ziemi Świętej" (I'm going to the Holy Land).

It may have been a coincidence, I thought, but as soon as those words were spoken it occurred to me that they were also the title of a poem by

Juliusz Słowacki, who more than a century before had predicted the coming of a Slavic pope, the one who would bring peace among the peoples.

In any case, the Lord heard the prayers of the pope, and the new millennium began for the Church under the pontificate of John Paul II.

Jubilee years were a tradition of the Old Testament, and they fell every seven years according to the Law of Moses—the Sabbath year, when the land was allowed to rest, slaves were set free, and debts were forgiven. Another, much more solemn jubilee was held every fifty years—the *Yobel*, from which the word "jubilee" comes—which was announced by sounding the ram's horn. Later, this jubilee year became a custom among the Christians, with Celestine being the first pope to inaugurate one. He designated it as a year of forgiveness, because the sins would be forgiven of anyone who went on pilgrimage to the basilica of Santa Maria di Collemaggio, in L'Aquila. The penitents had to come on August 28 and 29, beginning in 1295. Five years later, Pope Boniface VIII instituted the first jubilee to be celebrated every hundred years. For this, remission of sins would be granted to anyone who went on pilgrimage to the Basilica of Saint Peter, or to that of Saint Paul's Outside the Walls. The pilgrims included Dante, Giotto, and Charles de Valois, brother of the king of France, who went with his wife, Catherine. Fifty years later, Clement VI (the popes lived in Avignon by that time) decided that the jubilee should be celebrated every half century, and added another place where the indulgence could be received, at the Basilica of Saint John Lateran in Rome. It was there that Martin V opened the holy door in 1423. After this, all of the other doors were opened, including that of a fourth Roman basilica, Saint Mary Major.

Everything was meticulously prepared for the jubilee that came two millennia after the birth of Christ, and the pope's health was also taken into consideration. For example, the ancient ritual of the *recognitio* was performed ahead of time. It involved breaking down the walls erected in front of the holy doors, and usually this was done by the pope. But for the jubilee of the year 2000, the ceremony was moved forward by a few days, and the workmen were the ones to take a hammer to the bricks. Then a box was removed from the remains of the wall at each of the basilicas (containing coins and a parchment attesting to the sealing of the wall). After these contents were shown to the Holy Father, everything was ready for the ritual of opening the door. The holy door at the Vatican basilica was the first to be opened, on Christmas Eve 1999—twenty centuries after that blessed day. The pontiff followed the procession of clerics and laity, deacons and cardinals, all of them coming before the throne of Peter, the wooden throne where pious legend has it that the prince of the apostles had sat. His successor sat there now, and after he made the sign of the cross and invoked the most holy Trinity, the gospel was proclaimed, followed by the singing of the "Alleluia."

After the proclamation of the word of the Lord, there was silence again outside the basilica, and the pope approached the holy door. Climbing the steps in front of it, he intoned, "Aperite mihi portas iustitiae" (Open to me the gates of justice) and the choir responded, "Ingressus in eas, confitebor Domino" (I will go into them and give praise to the Lord). At the top of the steps was the door of salvation. He pushed against the doors with trembling hands, while from the other side two basilica employees pulled them wide open. The pope knelt at the threshold, and remained there for a few moments in prayer. It was a solemn liturgical moment. After he sang the acclamation and was helped to his feet, he returned to the throne. The doorjambs were decorated with flowers, while the incense burned and Eastern music played.

The pope then returned to the threshold to receive the book of the Gospels, which was displayed to the faithful outside and inside the basilica, and was then given to the deacon, while faithful from Africa blew elephant tusks. Then the choir began singing again, at which point the procession entered the basilica, moving toward the altar. Behind the cross there were the acolytes, the bishops and cardinals, the deacon with the book, and the other laypeople with lamps and flowers—and the pope, of course. At the altar, the book of the Gospels was placed on the throne, and the lamps and flowers in front of it, while the pope burned incense around them. It was the proclamation of the Great Jubilee, and the beginning of the holy year.

One by one, the pope opened the other doors of the Roman basilicas. On Christmas Day, he opened the door at Saint John Lateran, and the one at Saint Mary Major on New Year's Day. Last came Saint Paul's Outside the Walls, on January 18. But this did not mark the end of the celebrations, which were to continue for the entire jubilee year. One in particular, a penitential liturgy, was held about three months later at Saint Peter's, on March 12, 2000. Its purpose was to ask forgiveness for the sins of the Church, because in order to be truly holy, the Church needed to purify itself. Seven cardinals were asked to stand up and read seven confessions, asking forgiveness for the Crusades, the tribunals of the Inquisition, the treatment of slaves, witch hunts, the attitude toward the Reformation, and compulsory preaching. Cardinal Cassidy apologized for the sins committed against the Jewish people over the course of the centuries. When he had finished speaking, the pope recited the *Teshuvà*. It was certainly a gesture of repentance, but the curia was still hesitant to recognize those past faults in their entirety, so Cardinal Cassidy's words did not echo as profoundly as they should have. Instead of speaking of the faults of many Christians, he used the expression "not a few" and spoke of the violence the Jews had suffered "throughout history," while there were still people living with a detailed recollection of their tragedies, some of which had been inflicted by the Church.

But soon after this, John Paul II recited yet another prayer in that year of the Lord, when he was able to make the trip that he had been looking forward to for so long: his visit to the Holy Land. He told me that he wanted me to come along, and when I told Rosenberg that I would be going to Israel together with the Holy Father, Kurt was unable to restrain an expression of good-natured jealousy. Then he immediately began reciting the psalm that exalts Jerusalem as the pinnacle of joy.

I traveled aboard the papal airplane, in a section toward the back where the international reporters were also sitting—about forty in all, technicians, photographers, and journalists from all over the world. Toward the middle were the officials of the secretariat of state and the Vatican dicasteries, the directors of *L'Osservatore Romano*, and papal spokesman Navarro-Valls. Instead of the sky marshals I had seen on my last direct flight to Israel, there were about eight Swiss Guards and police officers, the most highly trusted, plus a doctor and a few of the sisters from the pope's apartment. At the front, behind a drawn curtain, were the pope and his immediate entourage, including Secretary of State Angelo Sodano and Bishop Stanisław Dziwisz.

On March 21, 2000, the papal party landed at the airport in Tel Aviv, where there was a welcome ceremony. Israeli president Ezer Weizman and prime minister Ehud Barak were in attendance. The pope's apostolic voyage had begun the day before, on Mount Sinai in Jordan, the mountain of the covenant, where Moses came into the presence of God and received the Law. As for Israel, the country was still in turmoil. Yitzhak Rabin had been assassinated a few years earlier, not by a Palestinian, but by a

Jewish extremist, following a rally in November 1995. Rabin, who had been so zealous for his country's good, died like Gandhi, at the hand of one of his own people. He had received the Nobel Peace Prize for the first accord with the Palestinian leaders, just as Peres and Arafat had. For his part, Arafat had been elected president by the Palestinians. He had then tried to reach a definitive agreement with the new prime minister of Israel, Benjamin Netanyahu, of the conservative Likud party. But then the Israeli settlements in the occupied territories resumed, and so did the fighting and terrorist attacks. In reality, they had continued even after the historic meeting in Washington. Muslims kneeling for evening prayers at the mosque in Hebron were killed. It was the last Friday in February 1994, and the prayer rugs were drenched with blood that day. The Muslims were shot by a Jewish terrorist, the follower of an ultranationalist group. The terrorist was killed as well, but only after taking the life of twenty-four Palestinians and injuring about a hundred more. There were other massacres that year, and then again in following years, like in Netanya near Tel Aviv, where eleven Israeli soldiers were killed by Palestinian terrorists. The peace reached in Washington seemed like nothing more than a house of cards.

The Holy Father arrived in Israel just shortly after the signing of an agreement between Prime Minister Barak and the Palestinian president, confirming another agreement that had been reached with the previous prime minister. It was called "land for peace." This time, the hope was that peace truly was within reach.

Over the course of a few days, the pope went to see everything that had been recommended to him. In Al-Maghtas, near Jericho, it seemed that he could glimpse with the eyes of his spirit Jesus being immersed in the waters of the Jordan, receiving baptism, and then setting off for the holy city of Jerusalem in order to die and rise again. He heard the choirs of angels singing in Bethlehem, in autonomous Palestinian territory, where Arafat came to greet him. The two went together to visit the refugee camps in Dheisheh. In the chapel of the Cenacle in Jerusalem, where the bread had been broken and the wine had been drunk at the Last Supper, he celebrated the Holy Mass. He was received by the chief rabbis of Israel in Hechal Shlomo, and told them the same thing he had said one day at the synagogue, that the Jews were the older brothers of the Christians.

That same day, he visited the president of Israel and then went to Yad Vashem, the mausoleum commemorating the victims of the Holocaust. I went with him, of course. In the Hall of Remembrance, the pope talked about his personal memories, about when the Nazis occupied Poland during the war, about his Jewish friends and neighbors, some of whom had died, while others had survived. He seemed to hear the echo of the heartrending cries of millions of slain Jews, wailing from the abyss of horror. In that concrete-walled building with its tentlike roof, they stood before a flame that is never extinguished. The pope went there to feed the flame, while two cardinals set down a wreath in white and gold, the colors of the Vatican. On the floor, the names of twenty-two extermination camps were engraved. I was in the front row, listening.

Next to me was a beautiful and elegant woman—Leah Rabin, the widow of the Israeli prime minister. We spoke with each other. She had been born in Könisberg in Germany, once a city of eastern Prussia, but her family had moved to Palestine in 1933, when she was just five years old. Israel did not yet exist, and the territory was still under the British mandate. She told me that she had met the pope a few hours earlier, in the presidential palace, and tried to describe the emotion she had felt. She also told me about the latest elections, saying that she had supported Peres after her husband's death, and she expressed her disappointment with Netanyahu, a revisionist who in her view was not good for the cause of peace. This was one of the reasons that she had supported Ehud Barak in the latest elections, because he belonged to the Labor Party, like her husband, and seemed more capable of resolving the Palestinian question.

The prime minister was also at Yad Vashem that day, and I met him a little later. Then someone tapped me on the shoulder. When I turned around, I saw my cousin Jerzy Huppert. Jerzy asked me if he could say hello to the Holy Father, and I brought him over and introduced the two. Lolek had often heard me talk about Jerzy, and even more about his father Ignacy, the brother of Grandma Huppert. He even knew about Ignacy's tragic death in Katyn, together with the other Polish officers whom the Russians had taken prisoner when they invaded Poland. The pope touched a hand to Jerzy's cheek and whispered something to him in Polish.

On March 24, 2000, the pope went to the Mount of Beatitudes, so named because the Messiah had given the Sermon on the Mount there, speaking about the poor in spirit, the meek, the merciful. Young people came from all over to greet the pope. The next day, he went to Nazareth and celebrated the Mass at the basilica of the Annunciation. Finally, in the

evening of March 25, he came to Jerusalem. Jerusalem! City of the mourn-
ful songs of the exiled children of Israel, city contemplated by Jesus from
the Mount of Olives, and also the land chosen by Allah, the homeland of
his many children.

I stayed at the King David Hotel, in the old city, a place dense with
memories. Under colonial administration, it had been the headquarters of
the British army. I imagined the lament of the bagpipes that must have
wound through the narrow lanes around the building on that evening in
May 1948 to announce that the British soldiers were leaving. That was the
end of the mandate and the domination that had lasted for thirty years.
Long before the British, the Assyrians and Babylonians had withdrawn
in the same way, as had the Persians and the Romans, the Crusaders, the
Arabs, and finally the Turks. The Turks were the ones who had driven the
English out of Palestine, the land between the fabled oil reserves of Iraq
and the Suez Canal, which the British would soon control just like the
Thames.

Now that the state of Israel was being created, before leaving, an
officer with red and gold insignia handed over the key to the Zion Gate,
one of the seven gates leading into the city of Jerusalem. God had been the
custodian of that key after the destruction of the Temple, and now the Jews
had it again, in the hands of a rabbi, Mordechai Weingarten. At attention,
the officer saluted him, and then left with the others. They had lived amid
those fortifications for a long time, immersed in the scent of the lavender
shrubs, and now they were leaving the city forever—leaving behind them
silence, the suddenly empty lobby of the King David Hotel, and also the
prospect of war. There were 160,000 inhabitants waiting for nothing else
than for them to leave, so they could begin slitting each other's throats.
That mutual hatred between Jews and Palestinians still raged on.

Unlike those memories of times past, that Sunday morning the hotel
lobby was full of people.

On the Temple Mount, John Paul II first spoke to the Grand Mufti
of Jerusalem and to the Muslims. Then he went to the Western Wall,
HaKotel HaMa'aravi, what remained of the destroyed temple. This was
the Wailing Wall, the holiest place on earth for the Jews, where for centuries they had wept over the dispersion of their people and where prayers
were recited or written onto pieces of paper stuffed into gaps between the
stones. When the pope arrived there, at about ten o'clock in the morning, a

large crowd had already gathered. There were Jews there, of course, but also Christians—and not only in the pope's entourage. The sun was out, and as always in Israel, the air was warm. I knew that the pope was going to pray in front of those stones. But before he did, his eyes met mine for a moment, and I saw a deeply moving expression of pain there. As I watched the pope walk away, suffering with each step, I shared in my friend's anguish. I wanted to put an arm around him, to support that body that had once been so agile but was now so labored. I knew I couldn't. Perhaps that illness, which was crushing the parts of him that had once been so lively, was itself part of a larger, inexplicable destiny. So I watched my friend's every move until he stood in front of the wall, made the sign of the cross, and began to pray. He had a piece of paper in his hand, and he placed it between the stones.

Thousands of years had passed since the destruction of the Temple so that this moment might take place. Before the pope backed away from the wall, he reached out and touched it, as if it were the face of a friend he did not want to leave.

God of our fathers, you chose Abraham and his descendants
to bring Your name to the nations.
We are deeply saddened by the behavior
of those who in the course of history
have caused these children of Yours to suffer
and, asking Your forgiveness, we wish to commit ourselves
to genuine brotherhood with the people of the Covenant.
Jerusalem, 26 March 2000
Joannes Paulus II

CHAPTER 25

THE HOLY WARS

T he holy door of Saint Peter's Basilica was again closed and then sealed off on January 6, 2001, marking the end of that jubilee. It had been a year truly rich with emotions, including for me, who, as a Jew, had had the privilege of accompanying John Paul II on his pilgrimage to the Holy Land.

Having returned from that voyage at the end of March, I had the opportunity to see my friend Lolek again on the occasion of his birthday, on May 18, 2000. His eightieth birthday fell on that jubilee year. To celebrate this event, there had been a Mass at Saint Peter's in the morning, attended by more than five thousand priests, and afterward a lunch served at the Domus Sanctae Marthae, the residence built in the Vatican to accommodate prelates passing through Rome. Sitting at the table with the pope were some of the cardinals dearest to him, including Sodano, Etchegaray, and Ratzinger, in addition to a dozen other prelates, also in their eighties. Sister Germana, the pope's personal cook, had urged that the ricotta and Parmesan gnocchi that he enjoyed so much not be left out, and her request was heeded. At the end of the meal, a giant pineapple cream cake made its entrance into the room, and although it seemed strange that there were no candles on it, it was decorated elaborately enough. John Paul II got to cut the first piece, obviously, and then lifted his champagne glass for a toast, as all of the cardinals sang "Happy Birthday" to him in their various languages. The evening ended with a concert in Nervi Hall, conducted by Gilbert Levine, himself Jewish. He had conducted another concert at the Vatican about ten years before, and during the rehearsal the pope had suddenly appeared before him. "Have you rehearsed enough? It'll be an important concert tonight, even the pope will be there!" He had personally requested that Levine conduct the concert held in 1994 to commemorate the Holocaust, just as he did for the celebration of his eightieth birthday. That evening's selection was a work by Haydn, "The Creation," a musical exposition of the first passages of Genesis.

That year of the Lord's grace did not, however, bring peace every-where, not even to the Holy Land, in spite of John Paul II's apostolic voyage there. What unleashed the hatred this time was something that happened at the end of September, when Ariel Sharon, the head of the Israeli nationalist Likud party, went with an escort of hundreds of Israeli police officers in riot gear to the Temple Mount in Jerusalem. In the sacred heart of this city, in the same place where the pope had prayed a few months earlier in front of the Wailing Wall, that political leader had gone to assert Israeli sovereignty over those sites, unleashing the violent reaction of the entire Arab world.

The tension in the air kept getting thicker. In July came the defini-tive failure of the Camp David summit, when even U.S. President Bill Clinton had been unable to strike an agreement between Israeli prime minister Ehud Barak and the president of the Palestinian Authority, Yas-ser Arafat. The discussions had stalled over the question of refugees and of the holy places in Jerusalem. The Temple Mount was one of these places, special for the Jews because the ruins of the ancient Temple of Solomon were there, but also for the Muslims, because the prophet Muhammad had been assumed into heaven from the rock on top of it, after Gabriel visited him one night and had him mount upon Burāq, a mule with the face of a woman. That same rock was then enclosed in the dome of the Mosque of Omar, also called the Dome of the Rock. So the presence of Sharon and of all those armed soldiers in the vicinity of the mosques seemed like an out-rage to the Islamic world, and led to a re-explosion of the conflict between Israelis and Palestinians.

The first victims came on the following Friday, the Muslim holy day, when at Haram el Sharif, a Muslim shrine, the imam whipped the crowd into a frenzy over Sharon's blasphemous action. The faithful began throwing stones, and after trying to defend themselves with nightsticks, the Israeli soldiers opened fire. By that afternoon, the ground around the Mount of Olives would also be dripping with blood. It was just the begin-ning. It was the Second Intifada.

From New York, a few days later, the Security Council of the United Nations officially condemned the excessive use of force against the Pales-tinians by the Israelis.

At the general audience that was held on October 11 that year, John Paul II said that he was heartbroken over the grave tension in the Middle

East, exhorting believers to pray that the peoples and leaders of that region might resume dialogue as soon as possible.

The day after his heartwrenching appeal, nonetheless, a group of Israeli soldiers in civilian clothes was arrested in Ramallah, and for three of them it was the end. The Palestinian crowd was enraged over the killing of a boy and his father a few days before, began shouting for vengeance in the name of Allah on behalf of those martyrs, and then entered into the Palestinian police station to get their revenge. One of the Israeli soldiers was thrown out of a window and kicked and beaten to death in the street, and his body set on fire. Then came the Israeli retaliation. The Cobra helicopters flew out of Jerusalem, launching rocket strikes on Ramallah and the police station, and then hit Gaza and Arafat's general headquarters. Israeli warships also opened fire, as the tanks began to advance in formation.

Sharon would go on to win the election in February 2001, adamant that Jerusalem was only for the Jews, that the settlements had to stay where they were, and that the Golan Heights could not be given back. And while the whole world would urge that the peace negotiations be restarted as soon as possible, a Syrian newspaper would write of the new Israeli prime minister: "He comes seated in the turret of a tank, with a dagger between his teeth."

I had an opportunity to discuss these painful events with Lolek. It was on the occasion of my birthday, on April 4, 2001, when he called to wish me a happy birthday and said that he had a present for me. When I arrived at his apartment, he gave me an old and very rare edition of *Quo Vadis?* in Polish. The words that he had written for me on the yellowed front page of that book brought tears to my eyes. We hugged each other tight. That book was so precious to both of us, part of our purest childhood memories, when we would linger over it sitting together at the little table in the kitchen of his house on Koscielna Street in Wadowice, lighting an old oil lamp when it began to get dark. It had united us back then, when we had just started high school, and it still continued to unite us now, although we were both in our eighties.

"We're a couple of old fogies," I remember him saying to me, "but you still look like a young guy. You still play tennis, don't you?"

"Of course," I said, "every Saturday morning at the Parioli club."

"Well, good," he replied, "may God keep you healthy as long as possible."

When we started talking about the recent unrest in Israel, I saw a wince of pain cross that face already harrowed by his long illness. He talked to me about the importance of international law for preventing conflict, about the need to respect the Geneva Convention and the resolutions of the UN, too often overlooked. He pointed out to me, "One state cannot impose itself on another through violence, it cannot occupy its territories through the use of force, because this is against international law."

I seemed to understand from what he said that he did not at all agree with the position taken by Israel toward the Palestinians in recent times, the excessive recourse to the use of force, which had already been condemned by the United Nations General Assembly as well as the Commission on Human Rights, which had also spoken of war crimes and crimes against humanity. He was also afraid that that conflict could increasingly become a clash among religions, reigniting the hatred of fundamentalist Islamic groups, which were not present solely within the Palestinian territories. From Egypt to Lebanon, from Yemen to Afghanistan, from Pakistan to India and other countries, there were various terrorist organizations established throughout the whole world and always ready to kill in the name of Allah. In order to prevent this, to avoid there being holy wars in the new millennium as in the past, it was fundamental to him that the three religions of Abraham should continue with the difficult journey of dialogue.

"As descendants of Abraham," he said to me again that time, "Jews, Christians, and Muslims all believe in the one God, the living God. Could this perhaps be a reason for hatred and disagreement rather than for union among these faiths?"

Obviously not, he thought. So much so that he immediately added, "These religions have the duty to respect one another, not to make war, and to proclaim to the world that there is only one God!"

This had always been his conviction, I knew it very well, but all the same I was struck by the force with which he had said it to me again. He also told me that it was the task of the Church to promote mutual understanding among the different faiths, according to the teachings of the Council, and that he would continue to persuade the followers of these other faiths of the goodness of fraternal coexistence, wherever he might meet them. This is what he had done in the past. During his countless apostolic voyages, he had often wanted to meet with representatives of

Islam and Judaism, just as he had granted audiences to so many of them at the Vatican, always moved by a profound respect for these religious traditions. And within the curia, special commissions with the task of studying them and making them better known had been set up for some time.

When we said good-bye a little later, he asked about my family, and told me to come see him more often. He seemed tired to me, perhaps worn out by the efforts of the jubilee that had just concluded. But he had certainly not lost his sense of humor:

"Even if you keep practicing every Saturday morning," he said to me when we were at the door, "your sister Tesia would still beat you at tennis!"

One month after that meeting he would be back out on the road for a jubilee pilgrimage in the footsteps of the apostle Paul, which would take him from Greece to Malta, with a stop in between in Syria, the land in which that saint had converted almost two thousand years before. It was a Muslim country, but when the Holy Father arrived he found waiting at the airport of Damascus a huge crowd, together with an honor guard and the young president, Bashar al-Assad, who had recently succeeded his father. The president belonged to the Arab socialist Ba'ath Party, and a few months earlier had made himself the talk of the whole world for his scathing accusations of Sharon and the Israelis, whom he had called worse than the Nazis. That day when he welcomed the pontiff to his country was no different, when he talked about the territories occupied by Israel in Lebanon, in the Golan Heights, and in Palestine, about the mistreatment of Christ by the Jews, about their offenses against Muhammad, and even compared the sufferings endured by the Palestinian people to those of Jesus. When I read his statements in the newspapers, I realized how much hatred there was in that region toward Israel, making the hope for peace in the Middle East even more elusive. All the same, however, I could not conceal my emotion when I read the following day that John Paul II had been received within the Grand Umayyad Mosque of Damascus. It took place on May 6, 2001. So the first pontiff to have crossed the threshold of a synagogue was also the first in history to have entered a temple of Islam. In order to do so, of course, he had to remove his shoes, after which a pair of white slippers was placed on his feet. He then shuffled laboriously over the enormous carpets covering the floor of that mosque. When it was constructed, many centuries before, the ancient cathedral of Damascus, where the head of Saint John the Baptist was kept, was destroyed. But since this prophet was just as important to the Muslims as to Christians, when the church was destroyed the chapel where the skull was kept was left intact. The Holy Father prayed for a few minutes in front of the chapel, leaning against a column with his right hand, his other hand resting on his cane, refraining from making the sign of the cross out of respect for his hosts. He had done the same in front of the Wailing Wall the previous year. Once he was outside of the mosque, the pope was seated next to the grand mufti, under a minaret dedicated to Jesus—the son of God for one, a great prophet for the other—and the al-Hashr sura from the Qur'an was sung, together with the many names of Allah. John Paul II struck his cane three times on the ground, one of his ways of expressing his happiness.

"*As-salámu 'aláikum*," he greeted those who were present. "May God be with you."

He went on to say that it was the task of Christians and Muslims to teach young people the way of understanding and respect, because violence destroys the image of the Creator in his creatures and could never be the fruit of religious convictions. While he was speaking, his voice mingling with the evening prayer of the *muezzin*, all the faithful gathered there listened to him in silence.

After centuries of offenses and wars between Christians and Muslims, even the presence of this pope within the mosque of Damascus was another sign of reciprocal forgiveness between the Church and Islam. It was another miracle that happened under the pontificate of John Paul II.

And it convinced me that the world could change, and that peace on earth truly was possible.

That same year, however, human cruelty would reveal itself to the world in the starkest manner possible. It was not yet nine o'clock in the morning on September 11, 2001, in New York when two airplanes brought death from the sky, smashing one after the other into the towers of the World Trade Center, which would become enveloped in flames and collapse. Shortly afterward, there would be news of a third airplane that crashed into a wing of the Pentagon, and of a fourth that fell without hitting its target, the White House in Washington.

This was how Islamic fundamentalism declared war on America and the West.

The leaders of almost the entire world condemned these attacks, and Palestinian leader Arafat was among these as well. At the general audience that was held the following day, John Paul II spoke of a dark day in the history of humanity, an affront to human dignity.

These events would quickly produce a villain and would be the prelude to more wars, the first not even a month later, in Afghanistan. The Saudi-born Osama bin Laden had gone there more than twenty years before to fight alongside the Mujahideen against the Soviets, then stayed there to found *al-Qaeda*, the Islamic fundamentalist organization believed to be behind the recent attacks. Because of his pursuit of *jihad*, or holy war, he had been kicked out of his own country, and after Sudan also refused him hospitality, the arid lands and bare mountains of Afghanistan had once again become his hiding place, all the more so after a twenty-five-million-dollar bounty was put on his head.

Just ten days after the massacre of the Twin Towers, the United States had issued an ultimatum to the regime of the Taliban, the fundamentalists in control of much of that territory, demanding that bin Laden and his followers be handed over. The demand was rejected. And so, after the failure of all diplomatic efforts, on the dawn of October 7, 2001, the invasion of Afghanistan would begin.

CHAPTER 26

TANKS ROLL
INTO BETHLEHEM

It was again in Assisi that the pope called on the faithful of all religions to pray for peace after the events of September 11, and again his heart-wrenching appeal was heeded. In procession came numerous rabbis and imams, Buddhists and Hindus, Sikhs and Shintoists and Tenrikyo. There were the patriarchates, the ancient Churches of East and West, together with African priests, and even a Zoroastrian, a Jain, and a Confucianist. It was January 24, 2002. They wound through those little streets in their official dress—elegant saris, long robes, purple cassocks, turbans. After this, everyone went to the basilica—the Christians to the lower basilica, the others to the friary. All offered their prayers. In the afternoon, they all assembled again outside the church, in the main square, at the center of which there was a big olive tree. They pledged their commitment to peace and condemned all war waged in the name of religion. This is what Saint Francis himself had done many centuries before, when he went to Egypt to preach peace to the crusaders and to the Muslims, even being brought into the presence of the sultan, who admired his faith and courage and showered him with gifts upon his departure. One of these gifts, a horn made of ivory and silver, was still kept inside the basilica as a witness to that friendship.

It was growing cold that early winter day, and then the first drops of rain began to fall. I was struck by the sight of the Jews and Muslims sitting next to one another under the huge tent that was protecting them from increasingly torrential rain. When the time for prayer came, the Jews recited psalms, and the Muslims invoked Allah while facing in the direction of Mecca. The ceremony continued, and a lit candle was placed on a tripod as a symbol of the commitment against all war. Then, after the Canticle of the Creatures, they all exchanged a sign of peace.

Meanwhile, in the Middle East, the hope that the way of negotiation might be resumed seemed ever more distant, above all on account of the growing number of attacks that since the beginning of the year had cost the lives of hundreds of innocent victims. In order to prevent such attacks, the IDF, the Israeli Defense Forces, began a military operation at the end of March named Homat Magen, Wall of Defense, with the aim of capturing terrorists, especially those of Hamas, Fatah, and al-Aqsa. The Israeli tanks besieged Ramallah and Arafat's general headquarters, with the aim of forcing him into exile. Then they pushed through Tulkarm and Qalqilya, until they reached Bethlehem, where there was gunfire on the churches and mosques. A group of armed guerillas sought refuge in the Basilica of the Nativity, breaking through the heavy door of the cloister of the Church of Saint Catherine and then navigating a series of internal passages leading to the basilica. They took some civilians and nuns hostage, as well as the Franciscan friars who were watching over the manger where the Virgin Mary placed Jesus after his birth. It was raining hard outside, while hundreds of armed Israeli soldiers were taking up position in the square and on the rooftops, and the muzzles of the Merkava tanks were aimed at the basilica. It was April 2, 2002. The next day, Nablus and Jenin would be invaded as well.

The following Sunday, John Paul II wanted to hold a day of prayer for peace in the Holy Land. "Whoever sheds the blood of man, by man shall his blood be shed," he said, quoting Genesis while standing at the window of his apartment. He prayed for the Greek and Armenian Orthodox who were also custodians of the basilica, and for the Franciscan friars who were being held hostage in the convent. (A few days later he spoke with one of these on the telephone, to give him courage.)

Vatican diplomacy was also activated. Archbishop Jean-Louis Tauran was given the task of persuading Ariel Sharon to prevent an armed assault within the basilica. There were private attempts to obtain safe passage for the Palestinian gunmen, with the suggestion that they be transferred to Gaza in an international convoy. Israel did not accept this compromise, but reiterated that the holy places would not be profaned. Within the apostolic palace, nonetheless, these concerns remained. The Israeli embassy to the Holy See, in fact, had stated in an official document that the Palestinians had violated international norms by entering the convent with weapons, making this a legitimate military target. The risk of a raid therefore remained high.

The military operations conducted by the Israeli army in Palestinian territory were also an obstacle to the efforts of Arab nations to attain peace in the Middle East. By a quirk of fate, these began on the very day after the approval of a historic document by the Arab League, unanimously endorsed by the twenty-two member countries. Prince Abdullah of Saudi Arabia had proposed it, and it provided for the resolution of the conflict with Israel in exchange for the restitution of the territories occupied in 1967, the creation of a Palestinian state with its capital in East Jerusalem, and the return of refugees according to UN resolution 194. It also included a collective commitment to consider any aggression against one of the states of the League as an attack on the national security of all Arab states. And this was a clear sign that another war was in the air, this time with Iraq. After the attacks of September 11, this country had also become a threat to international security, because of its presumed support for Islamic terrorism and for al-Qaeda in particular. The United States had led a military intervention against the regime of Iraqi President Saddam Hussein before, in the 1990s, and now a second conflict in that country was likely. Moreover, it was no accident at that same summit that the leaders of the Arab League had obtained the commitment of all to reject threats of aggression against any Arab country, especially Iraq, calling for respect of sovereignty, independence, and security.

When I saw Lolek during those terrible days of the siege of the Basilica of the Nativity, as usual he had words of faith and hope. He was also convinced, however, of the need for Israel to free those holy places from its military presence, since this would make any negotiations more difficult. I tried to tell him that the Palestinians themselves had gone into the convent armed, and he showed his disapproval of this as well. I did not stay with him very long that time, because I saw how much suffering the effort to speak brought him. His head was bowed so low that I had to bend down to see his face.

Nevertheless, it wasn't long after that last meeting that the bells at the Basilica of the Nativity began to ring again, marking the end of the siege, which had lasted thirty-nine days. It was May 10, 2002. After extensive negotiations an agreement had been reached on the fate of the Hamas and al-Aqsa terrorists barricaded in the convent. The thirteen considered the most dangerous were the first to stoop down to pass through the Door of Humility into Manger Square, accompanied by a Franciscan friar. One of them knelt down in the direction of Mecca. Then they were put on a bus and taken by escort to the Tel Aviv airport, where a British plane would transport them to Cyprus, and the start of their exile. The other militants, twenty-six in all, were destined for the Gaza Strip. The hostages came out last. They were taken first to the settlement of Gush Etzion, not far from the city, and were then taken back home. Only the Armenians, the Greeks, and the Franciscans remained inside the basilica, its constant custodians.

Summer came hotter than ever that year, and with it a very special invitation. I knew that the Holy Father was planning to go to Poland around the middle of August, for the dedication of a shrine in Kraków. Our old classmates also knew about it, the few of them who were left, and they organized a lunch with Lolek. Stanisław Jura called me for the occasion: "Are you coming? You'll see, it'll be great to remember the old times together!" Unfortunately, I could not make it on that date, in spite of Jura's efforts to persuade me, promising that he would see to it that my table was supplied with the best Polish vodka. I was greatly saddened, during that telephone call, to learn that another childhood friend had left us, Antoni Bogdanowicz, who for many years had sat at the same bench as Lolek. He had died the previous Christmas Eve. Our dear Antoni. I told Jura to write at our friend's grave that for me as well a flower was gone, and to tell me everything about that reunion as soon as it was over. He promised me that he would do both of these.

Being a man of his word, he called me on the very night after that get-together in the dining room of the archbishop's residence. As a good Pole, he did not miss a certain detail: "Poor Lolek," he said, "didn't drink anything at all, not even a glass of white wine. Just some strange potion. Speaking of which, since you see him so often, do you have any idea what that stuff is?"

"How would I know?" I replied. "It must have been some mixture of medicines. But let's not waste any time talking about things like that. Tell me, how did it go?"

He then began to tell me every detail of that lunch, from the classmates present—six in all, not counting a dozen fellow students from other classes—to the menu, strictly based on traditional local dishes, with cold fish as an appetizer followed by roulade with macaroni in sauce. Bninska, another childhood friend, had flown in from Florida, as had Hagengruber, the old pastry chef of Wadowice, who had also immigrated to the United States.

"Halina was there too, you know? She really wanted me to tell you hello."

He was talking about Halina Kwiatkoskwa, the daughter of the principal of the Krolikiewicz school, who had taken her husband's name. At school she shared Lolek's passion for the theater, which had then become her life's work. Halina had reminded the pontiff of the time when they had performed in Antigone together, and Jura told me that Lolek was truly happy to look back over those days of his youth. They also talked about the soccer games, of course, the ones played between Jews and Catholics, and someone reminded Lolek of his nickname as goalkeeper, "Martyna," an outstanding player active between the two world wars. Amid all the talk, they did not forget the mountain excursions, the skiing, and since Hagengruber was there, it was Lolek who mentioned one of his favorite little indulgences: "Ah," he sighed, "your *kremówki*, how many bellyfuls of those I had!"

We had graduated in 1938, so the next year was going to be the sixty-fifth anniversary, and those old classmates agreed to meet again on that date, hoping perhaps to have it in Rome or Castel Gandolfo. Before he left, John Paul II gave them all a blessing.

CHAPTER 27

ALL THE BELLS
OF THE WORLD TOLLED

A t the end of 2002, the risk of a war in Iraq became more and more real, after the United States accused Saddam Hussein of secretly producing weapons of mass destruction.

John Paul II did all he could to prevent this conflict. He met with heads of state, ministers, and UN representatives, and even mobilized some of the most skillful Vatican diplomats. In February 2003, he sent Cardinal Etchegaray to Baghdad, giving him a letter to be delivered by hand to Saddam Hussein, to persuade him to collaborate with the international authorities and authorize inspections. A few days after this mission the cardinal was received in person by the Iraqi deputy prime minister, Tariq Aziz. Cardinal Pio Laghi, for his part, was sent by the pontiff to meet with President Bush in Washington. Days of fasting and prayer for peace were also held.

One of the things that struck me about Lolek in those days was that he seemed to be doing better, to have regained a bit of his former strength, which recently seemed to have left him for good. There were rumors of a strange concoction based on papaya, maybe the "potion" that Jura had mentioned, but I was certain that this was not what was bringing him relief. Maybe he was being bolstered instead by the various medications that he was taking, the beneficial effects of physical therapy for his knee, and perhaps also the speech therapy exercises he had decided to do in order to speak more clearly. Nonetheless, I was soon convinced that in addition to his medical care, there was also his determination not to spare himself at such a delicate moment for the world.

Cardinal Pio Laghi came back from Washington, and the pope talked with him for several hours. Unfortunately he was not the bearer of good news, telling the pontiff that although President Bush said he understood very well the concerns of the Holy Father, the United States had given Saddam Hussein an ultimatum of forty-eight hours, and there was no turning back.

The following Sunday, March 16, John Paul II appeared at the window of his apartment for the customary recitation of the Angelus. He addressed the leaders of Iraq, who had the duty of collaborating with the international community to prevent an armed intervention, and also the member countries of the United Nations Security Council, to whom he quoted the Charter of the United Nations, which authorizes conflict only after all peaceful means have been exhausted. After the usual greetings, he then reminded everyone that he belonged to a generation that had lived through the Second World War, and thanks to God had survived it, so that he felt the duty to conclude: "Never war again!"

This was his last-ditch effort to prevent a conflict already announced.

A few days later, during the night of March 20, the first bombardment of Baghdad began.

In May, Lolek celebrated his eighty-third birthday.

The president of Poland, Aleksander Kwasniewski, came for the celebration, as did many of the pope's fellow countrymen, almost twenty thousand of them. They brought him a cross made of salt from the mines of Wieliczka, a valuable Gutenberg Bible, and honey and poppy seed cakes. They also made a donation for the victims of the conflict in Iraq.

In the meantime, Baghdad had already fallen, with the military operations practically concluded after less than two months, although now the country was being torn apart by a terrible civil war.

The following month, Lolek left for Croatia, and for him it was a record-making voyage, the one hundredth since he had been elected pope. What was striking this time was the appeal he made to the Croatian faithful who had come to listen to him, asking them to pray for him in life and after his death.

He had said this, I believe, because he felt very weak again. And I think he was weak partly because he never exempted himself from his duties. Just a few weeks after he returned, he departed again, this time to Bosnia and Herzegovina. It was only in July, as I recall, that he allowed himself a little rest, at the request of his doctors, and went to Castel Gandolfo, on Lake Albano. He was comforted by his outings almost every afternoon in his wheelchair, along the little pathways of the park. Feeling a little bit better, he wanted to go to Abruzzo, to the Gran Sasso mountain.

It was the place where he went skiing after he was elected pope, often with me. Now that he was going back, an armchair was set up for him in a clearing, and he sat there praying and meditating.

That summer in Jerusalem, a bomb exploded on a bus, killing twenty people. Five of them were children. The massacre was committed by the imam of a mosque, disguised as a Hasidic Jew, with the sidelocks, the hat, and long black robe.

To prevent Arab terrorists from making constant incursions into Israel, the government of Ariel Sharon decided in October to go ahead with a project already approved in the past, the construction of a wall along the border with the West Bank. These were real and proper monoliths of reinforced cement, twenty-five feet high, which were to stretch across a length of more than two hundred miles.

Israel's decision had prompted an international controversy. Washington had been against the project from the beginning, and John Paul II himself had criticized it harshly, convinced that raising such a barrier would weigh heavily on the possibility of a resumption of negotiations in the Middle East, which were becoming all the more fundamental at such a delicate moment for the entire world.

On October 16 of that year, the pope reached another milestone, the twenty-fifth anniversary of his pontificate, one of the longest in the history of the Church. To celebrate, a Mass was held in Saint Peter's Square, where an altar was set up in front of the basilica. It was six o'clock in the evening. A quarter of a century before, at that time, Cardinal Pericle Martini had introduced the world to a Slavic pope. As Lolek spoke now, his voice sounded different than it did back then. He started telling about the moment of his election, when he agreed to be the successor of Peter, but then he was no longer able to continue his speech, and had to stop. A monsignor continued reading for him. Lolek wanted to resume speaking only at the end, at the moment of the final prayer. He said, "May all be done according to your will!" He was making it clear that he did not intend to abdicate, in spite of the many who maintained that he should do so.

The civil war, in the meantime, continued to stain Iraq with blood. On November 12, Italy also had to mourn its dead, the carabinieri and soldiers of the contingent stationed in Nassirya, who died in an attack along with civilians. But all of the massacres were not confined to that desert. Two days after that tragedy, in Istanbul two car bombs exploded near two synagogues in the neighborhood of Beyoglu Kuledibi, killing twenty-three and injuring hundreds. On March 11, 2004, it was Spain's turn. This time the bombs were placed on four trains, in four different stations in Madrid, and killed two hundred people, injuring several hundred. The first suspicions were directed at ETA, the Basque separatist organization, but in the following days responsibility for the massacres was claimed by al-Qaeda.

The Monday after the events in Madrid, a large crowd gathered beneath the pope's window. In the middle of it, a few flags with the colors of Spain waved gently. The square looked like a fortified compound, with hundreds of police officers spread everywhere because of the danger of attacks. John Paul II harshly condemned those attacks, his voice shaking with emotion at times. At noon, silence fell over that square for three minutes, as in the rest of Europe, in memory of the victims.

I had a chance to see Lolek afterward. He practically didn't use his legs at all anymore, but he had command over his ability to speak, and this was what really mattered to him.

"This gives me more time to pray."

I knew from previous discussions with him to whom, at this critical time, he would pray most of all: Our Lady of Fatima. He was devoted to Her and convinced that the bullet that was intended to kill him in Saint Peter's Square—fired on the feast of Our Lady of Fatima—was diverted by the Madonna's divine power. We had talked about this and the story of Our Lady of Fatima several times and even I, a Jew, found the whole story completely explicable. He had been to Portugal to the Shrine of Our Lady several times to pray for the peace of the world, and he had arranged to have the bullet fired at him embedded in the crown of her statue there. Also, during the last Jubilee, he had left his dearest possession—the ring that Cardinal Wyszyński gave to him when he was elected pope. He put it in the little casket, placed at the foot of his beloved "Madonna of Fatima."

He told me that he had had to accept a reduction in his public appearances and in the length of his speeches, to avoid becoming too tired. It seemed that his health had already benefited from these adjustments to his daily routine, and he confided in me that he would be traveling again soon. A life of seclusion in the apostolic palace had never been for him. I knew this. After his recent references to death, perhaps flashes of melancholy that had seized him in the most difficult moments of his recovery from illness, I saw no further traces of such thoughts, yet he was burdened by his keen awareness of the recent tragedies. He was more convinced than ever that terrorism had to be defeated, but not with wars, which risked fostering ongoing violence. He told me again about his opposition to military intervention in Iraq, and the need for a more active participation of the United Nations during this chaotic phase in the country's history. He called it the "big family" of the United Nations.

On June 4, 2004, President Bush came to Italy to commemorate the sixtieth anniversary of the liberation of Rome. I remembered the images of those days, as in a black-and-white film, when I was on leave, staying at the Hotel Flora on one of the most beautiful streets of the city. That same day Bush was received at the Vatican by the Holy Father. They first had a private conversation that lasted about fifteen minutes, and then they talked in public, in the Sala Clementina, in front of about a hundred people. The pope recalled the sacrifice of the American soldiers who had died in the Second World War, but then he began to talk also about Iraq and the Holy Land, clarifying once more the position of the Holy See on preventive war and the role of the United Nations. In the grand Renaissance-style hall, the American president listened to him without ever changing his expression. He did not do so even when Lolek called for respect of fundamental human rights, a clear allusion to the recent scandals at the prison of Abu Ghraib, near Baghdad, where Iraqi prisoners had been tortured by U.S. soldiers. His speech was very direct. By the end the pope had examined every point that was close to his heart, not for the sake of provocation, but simply as a man of peace. When Bush made his speech, he did not reply to any of the pope's remarks, but simply recognized him for the work he had done over his lifetime. For that president, for America, Lolek was also the one who had defeated communism, a hero.

During the meeting with the American president, Lolek had acted like a great world leader, but had also given the impression of being very tired. He had looked as if he had trouble breathing, and his voice was extremely weak, so weak that at times it was impossible to hear what he was saying. But instead of resting, the next morning he was ready to get on the papal airplane that would take him to Bern, Switzerland, with an agenda packed with appointments over the next seventy-two hours. I wasn't surprised—travel was almost therapeutic for him. That summer he also went to Lourdes. While he was delivering a homily in front of three hundred thousand pilgrims, he had to stop suddenly and call out for help in Polish. He was brought a glass of water, which helped him to regain his composure.

That was his last apostolic voyage. For a little while longer, his body permitted him to follow his normal routine, celebrating Mass, reciting the Angelus every Sunday, even granting an audience to the new Iraqi prime minister, Ayad Allawi, in November.

Since the end of January 2005, however, his health seemed to deteriorate tremendously.

Because of his troubled breathing, it was decided that he should be hospitalized at the Gemelli, where he was in treatment for ten days. But once he was released, it was soon clear how fleeting any hope for his recovery was. One evening he had another terrible crisis, tremors so violent that each time it seemed he wouldn't make it. A consultation among his physicians was organized, from which the decision came to perform a tracheotomy on him. He was told that he would be unable to speak for a while.

The following Good Friday, he was unable to officiate at the Stations of the Cross at the Coliseum and to see the thousands of candles lighting up the Palatine Hill. In order to allow him to follow it, a television set was put in his private chapel. On Easter Sunday he came to his window, thinking that at least he would be able to impart the blessing Urbi et Orbi. It was clear that he was trying to say something, but being unable to produce any audible words he simply made the sign of the cross three times and withdrew.

I went to see him that day with my family. My granddaughter Stefania had come from London with her husband Edward and their little daughter. Our dear Dziwisz introduced us as always, and since it was almost lunchtime a few sisters bustled around the room. I brought before Lolek the pretty little dark-haired girl, her face round, her cheeks full:

"Your Holiness," I said to him, "do you see how she has grown?"

It was Chiara, my great-granddaughter, whom he had baptized five years before. She took a few steps toward him, bowed down, and kissed his trembling hand. Everyone greeted him like that, and whispered something to him. I don't remember what I said. Mingled together with that scene, I saw pass before me an entire life lived together with him, the most familiar objects and places, the people dearest to us. I had played with him, I had shared sadness with him, and the most beautiful moments of young love. I had enjoyed talking with him about anything, anything at all. I had had the memory of admiration and nostalgia during the years in which I had lost contact with him. I wanted to hug him. A photographer who documents every moment of the pontiff's public life asked us all to squeeze in around him. We posed and smiled, and that last photo was taken. It really was the last.

Lolek, my beloved Lolek, passed away a few days later, on the evening of April 2, 2005. Outside in Saint Peter's Square, thousands of the faithful were standing vigil with prayers and songs. They had stood there day after day, one beside another, some of them not wanting to resign themselves to the thought of death, and perhaps hoping that a miracle might take place at the last moment. It didn't. After the announcement of the death of John Paul II was made in front of the basilica, the cardinals intoned the *De Profundis* from the steps leading into Saint Peter's. The bell of Saint Andrew rang out its solemn, lingering peals. In Rome, all the bells were ringing. The bells were ringing all over the world.

INDEX